SEEKING WESTERN MEN

Seeking Western Men

Email-Order Brides under China's Global Rise

MONICA LIU

STANFORD UNIVERSITY PRESS

Stanford, California

Stanford University Press
Stanford, California

Printed in the United States of America on acid-free, archival-quality paper

Library of Congress Cataloging-in-Publication Data

Names: Liu, Monica (Sociologist), author.
Title: Seeking Western men : email-order brides under China's global rise / Monica Liu.
Other titles: Globalization in everyday life.
Description: Stanford, California : Stanford University Press, 2022. | Series: Globalization in everyday life | Includes bibliographical references and index.
Identifiers: LCCN 2022007409 (print) | LCCN 2022007410 (ebook) | ISBN 9781503632479 (cloth) | ISBN 9781503633735 (paperback) | ISBN 9781503633742 (ebook)
Subjects: LCSH: Intercountry marriage—China. | Marriage brokerage—China. | Mail order brides—China. | Foreign spouses—Western countries. | Online dating—China. | Women—China—Social conditions. | Women—China—Economic conditions.
Classification: LCC HQ1032 .L585 2022 (print) | LCC HQ1032 (ebook) | DDC 306.84/50951—dc23/eng/20220225
LC record available at https://lccn.loc.gov/2022007409
LC ebook record available at https://lccn.loc.gov/2022007410

Cover design: Michel Vrana
Cover images: iStock
Typeset by Elliott Beard in Minion Pro 10/14.4

For Michael Nguyen. Thank you for seeing the best in me.

Contents

Acknowledgments   ix

INTRODUCTION   1

1 WHY DO CHINESE WOMEN   35
   SEEK WESTERN MEN?

2 PROVIDER LOVE   71

3 TRANSNATIONAL BUSINESS MASCULINITY   93

4 EMBRACING DOMESTICITY   115

5 BODY OF A WOMAN, FATE OF A MAN   142

6 SURROGATE DATING   164
   Translators behind the Screens

EPILOGUE   189

   Notes   201
   References   213
   Index   233

Acknowledgments

I owe my greatest debt to my respondents, whose willingness to share the most private aspects of their lives enabled me to write this book. Given the sensitivity of my research topic, I will refer to them by their pseudonyms here. First, I am eternally grateful to Helen, a longtime family friend, for introducing me to the Chinese dating agencies. I am also deeply indebted to Ms. Fong and her husband, who took the risk of letting me conduct research at their company despite the precarious legal status of the transnational dating industry in China. I also thank the managers, Ms. Mei and Mr. Li, for their heartfelt support and assistance over the years. Finally, I convey my sincere gratitude to all the men and women who participated in my study. This research journey was an unforgettable experience that has forever transformed my worldview and inspired me to become a lifelong writer.

Many people at the University of California, San Diego (UCSD) have provided me with intellectual and emotional support over the years. I thank Richard Madsen for giving me unconditional encouragement, from the moment I first arrived as a new student until I became a professor myself. Richard taught me to pursue a big-picture perspective and to connect macro-level trends with everyday interactions. He pushed me to follow my passion, trusting me to find my own way in moments of uncertainty. His wisdom, generosity, and kindness will always be remembered. I am also indebted to John Skrentny, who taught me how to clarify my theoretical framework and encouraged me to think more deeply and boldly. During moments of self-doubt, John's faith in me enabled me to maximize my potential as a scholar. I am forever grateful to Christena Turner as well, for giving me detailed advice on the various forms of writing this project necessitated throughout its development. As a seasoned ethnographer, she gave me advice on how to handle difficult respondent questions that proved invaluable, particularly given my unique positionality as a Western-trained scholar conducting research on a sensitive topic in China.

In addition, at UCSD, I express my sincere gratitude to Yen Le Espiritu, Weijing Lu, Barry Naughton, Akos Rona-Tas, Na Chen, Lizhu Fan, and Lei Guang for sharing their expertise and critically engaging with my work. At the National University of Singapore, I greatly appreciate Melody Lu, who connected me with various marriage migration scholars and provided me with hard-to-find academic sources on this subject. At the University of Washington (UW), Seattle, I am deeply indebted to Stevan Harrell for many years of support and mentorship, from my days as an undergraduate in his anthropology class to the latter part of my graduate school career, when he provided me with institutional affiliation as a visiting scholar at UW.

At Carleton College, where I was a visiting assistant professor of sociology, I thank Annette Nierobisz for reading my manuscript and organizing an on-campus research presentation, thereby encouraging me to continue writing while juggling my first teaching job after graduate school. At the University of South Florida, where I was a postdoctoral fellow in the Department of Sociology, I am indebted to James Cavendish, Jingping Du, Beatriz Padilla, and Kun Shi for their wonderful guidance and support. I also thank Fangheyue (Amber) Ma for the brilliant conversations and delicious home cooking. At Colgate University, where I was a visiting assistant professor of sociology, I am grateful to Michelle Bigenho, Chris Henke, Carolyn Hsu, Alicia Simmons, and Song Yang for their mentorship. I am also indebted to Yness Abdul-Malak, Jonathan Hyslop, and Chandra Russo for critiquing my manuscript. (Yness, I will always remember our heartfelt conversations, and I miss the days when we picked up lunch together at the Merrill House.)

After several years of visiting assistant professorships and postdoctoral fellowships, I feel extremely fortunate to have found an academic home in the Justice and Society Studies Department at the University of St. Thomas, Minnesota, where I am in the company of colleagues who have offered me a most congenial and supportive environment. I am deeply indebted to Tanya Gladney, my department chair, who, despite her busy schedule, always made time to address my concerns and support my research in any way she could; remarkably, she made starting a new tenure-track position during a pandemic a seamless transition. I am also grateful to Amy Finnegan, Richard Greenleaf, Jessica Hodge, Michael Klein, Patricia Maddox, Obasesam Okoi, and Xiaowen Guan for their mentorship and assistance. Finally, I owe an eternal debt to the institutional support of Yohuru Williams, Mark Stansbury-O'Donnell, and Kristine Wammer.

Undertaking the research for this book was costly, as I traveled both within China and throughout various parts of the United States. I would like to express my gratitude toward the organizations and institutions that awarded me generous grants and fellowships. UCSD provided me with four years of support via the Eugene V. Cota-Robles Fellowship, alongside several grants that together covered the costs of traveling to China to conduct preliminary research. The grants were awarded by the Department of Sociology, Dean of Social Sciences, and Institute for Comparative and Area Studies. I am also grateful to the University of California for granting me the Pacific Rim Research Program Mini Grant. The Fulbright Foundation provided me with the funds that enabled me to spend a full year conducting research in China (2011–12). With generous additional funding from the University of California, the University of South Florida, the Confucius Institute, and Colgate University, I was able to conduct follow-up research and finish writing without interruption.

While conducting research in China, I was fortunate to have been supported by various people and institutions. I express my gratitude to Changcheng Zhou for providing me with an academic home in China, serving as my faculty mentor, connecting me with local scholars, and being my tour guide. I will always remember the enlightening conversations and exciting times we had at the dinner banquets and social events he hosted. I also thank Qi Wu for assisting me with my research and IRB application, and Huiping

Wang for helping me acquire demographic data from the local government office. In addition, I am grateful to Janet Upton from the Fulbright Foundation and Xuan Zhang from the US Consulate General for assisting with my day-to-day living and for helping me arrange for sick leave when I was in China. I am also deeply indebted to Dr. Hongbo Wang for providing me with compassionate treatment when I fell ill. Moreover, I am lucky to have connected with Tricia Wang and Ian Gross, two fellow Fulbright scholars whose company and support were invaluable to me as I navigated research abroad, a sometimes isolating endeavor.

Over the years, many of my friends, colleagues, and assistants have closely read different parts of my book and offered essential critiques. I benefited immensely from the assistance of Shaohua Guo, Ling Han, Ellen Lamont, Jun Lei, Stephen Meyers, Abigail Ocobock, Jessi Streib, Jaclyn Wong, Cynthia Zhang, and Shuxuan Zhou. Moreover, Colgate University's Faculty Research Council Publication Expenses Grant enabled me to hire student assistants and professional book editors, while the University of St. Thomas's Faculty Research Grant gave me the course release I needed to complete my manuscript revision. Here I gratefully acknowledge my amazing student assistants from Colgate University: Kate Hinsche, Lauren Hutton, JY Khoo, Gabby Malloy, Tristan Niskanen, and Nizhoni Sanez. In particular, I am indebted to Lauren Hutton, a skillful writer with a magnificent ability to map data to theory, for her significant contributions to the book. Finally, I am grateful to my editors, Elizabeth Ridley and Roberta Raine, for perfecting this manuscript and making it accessible to a popular audience.

I had the privilege to present various portions of this book to numerous audiences, including those who attended the Asia Research Institute Transnational Mobility Workshop at the National University of Singapore; Department of Sociology Lecture at Wuhan University; China Studies Colloquium at the Jackson School of International Studies, University of Washington, Seattle; Department of Sociology and Anthropology Lunch Lecture Series at Carleton College; Department of Sociology Colloquium at the University of South Florida; Division of Social Sciences Seminar Series at Colgate University; and the Wednesday Gender Seminars at the Chinese University of Hong Kong. Portions of this book also appear in the journals

Men and Masculinities, Qualitative Sociology, and *Signs: Journal of Women in Culture and Society.*

At Stanford University Press, I am grateful to Rhacel Parrenas, editor of the Globalization in Everyday Life Series, for being a strong advocate for my project from day one. I also thank Marcela Cristina, the acquisitions editor, for reading various drafts of this manuscript and patiently addressing all my questions. Moreover, I convey my gratitude for Sunna Juhn and the entire production team at Stanford University Press. I could not imagine a smoother publishing process.

Last but by no means least, I express my gratitude to my friends and family. Without their support over the years, I would not have had the motivation to complete this project. I am deeply indebted to Julia Meszaros, my intellectual companion who stood by me on every step of this journey. I would not be where I am now without her selfless help. In addition, special thanks to Gabrielle Chang, Shaohua Guo, Jun Lei, Jomo Smith, and Qian (Angel) Zhang for their unwavering support and inspiring conversations. I also take this opportunity to thank my parents, Xiaolan Liu and Yixin Zhang, for their deep love and encouragement. In China, I thank my aunts Xiaohong Liu and Xiaohui Liu, my uncles Dengyun Huang and Ping Huang, and my cousin Yingfei Huang for taking such good care of me when I was in the field. Moreover, I am deeply indebted to my grandparents Shanxue Liu and Shuyuan Chen, who taught me the value of compassion, integrity, and commitment. They were the first to show me what unconditional love looks like, having made every sacrifice imaginable to raise me and improve my well-being in any way they could. Finally, I thank Michael Nguyen for his love and care, for seeing the best in me, for lifting me up when I could not reach, for all the sacrifices he made to support my career. Without him, I would never have been able to come this far in life.

SEEKING WESTERN MEN

INTRODUCTION

ONE HOT, SUNNY AFTERNOON IN June 2008, I found myself on an airplane heading from Los Angeles to China. I was excited, especially about seeing my grandparents, aunts, and cousin—the extended family I grew up with before immigrating to Boston at the age of eight. Moreover, I was excited about the prospect of starting a new research project. At the time, I was a first-year PhD student in the Department of Sociology at the University of California, San Diego and embarking on a research journey that explores global internet dating and cross-border marriage between Chinese women and American men.

On the plane, I picked up a Chinese newspaper left in my cabin seat and started browsing. Soon, the personals section, which featured photographs of a few middle-aged women, caught my eye. The women described themselves as caring, gentle women who sought financially stable, family-oriented men residing overseas. At this point, Jeff, a businessman from Beijing with whom I had chatted earlier, glanced over my shoulder and said in a cynical tone, "Don't believe in those ads for a moment. You know, those women are all *lao you tiao* [deep-fried dough sticks], exceedingly difficult to date." His words struck me, particularly his use of the term *lao you tiao*, which in Chinese refers to people who are slick, cunning, and worldly. In the context of dating and marriage, the term is usually used to describe sexually experienced men who prey on young women. Somehow, I could not associate *lao you tiao* with divorced mothers seeking to rebuild their families.

Now, readers may wonder how a young graduate student such as myself became interested in this niche-sounding topic prior to my airplane encounter with Jeff in 2008. Having majored in business administration during college, I entered my PhD program with an interest in economic sociology and hoped to examine Chinese business culture. Yet, my plans changed unexpectedly because of an old family friend named Helen. Back in 2005, Helen was in her mid-fifties and had just gotten divorced in China. She decided to join an internet dating company that connected local women with men from English-speaking Western countries. With the help of translators at her agency, Helen exchanged hundreds of emails with a retired American engineer. Yet, when he asked to meet in person, she hesitated, as she had never dated a foreign man before. Feeling nervous, she called up my father, her old friend who had immigrated from China to the United States twenty-some years ago.

The next time I heard about Helen, through my father in 2007, I was shocked to learn that she had married and moved to Seattle. She completely reversed my previous assumption of a so-called mail-order bride as someone young and never married, based on what I had seen on TV. Beyond my interest in economic sociology, I was also fascinated by China's gender issues, so I decided to give Helen a call to learn about her experiences. I was pleasantly surprised by her warmth and eagerness to share, and we engaged in a series of telephone conversations over the next few months. I learned that the other women Helen had met at her dating agency were also middle-aged and divorced. Moreover, some of them valued Western men for being less promiscuous and more family-oriented than their nouveau-riche Chinese ex-husbands, even though the Western men were less wealthy by comparison. Intrigued, I asked Helen if I could visit her agency.

Helen soon connected me with Ms. Fong, her agency owner. Introducing myself via email as a Chinese American PhD student, I expressed my desire to interview her clients and possibly publish a research paper based on my findings. Although Ms. Fong agreed to let me visit her company, her replies were lukewarm, often just single-word responses such as "okay," "yes," or "maybe." While Ms. Fong's agency was headquartered in a major coastal metropolis that I call "Lingshan" by pseudonym, she co-owned two other agencies, both of which were in my Chinese hometown, a mid-sized inland city that I call "Tunyang" in this book. Ms. Fong also put me in touch with Ms. Mei and Mr. Li, the managers at those two agencies.

Right after classes ended in June 2008, I was China-bound. At this time, I had secured travel funding from my school to conduct pilot research on this project. My research journey began on my third day in Tunyang, on a hot, humid summer morning. I had barely slept the night before, thanks to both jet lag and bloodthirsty mosquitoes that buzzed in my room all night. As soon as dawn broke, I hopped in a taxi and headed toward Ms. Mei's agency, thirty minutes away from where I was staying at my grandfather's home. Her office was located inside one of the tallest skyscrapers in Tunyang's central shopping district. A giant billboard featuring Kate Winslet in a Lancôme ad hung outside the building, while various department stores, bars, lounges, and business offices occupied each floor.

Upon my arrival on the twenty-eighth floor, I saw an open office occupied by young women sitting in cubicles, typing away on their computers. Inside, another suite featured two mahogany desks, a flimsy-looking orange couch, and a floor-to-ceiling window that opened partially to the smog-filled air outside. This was Ms. Mei's office, which she shared with her secretary, a bright-eyed young woman in her early twenties who wore large, black-rimmed glasses and spoke fluent English. Ms. Mei was a voluptuous lady in her fifties, with shoulder-length hair dyed chestnut-brown. She was dressed tastefully, in an expensive-looking black suit along with fine jade jewelry. Although her formal attire made her look unapproachable, her voice was cheery and earnest. Unlike the more standoffish Ms. Fong, Ms. Mei was extremely warm and receptive to having me visit as a researcher. Before leaving the office that day, she even treated me to her homemade pancakes and stuffed some in my purse, as if I were an old friend from abroad.

MY FIRST SUMMER ON-SITE

I spent the first two weeks of June at Ms. Mei's agency, which was always crowded with clients. Just as Helen had said, most of these women were middle-aged (older than forty) and divorced (for more detailed demographic information collected in 2012, see figures 1 and 2). I had my first on-site conversations with Joanne, a tall, elegant lady in her forties who wore a Louis Vuitton necklace and a special fragrance. When I complimented Joanne on her perfume and jewelry one day, she smiled and said she had received both as presents from an American man she had been dating for the past year. Surprisingly open to sharing intimate aspects of her life with me, Joanne told me she had had difficulty becoming aroused when her American beau visited China. Joanne, who was undergoing early menopause at the time, attributed her sexual problems to the stresses she had endured as a single mother over the years, after her Chinese ex-husband had gambled away her business.

At that moment, Scarlett, a skinny woman in her fifties who wore heavy makeup and a form-fitting black nylon dress, chimed in and said, "Ladies, I'm past menopause, but I have still got strong desires! So many men tell me my body is amazingly sexy and they all want to make love to me!" Scarlett made a few erotic dance moves around the room before sitting down to tell us about her experience dating Western men. The first man she mentioned worked for the American FBI, and she supposedly rejected him because he was too stingy. She liked the second man and wanted to marry him, but failed her fiancée visa interview at the British consulate in Beijing because she forgot how to pronounce his last name. At Scarlett's admission, everyone in the room broke into hysterical laughter. They were so loud that Ms. Mei rushed over to remind us of the translators working next door.

As I spent more time on-site, I noticed that the women I met were extroverted, worldly, and perhaps even a bit jaded with life, far from the stereotypical Western media image of an Asian "picture bride"[1] as introverted, girlishly innocent, and sexually inexperienced.[2] Moreover, their desire to seek marriage migration was rooted in their grievances with Chinese society. In particular, they were frustrated by China's rising rate of extramarital affairs and divorce, exam-focused system of education, and privatization of social security and health care, which made these services increasingly

FIGURE 1. Female client age distribution, May 2012 (n=1740, Tunyang and Lingshan combined). *Source:* Author created.

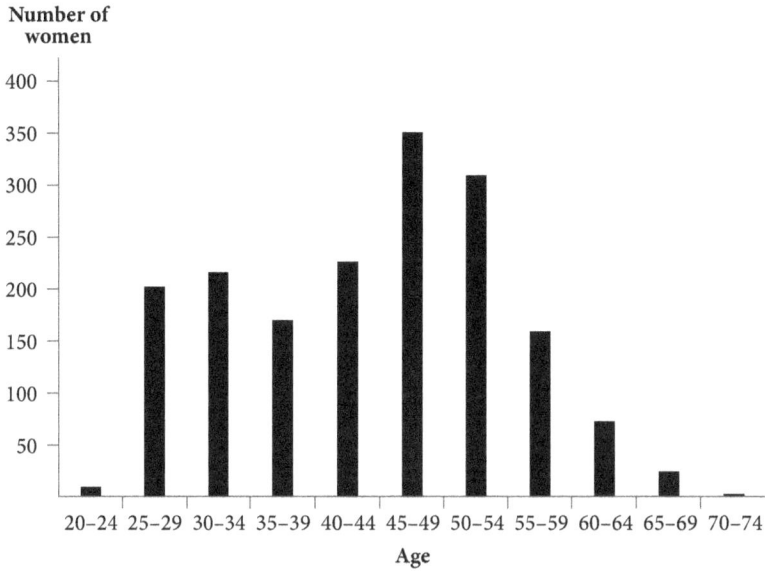

FIGURE 2. Female client marital status, May 2012 (n=1740, Tunyang and Lingshan combined). *Source:* Author created.

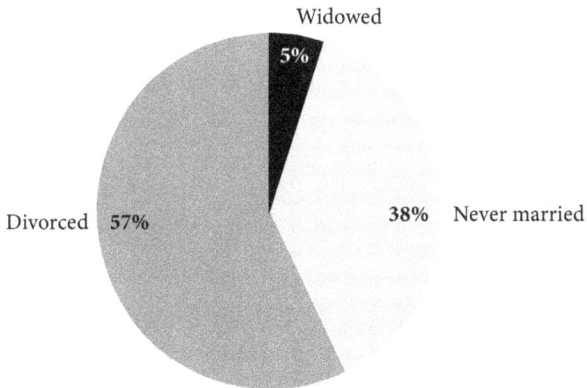

unaffordable. Specifically, those concerns came from three distinct groups of women: ex-wives of nouveau-riche men who were financially well-off but emotionally disturbed by their ex-husbands' infidelity; single mothers who wanted their children to study overseas but could not afford it; and lower earning women who were approaching retirement age and sought better social services abroad. Soon, I realized this was a robust place to observe how macro-level structural changes in postreform China fostered women's desires to migrate. Their stories and narratives shed light on the aftermath of sweeping policy changes and social transformations in China, including the 1966–76 Cultural Revolution,[3] the collapse of state-owned enterprises during the 1990s,[4] and the meteoric rise of new rich businessmen and their mistresses.

Interestingly, the dating agencies provided much more than just networking opportunities for these women. In fact, they served as important relationship counseling centers. This became apparent when I visited Mr. Li's agency, which had far fewer clients than Ms. Mei's agency, even though both were in the same city and followed the same business model. Later, I learned that Mr. Li's agency was less popular because many women felt uncomfortable sharing with a man the intimate details of their dating life. In contrast, Ms. Fong's and Ms. Mei's position as previously divorced women enabled them to build excellent rapport with their female clients, thereby putting them in a better position to market their businesses. Unlike transnational dating agencies in other countries, such as Ukraine or the Philippines, which offer free membership to women,[5] the agencies I studied charged their female clients US$1,000 each year. Hence, Chinese female clients were valued not only for their ability to attract revenue from Western men, but also for their own purchasing power as rising consumers in China's new market economy.

Beyond the lives of the couples, I was also curious about how their translators facilitated their email exchanges. I gained a concrete understanding of the translators' work during the last few days of my 2008 summer research trip, when I visited Ms. Fong's agency in Lingshan. Since Lingshan is located six hundred miles away from Tunyang, I traveled there by train with my father, who happened to be in China and decided to come on this excursion with me. While Tunyang is considered a "second-tier city," Lingshan is a "first-tier city," meaning that it is a wealthy megalopolis with huge economic, cultural, and political influence in China. Clean and modern, Lingshan had wide streets and a newly built subway system. While bicycles and motorcycles weaved between cars in Tunyang, here they stayed in their own lane and pedestrians actually used the crosswalk.

Ms. Fong's agency stood in a tall commercial building at the city's edge. At her suggestion, my father and I checked into a hotel where Western clients who visited her agency often stayed. That evening, we met at a small restaurant specializing in northern Chinese cuisine of buns and spicy cabbage with pork. Ms. Fong was a shapely lady in her early forties, with creamy white skin and almond-shaped eyes. That day, she came in a gray jogging suit with her long black hair tied back in a high ponytail. She was much more outgoing than I had expected, with a radiant smile and lots of energy. While she initially held some reservations, worried that I was a Western reporter who might portray her agency in a negative light, she relaxed as we got to know each other. Like my father, Ms. Fong was born into a Communist cadre family in Tunyang, the city where she had spent much of her youth before moving to Lingshan. As we chatted further, she came to realize that my uncle was her former neighbor and supervisor at the state-owned enterprise where she once worked before quitting to pursue a career in business.

The next day, Ms. Fong took me to her office, which looked much more spacious than Ms. Mei's and Mr. Li's agencies and had twice as many translators. However, fewer women came on-site, while most of their communication with their translators took place via phone or instant messaging. According to Ms. Fong, most women in Lingshan were busy career professionals who worked during the day and took part in the city's bustling nightlife, thereby having little time or interest in using the agency as a social space. Nevertheless, she arranged for me to meet with some of her clients. To help me learn more about their mate-selection criteria, Ms. Fong had me converse with them and then help them write introductory emails to Western men.

After spending three days on-site and writing more than one hundred letters, I was surprised and embarrassed to learn that I could not elicit a single reply, despite my native command of English. By contrast, the translators' letters, filled with grammatical errors and Chinese-style "teen-age talk," fared much better with the men. These translators, mostly female, were fresh out of college. Some had never even been involved in a romantic relationship. Ms. Fong told me she liked hiring young women, particularly those from rural areas, because they were creative and hard-working. As rural migrants hoping to make it in the big city, they worked late into the night, on weekends, and during holidays. Interestingly, this group of youth born in the 1980s and 1990s took charge in brokering the desires, aspirations, and dreams of middle-aged men and women across cultural and geographical borders.

Throughout my three-week stay in China that summer, I was on-site at the dating agencies from 9:00 a.m. to 8:00 p.m., and then stayed up well past midnight writing up fieldnotes in my hotel room. Despite the long hours, it never felt like grueling work because I was utterly fascinated by the material. I knew I was observing something socially significant, and I felt compelled to record my findings. After getting a glimpse into China's social problems through my initial observations in 2008, I set out to formally research these dating agencies.

OVERVIEW OF THE BOOK

By 2012, agencies like those of Ms. Fong, Ms. Mei, and Mr. Li, which facilitate email exchanges, romantic tours, and marriages between women from developing countries and men from economically advanced countries, constituted a US$2 billion global business equal in size to the entire domestic online-dating industry in the United States.[6] Drawing on data that I collected in both China and the United States over a span of eleven years (2008–19), this book examines why Chinese women seek Western men and how their translators mediate their courtship, and looks at the outcome of their postmarital lives abroad. I have interviewed and observed the female clients, the staff at their dating agencies, and the men who traveled to China to meet them. I have also analyzed the couples' online dating profiles, as well as the agencies' websites and blogs. Following the women's marriages and migration, I also interviewed some of them in their new homes abroad.

My work is situated against the backdrop of a changing global economic order, marked by China's rapid ascendance and a relative decline of the

West.[7] Although I did not realize it at the time, I was conducting research during a period when the relationship between China and the West was taking a major turn. The 2008 global financial crisis had rocked the United States, Europe, and Oceania, leading to reverberations that my Chinese respondents could immediately feel. For example, on-site I heard about Western men dropping out of online courtships or even wedding engagements because they had suffered a sudden job loss, bankruptcy, or even home repossession. The crisis had a much more limited impact on the Chinese economy,[8] and few women I met on-site suffered from it financially.

Following in the footsteps of sociologists such as Kimberly Hoang and Viviana Zelizer, I examine how market forces inextricably intertwine with intimacy. Specifically, I chronicle how the shifting global economic order reshaped Chinese women's perception of Western men and marriage migration. I also examine the ways in which the commercial agencies market Western men to their Chinese female clients, given Western men's newly declining economic power within a global context. My work stands in contrast to previous scholarship, which focuses primarily on how commercial agencies market third-world women as marriageable entities to first-world men.[9] I analyze how the women's own gender ideologies and economic positions within China shaped the outcome of their relationships with Western men. Thus, unlike many existing works that address how Western forces influence China, this book highlights how endogenous changes within China shape international marriages and the transnational dating industry. I treat China not only as a location where globalization takes effect, but also as a site where new gender norms are being produced and making a significant impact on the rest of the world.

In addition, I explore how the translators capitalized on their knowledge of China's contemporary sex culture and youth culture to help their female clients build attractive online personas, through a process I call "surrogate dating." Looking beyond how translators shaped their clients' marital outcomes, I also explore how joining the industry altered the translators' own life trajectories. I discuss the new opportunities they acquired for upward socioeconomic mobility, alongside the emotional burden they had to endure while performing surrogate dating on their job.

STRUCTURE OF THE DATING AGENCIES: A GLOBAL BUSINESS CHAIN

As of 2012, Ms. Mei's, Mr. Li's, and Ms. Fong's offices had a combined total of 1,740 female clients. The agencies were not individual entities, however, but rather part of a larger commercial chain in the global marriage-brokering industry. Instead of recruiting male clients on their own, they partnered with a foreign company that was responsible for seeking Western men and for providing the email platform through which these men contacted the Chinese women. The male supplier company they partnered with had 1.6 million registered men and worked with various local female supplier agencies not only in China but also in Southeast Asia, Eastern Europe, and Latin America (see figure 3). Among the male clients, Americans predominated, followed by British, Canadians, and Australians. These male clients tended to be politically conservative, and many came from rural areas.

With regard to race, most men I saw on-site in China were Caucasian. I met a few Latino or Native American men, but no Black men. This is because the translators do not entertain emails from Western Black men, on the basis that the Chinese clients will not be interested in pursuing a relationship with them. These women's reluctance to date Black men can be traced back to China's longstanding history of anti-Black prejudice.[10] Today, Black men still fall to the bottom of China's transnational dating market, despite the potential desirability of their citizenship, wealth, or character.[11]

Although the Chinese women rejected Black men, they did not discriminate against other racial groups. To them, the term "Westerner" encompassed Caucasians, Latinos, and Native Americans. Occasionally, some clients referred to Western men of Northern and Central European ancestry as "pure white," and Latino men, men of Southern European ancestry, and Native Americans as "non–pure white." However, based on my observation, being "pure white" did not boost their desirability. For example, some women considered an American man of Sicilian ancestry to be "non–pure white," "less hairy," and "more Asian-looking" than the typical Caucasian male, and therefore "more pleasing to the eye." For example, Daisy, a female client, found Anthony, a Floridian business owner of Native American ancestry, to be particularly sexy, although many other, non–Native American men wrote her. On the whole, my observations show that for male clients who were not Black, race appeared to have little effect on their marital prospects at the agency, while class mattered much more.

FIGURE 3. The global business chain. *Source:* Author created.

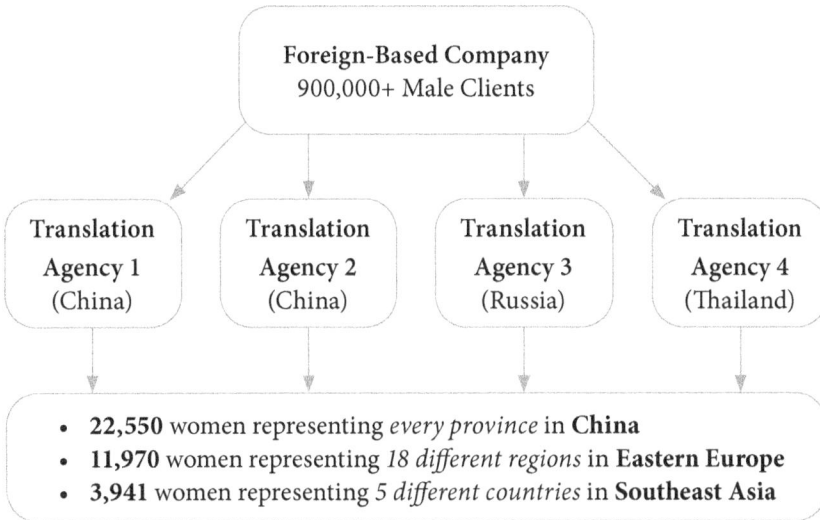

Foreign-Based Company
900,000+ Male Clients

| Translation Agency 1 (China) | Translation Agency 2 (China) | Translation Agency 3 (Russia) | Translation Agency 4 (Thailand) |

- **22,550** women representing *every province* in **China**
- **11,970** women representing *18 different regions* in **Eastern Europe**
- **3,941** women representing *5 different countries* in **Southeast Asia**

While the foreign companies recruited the male clients, local agencies like Ms. Mei's were in charge of recruiting female Chinese clients and translators, who helped the women create online profiles, write emails to the Western men, and translate their phone calls and webcam meetings. Female clients paid a flat US$1,000 annual membership fee, while male clients paid US$5.00 to US$10.00 per email written or read. Despite the public's concern over the potential for human trafficking, I did not witness such danger in my research. The translators in my study did not pair couples themselves, but instead let the women choose men from the agency's database before sending out introductory letters on the women's behalf. In all ensuing email exchanges, translators would ask women to provide their response in Chinese first, and they always sent the women a copy of the men's original letter.

Couples typically correspond for several months before some men take weeklong trips to visit their potential brides; the translators also facilitate communication between couples during the visits. Figure 4 outlines this courtship process. Interestingly, most men never visit the women with whom they exchange emails. As a result, each agency has only three or four male visitors on-site per month. Due to the small number of visitors, the

FIGURE 4. The courtship process. *Source:* Author created.

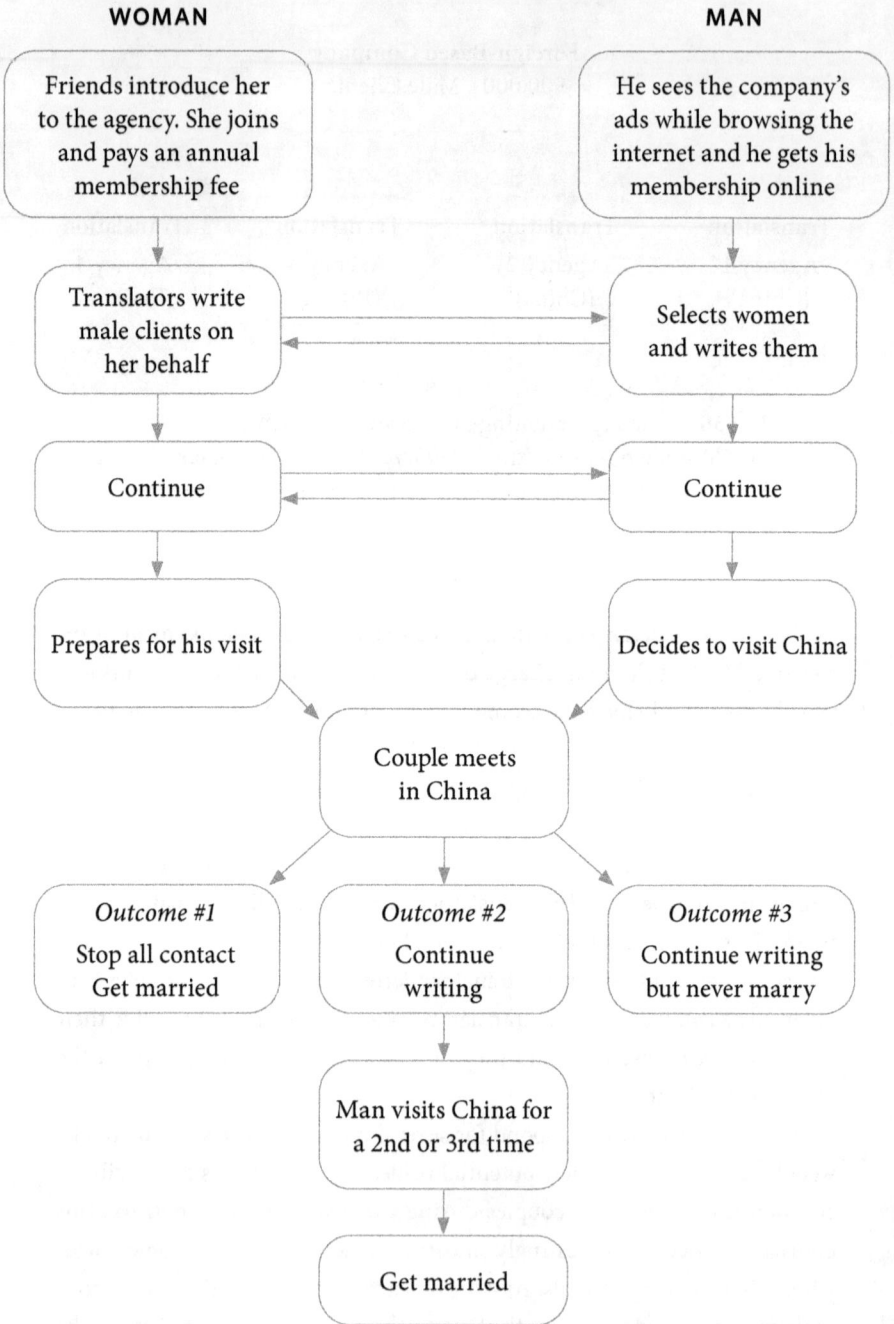

WOMAN	MAN
Friends introduce her to the agency. She joins and pays an annual membership fee	He sees the company's ads while browsing the internet and he gets his membership online

Translators write male clients on her behalf → Selects women and writes them ← (mutual arrows)

Continue ↔ Continue

Prepares for his visit / Decides to visit China

Couple meets in China

Outcome #1
Stop all contact
Get married

Outcome #2
Continue writing

Outcome #3
Continue writing but never marry

Man visits China for a 2nd or 3rd time

Get married

company I studied did not offer large-scale group tours to the men, unlike some other transnational dating agencies. Among couples that got married, the typical time lag between their first email exchange and their marriage engagement was two years. Across her three agencies, Ms. Fong reported a combined total of more than two thousand marriages over the course of thirteen years (2000–2013), 40 percent of which consisted of couples that settled in the United States (the remainder in Western Europe, Canada, Australia, and New Zealand).

WHY STUDY CHINA?

In the past few decades, China has undergone dramatic social, economic, and cultural changes. It is therefore a prime location to observe how macro-level sociostructural shifts reshape people's private lives. Historically, the Chinese family structure is rooted in patriarchy.[12] Most women had no access to schooling and lacked economic roles outside the home until 1949,[13] when the newly established socialist state required all women to partici-pate in labor production outside the home.[14] At this time, the state pro-vided social services, such as childcare assistance, to urban women.[15] Yet in the postreform era (1979–present), the state withdrew such services and relocated care responsibilities back to the private sphere as part of women's unpaid work at home.[16]

In addition to increasing gendered division of labor within the house-hold, labor market dynamics were also changing. As China transitioned toward a market economy, employers increasingly prioritized efficiency over equity[17] and favored hiring men over women.[18] Moreover, the newly emerging private business sector started engaging in "beauty economy" market practices,[19] where only attractive women below the age of thirty get hired in the retail industry. In addition, middle-aged women were dispro-portionately affected by large-scale SOE (state-owned enterprise) layoffs during the 1990s.[20]

Although a small subset of women did benefit from the reform and achieved financial success at an *individual* level—either by developing successful careers or by marrying wealthy men[21]—women as a *group* still experienced an overall decline in status as wealth became concentrated among a small subset of men.[22] In light of rising labor market competition, increasing gender discrimination in the workplace, and booming desires for consumption,[23] many women have come to view their bodies as valuable commodities to be exchanged for income and security.[24] In China today, masculinity is centered on a man's ability to make money,[25] while beauty and femininity have become essential to women's gender identity.[26]

Beyond the labor market, women also faced challenges on the marriage front. Divorce rates in urban areas rose from 2 percent in 1970 to 27 percent in 2013.[27] Upon divorce, older women face a highly competitive dating market since many young, never-married women who want a breadwinner husband seek men significantly older than themselves.[28] Interestingly, although China's ratio of marriage-age men to women stands at almost three to one,[29] this gender imbalance, which results from the 1979 One-Child Policy, does not apply to most of my respondents, who were born before 1979.

In response to changing social, economic, and cultural structures that have become increasingly inequitable to women, two strands of local feminism have emerged in China. The first one, called "noncooperative C-fem,"[30] encourages women to retain their financial independence and choose a career over marriage and childbearing when faced with conflicting obligations.[31] This strand of feminism appeals more to women born after China's One-Child Policy came into effect. Growing up as only children, these women had better access to higher education and better career prospects than their predecessors. By contrast, the women in my study, most of whom were born before 1979, do not identify with noncooperative C-fem.

Instead, my respondents identify with a second strand of Chinese-style feminism that scholars Angela Wu and Yige Dong call "entrepreneurial C-feminism."[32] This model encourages women to abandon traditional virtues such as submissiveness and self-sacrifice, but it does not associate female empowerment with participation in the paid labor force. Instead, women are encouraged to capitalize on and cultivate their sexual attractiveness, including their femininity and domestic skills, to maximize their material gain. Popular adages that emerged in the postreform era speak to this strand of feminism: "Women conquer the world through conquering men"; "A man shows his love for a woman by handing her his wallet." The idea here is that, rather than gaining direct access to power through the paid labor force, women are better off using their feminine appeal to control men.

Entrepreneurial C-fem resonated with many of my respondents, who lived in a time when China became governed by a market logic that emphasized women's economic dependence on men and their sexual objectification by men.[33] Under such conditions, many women aimed to achieve leverage over men by cultivating their attractiveness through performing conventional femininities, rather than by competing with men directly in the labor market.[34]

While modernization theorists assumed that women would develop more Western-style liberal outlooks on gender as China grew economically, the 1949–79 intervention of state socialism altered this trajectory. China took an unorthodox path toward modernization, in which a revival of traditional patriarchal ideology emphasizing feminine youth and domesticity emerged simultaneously alongside economic expansion. Thus, my respondents' gender ideologies and their subsequent marital trajectories differed from those of many other marriage migrants, who came from countries that did not experience the same postsocialist backlash against women's participation in the paid labor force.

CHINESE WOMEN AND WESTERN MEN IN A CHANGING GLOBAL ECONOMIC ORDER

Throughout this book, I refer to my respondents as "Chinese women" and "Western men." As a reminder, these people do not necessarily represent the average cisgender woman in China or cisgender man in the West. In fact, they may not even represent the typical Chinese marriage migrant, given that it is mostly women without English skills who opt for translator-assisted dating, while women fluent in English would join dating sites such as Match.com or eHarmony on their own. Similarly, most men residing in Western countries do not specifically seek foreign wives. Hence, rather than being the "average" man or woman, my respondents represent a unique subset of the population in their home countries. Nevertheless, one experience they share is the fact that structural changes brought on by globalization have dramatically altered their livelihoods. Let us now examine some of the transformations that motivated these people to seek a foreign spouse.

Unlike the 1980s and 1990s, today the West is no longer the world's sole center of wealth. Alongside the global integration of financial markets, an affluent capitalist class is emerging in both Western and non-Western countries.[35] By 2020, there were 614 billionaires in the United States, followed by 456 in China, 114 in Germany, 102 in India, and 99 in Russia.[36] Moving away from the binary construction of the rich West and poor Global South, geographer David Harvey[37] urges us to reenvision the world system as one demarcated not only by nationality but also by access to wealth. Today, the increasing polarization in wealth distribution has led to an emergence of both "haves" and "have-nots" in every nation. These macro-level structural shifts have had a significant impact on the motives and aspirations of the women and men in this study.

Brides under China's Global Rise

As previously stated, China has transitioned from a poor socialist state to the world's second-largest economy. However, not all women benefited equally from China's reform. My female respondents include both economic "winners" and "losers" of globalization. Some became millionaires, while others were pushed into the contingent employment sector, earning less than US$5.00 per day. Among both the wealthy and poor women, one common factor that motivated them to seek marriage migration was age discrimination, when they found themselves too old to be considered desirable by men on their local marriage market. Additionally, working-class women in service industries faced age discrimination not only on the marriage market but also on the local labor market.

While my respondents often cited "gender equality" or "women's rights" as their top reasons for seeking marriage migration, it is important to note that their conception of equality differs from middle-class, Eurocentric feminist assumptions. For example, they envision "respect for women" as men opening doors and saying, "Ladies first," which is exactly what some Western feminists flag as evidence of gender inequality. Subscribing to entrepreneurial C-fem, my respondents differ from many other marriage migrants, such as the highly educated Vietnamese brides described in sociologist Hung Cam Thai's *For Better or for Worse: Vietnamese International Marriages in the New Global Economy* (2008), who sought men with a more Western-style, "liberal" outlook on gender. By contrast, many of my respondents wished to perform conventional femininity in exchange for men's financial support. In fact, they pursue Western men only because they can no longer strike such a patriarchal bargain in China. Among my wealthier respondents, many had been abandoned by their Chinese ex-husbands, who became newly rich entrepreneurs and wanted to "upgrade" to a younger wife. Among the poorer women, many had divorced their Chinese ex-husbands who could not provide for their families after losing their state jobs and who later resorted to gambling, drinking, or substance abuse.

In their pursuit of marriage migration, my Chinese respondents are not trying to *escape* a patriarchal bargain, but rather hoping to find an *alternative version* that maximizes their interest. They want a gendered economic deal where men still serve as primary household providers, but women need not be submissive or youthful. Essentially, they hope to find a husband who foots all the household bills and at the same time remains devoted and caring to his aging homemaker wife.

Grooms under Western Decline

While the Chinese women's motives and expectations have been shaped by macro-level changes in economic structure and cultural norms, so have the livelihoods of the Western men. In the United States and Western Europe, globalization has also created both winners and losers. While highly educated, highly skilled workers in finance and consulting industries are accumulating significant wealth, those working in the agricultural, manufacturing, and small-business sectors have experienced diminishing wages and a decline in socioeconomic status.[38]

In contrast to the more economically diverse Chinese female clientele, the majority of the Western male clients belong to the have-not sector of their society. A random sample of 1,000 male client profiles shows a self-reported salary of US$15,000–$34,000 among 29 percent of the men and US$35,000–$49,000 among 21 percent of the men, while less than 7 percent earned above US$150,000 (see table 1). To put this in context, the average annual salary for a man in the United States in 2014 was US$50,383.[39] My interviews reveal that the motives of these men for seeking Chinese brides overlap with findings from existing scholarship on global internet dating. That is, these men associate their own lack of success on their local marriage market with forces of global capitalism and feminism, which they believe have made Western women overly independent, materialistic, and self-centered.[40]

Many of my male respondents were born between 1940 and 1960. During this period, the booming of industrial and manufacturing sectors made it possible for many men—including working-class men—to support a stay-at-home wife.[41] Starting in the 1980s, however, Western economies shifted away from industrial production toward service and information. Automation, globalization, and corporatization have contributed to the dramatic decline of agriculture, manufacturing, and small business. Subsequently, men's ability to serve as primary household providers has also declined.[42]

Beginning in the 1980s, the traditional breadwinner/housewife model of marriage started fading, while a new model of partnership marriage,[43] which emphasizes more equal sharing of breadwinning and homemaking responsibilities between couples, emerged. It is important to note that partnership marriages benefit upper-middle-class men more than working-class men. This is because male doctors, lawyers, and investment bankers already occupy the upper echelons of their society, so they are less likely to feel emasculated by their perceived loss of power in partnership marriages. In fact, upper-middle-class men experience a net gain from partnership marriages, which allow them to form "power couple" alliances with similarly high-earning women, thereby doubling their wealth and passing these advantages on to their children.[44]

In contrast, most working-class men view this changing economic landscape as a threat to their masculinity. Numerous sociology studies show that marriage rates have declined among working-class men and poor men, primarily because women within their own class find them too poor to be marriage worthy.[45] Having slipped down the socioeconomic ladder, these men struggle to hold onto what privilege they have left by pursuing so-called traditional marriages, possibly with foreign brides, as they think this will allow them to exert more dominance and control at home. There are also some middle-class men who, despite being financially stable, still feel out of place within the new gender norms of Western societies, dominated by feminists who are supposedly destroying the family and nation through their "spoiled behavior" and materialism.[46] As we can see, both the Western men and Chinese women have their own fantasies of what an ideal

TABLE 1. Male clients' self-reported demographic information (n = 1,000). *Source:* Author created.

Age	*	Marital Status	*	Education	*	Popular Occupations	* / **	Income (US$1,000)	*
< 30	28%	Never married	53%	High School	24%	Sales/Marketing	19%	15–34	29%
30–39	35%	Divorced	33%	Vocational	10%	Technical	14%	35–49	21%
40–49	20%	Separated	10%	Associate	30%	R&D Engineering	7%	50–74	22%
50–59	11%	Widowed	4%	Bachelor	17%	Retired	7%	75–99	13%
60–69	5%			Postgrad	19%	Upper Mgmt./Executive	5%	100–149	8%
>69	6%					Home Business	5%	150+	7%

*Margin of error = 4% (p < 0.05).

**Note that only 751 out of 1,000 men indicated their occupation. The percent calculation in the occupation column applies to 751 men only.

partner looks like. Their translation agencies, in turn, are on a mission to construct idealized images of Asian femininity and Western masculinity that cater to their clients' imagination.

China's ascendancy and the relative decline of the West threaten the geopolitical dominance of the West as well as the status of the Western men who benefit from white supremacy. At the same time, China's reform and newly opened economy have left many older women behind in both the marriage and labor markets. These women mourn their previous status as beloved wives of once-loyal husbands, or as beneficiaries of dependable state jobs. Transnational relationships offer a kind of loophole for people who feel newly disadvantaged by the forces of global capitalism that permanently altered their economic opportunities and gender roles in the West and in China.

The migrant marriage industry between Chinese women and Western men thus surrogates for what the participants see as the failures of capitalism. The women can now opt out of China's marriage and labor markets— ones that are difficult for them to succeed in—and instead resort to domestic roles in a new relationship abroad, where their performed femininity allows them to remain provided for and cherished, despite their older age. Meanwhile, men who may not be considered good providers by Western women can now cement their masculinity by maintaining historic racial and geopolitical imaginations of elitism in their own marriages. These men embed themselves in a nostalgic understanding of the white working class, a certain glory no longer afforded to the auto industry worker or coal miner today.[47] Put broadly, these relationships allow for a fulfilled sense of self necessary for a positive quality of life and self-image, which a changing world order has seemingly taken away from those left behind by the forces of global capitalism.

SURROGATE DATING: TRANSLATORS BEHIND THE SCREENS

Beyond the lives of the transnational couples, this book also delves into the day-to-day lives of their translators. I explore how economic changes in post-reform China shaped the global dating industry and altered the staff's livelihoods. I show how the industry has created new opportunities for rural migrants to achieve upward mobility by working as translators and later becoming homeowners, entrepreneurs, or even marriage migrants them-selves. Moreover, while the media depict global dating agencies as ruthless exploiters or even human traffickers in disguise, my work reveals why these portrayals are oversimplified. I highlight the process through which the young translators struggle to balance their profit-making goals with their conscience while living in a "values vacuum" following the collapse of a strong public moral ideology in postsocialist China.[48]

Many scholars believe that China is in a state of moral decay because traditional values and religions have been upended,[49] while Deng Xiaoping's pragmatic push for economic reform led moneymaking and materialism to become the nation's most conspicuous public values.[50] Living within this context, many female clients pursued dating strategies that undermined the traditional norms of fidelity and earnestness. Recall that these female clients are primarily middle-aged, and many have experienced traumatic life events, such as infidelity, divorce, domestic abuse, or career failure. In contrast, more than 90 percent of the translators are in their early to mid-twenties. On one hand, these translators are valued by the industry for their youth and emotional inexperience, as these qualities help them write letters with a "freshness and innocence" that the middle-aged clients lack. Yet, on the other hand, these qualities also render them unprepared for their clients' lying, cheating, and "gold digging," so that they often feel perturbed and sometimes outraged, as they bear witness and even contribute to be-havior that they find morally despicable.

KEY REVELATIONS ABOUT RACE, CLASS, AND GENDER IN A GLOBAL CONTEXT

This book addresses a variety of sociological issues, including race, class, gender, globalization, and immigration, offering several key theoretical insights. First, this work challenges readers to rethink the relationship between race and class in a new world order, where wealth is decentering across continents and world regions but becoming polarized within each nation. Under such conditions, does Western masculinity still command some degree of hegemonic power in China, despite China's global rise? I confirm that it does by showing how the agencies market their Western male clients as morally superior to Chinese men, despite their relative lack of wealth. The fact that this portrayal sells in China reflects the continued superiority of Western culture within the Chinese imagination.

However, I also chronicle moments during which Western masculinity starts to lose its hegemonic power. This typically happens in the latter phase of the courtship process, when couples go offline and meet face to face. I show the process through which some women quickly rejected their working-class Western suitors once they realized that these men did not embody the type of elite masculinity they were seeking in a partner. Instead, some of those women chose to continue dating their local Chinese lovers, even if those men were married and reluctant to leave their wives. This is because the women's Chinese lovers had refined tastes, lifestyles, and sexual know-how that their foreign suitors lacked.

In Western countries, race remains an important marker of status independent of class, because ethnic minorities still hold significantly *less* economic, political, and social power than the white majority, despite the accomplishments of some racial minorities at an *individual* level. In Asia, however, the old racial hierarchy that featured white men on top is now being realigned in light of a changing global economic order,[51] as shown by the Chinese women's preference for their wealthy local lovers over their modest-earning foreign suitors. Hence, my work captures a shift in the relationship between race and class as an affluent capitalist class emerges in both Western and non-Western countries.

Second, this book has important implications for how we understand and theorize global migration, and in particular, the way we think about new differences of wealth between sending and receiving countries. Today, China occupies a unique position on the world stage. On one hand, it is an emerging world superpower projected to overtake the United States to become the world's largest economy by 2028.[52] On the other hand, China's growth has been uneven, and the nation is still considered a developing country based on its GDP per capita. Given China's economic diversity, we can no longer make generalized predictions about Chinese migrants on the basis of macro-level economic trends alone. Instead, we must focus on intragroup differences.

While most empirical studies examine marriage migrants from only one particular class when looking at a specific country,[53] I illuminate class differences among women of the same nationality by comparing the experiences of both "financially flexible" and "financially burdened" women. Clients whom I call financially flexible have medical insurance and guaranteed retirement funds, are not burdened by the costs of child-rearing, and are not in debt. By contrast, clients in the financially burdened category include women in the contingent employment sector who seek access to better social services as they approach retirement age, as well as women who have other imminent financial needs due to circumstances such as debt incurred from business failure.

My results show that the majority of the financially flexible women rejected their Western suitors, while the financially burdened women married them at significantly higher rates. In fact, many of the latter even compromised on other aspects of marriage, such as romantic attraction or sexual compatibility, because they were desperate for financial security or a US "green card." (Having a green card, officially known as a Permanent Resident Card, allows a person to live and work permanently in the United States.) Upon moving abroad, the financially burdened women were also more likely to tolerate abusive marriages, while the financially flexible women could afford to end things quickly if they felt unhappy.

Thus, rather than portraying China's global rise as a uniform process of empowerment for Chinese women and disempowerment for Western men, I show that these dynamics depend on the men's and women's comparative class positions. For this reason, I treat financially flexible women and financially burdened women as separate groups even though we call both groups "Chinese marriage migrants." Despite their shared nationality and shared goal of marriage migration, their distinctly different financial positions give them dramatically different levels of power. Their divergent marital trajectories reveal that as wealth decenters across continents but becomes increasingly stratified within each nation, class becomes an increasingly significant marker of privilege over other factors, such as nationality or citizenship status.

Third, this work challenges readers to reflect on Euro-American, middle-class feminism and its applicability to non-Western women. While modernization theorists assumed that Chinese women would adopt a more Western-style, liberal outlook on gender as China's economy grew, in reality, thirty years of state socialism altered this trajectory. China's path to modernization is unorthodox in the sense that gender essentialism has actually revived alongside economic development. Subscribing to entre-preneurial C-feminism, many of my respondents rejected Western-style "egalitarian" marriages. Instead, they pursued a Chinese-style feminism that pushed women to abandon traditional virtues, such as submissiveness and self-sacrifice, while simultaneously capitalizing on their domestic skills and sexuality in order to profit from the marriage market. As previously discussed, this new strand of feminism emerged in postreform China as a response to the nation's newly gendered structure of power. By exploring how this Chinese-style feminism affected these women's relationships with their Western husbands, I highlight the process through which endogenous changes within China's local gender order take on a global presence and shape intimate relationships across borders.

The experience of China's email-order brides is not unique; it resem-bles that of marriage migrants from other postsocialist economies. Just as it did in China, the restoration of capitalism in Eastern Europe and the former Soviet Union led to the emergence of a new class of male business elites and "a sharp worsening in the social position of women."[54] At the same time, traditional gender ideologies are also reemerging as a pushback against the socialist past. Subsequently, women in these places employ a gender strategy similar to entrepreneurial C-feminism, where they are only interested in using their beauty and sexuality to date American men for free meals, gifts, and monetary gain, but have no intention of actually marry-ing and moving abroad.[55] Unlike the situation in the 1990s, today their de-sires to marry Western men have waned considerably as wealthy local elites emerged.[56] In fact, sociologist Julia Meszaros notes that the transnational dating agency she studied has canceled its American tour group to Russia, partly due to the women's lack of interest. The Russian experience confirms my assertion that, as wealth gaps between Western and non-Western coun-tries lessen, class becomes an increasingly significant marker of privilege over other factors, such as nationality or citizenship status.

Finally, this book challenges readers to reexamine the social role of businesses in societies undergoing transition. While people often question businesses for engaging in unethical practices, while excusing consumers from similar concerns, this book explores the reverse. I highlight the process through which the agency staff serve as crucial moral gatekeepers of their clients during the dating process. Why are Chinese businesses taking on the role of social moral regulation? I argue that they do so because China is going through a state of anomie[57] in which traditional morals, values, and ideologies have been upturned without a replacement system. Fueled by a culture of rampant materialism, many clients are pursuing dating strategies that undermine norms and values that support the institution of marriage. In societies undergoing rapid transition and experiencing subsequent moral chaos and dysfunction, meso-level institutions, such as dating agencies, are stepping up to police their clients. I argue that the agencies do so not only for the pragmatic purpose of maintaining profit, but also to fulfill their innate human desire to serve social justice.

METHODOLOGICAL APPROACH

This book draws from data I collected over a span of eleven years (2008–19), including nineteen months of on-site fieldwork in China, alongside additional research in the United States. After acquiring institutional review board (IRB) approval, I completed pilot research in China during the summers of 2008–10, and then embarked on a full year of fieldwork in 2011–12. After leaving China, I maintained contact with my respondents via email or online instant messaging to follow their marital status up to 2014 and beyond. From 2010 to 2019, I also traveled to different US states to visit women whom I initially met in China but who later married and migrated to the United States. Moreover, I revisited the agencies during the summers of 2017–19.

This book is based on my extensive observations and in-depth interviews with 61 female clients, 20 male clients, 30 translators, and 6 managers. I was also given access to the agencies' intranet, and some of my demographic data draw from this source. In addition, I conducted content analysis on 154 blog articles that the managers wrote. These articles describe how couples meet and marry, as well as the women's postmarital lives abroad. They serve as crucial promotional tools for the agencies to attract female clients.

Maintaining respondent confidentiality is of utmost importance to me, given the murky legal status of the industry. Officially, cross-border matchmaking is illegal in China due to the government's concerns about human trafficking.[58] To work around this, the agencies enlist themselves as cultural mediation companies rather than "matchmakers," and the government has therefore issued them official work permits. Nevertheless, the state could also claim they are matchmakers in disguise and shut them down at any time. Given this situation, I decided to use pseudonyms for the cities in this book.

Maintaining confidentiality mattered for the clients and translators as well. Some women wanted to keep their agency membership a secret from their ex-husbands, lovers, family, and friends, while some translators felt embarrassed to be working in the online dating industry and thus hid the nature of their jobs from their family and friends. Thus, I also used pseudonyms for my respondents.

Due to the highly private nature of my research topic, I did not recruit subjects by randomly selecting their names from a list and cold-calling them. Instead, I recruited some subjects after meeting them on-site. In addition, I sometimes volunteered to teach English to the female clients—a service normally provided by the translators—and I met some respondents this way. Others were selected through snowball sampling, meaning that some currently enrolled respondents helped me recruit more participants by referring their friends. Moreover, the staff sometimes stepped in to connect me with clients who did not visit the office regularly. One limitation of my sampling method is representativeness. For example, I later discovered that men and women who experienced relationship problems and wanted assistance were more likely than others to join my study.

Most interviews were informal and covered basic background questions as well as intimate questions about the men's and women's previous family life, why they sought a foreign spouse, the current state of their relationship, and their expectations about their future marriages. Examples of questions for the staff, which were tailored to my research interest, include: How do you view yourself as the moral regulator of the company, or how do you think joining this agency changed your view on gender and marriage? Rather than interviewing each subject only once, I conversed with them regularly, both in person and via phone or online instant messaging. Many clients who were involved in ongoing romantic relationships reached out to me frequently. When meeting in person, we engaged in various activities together, such as shopping, dining out, or taking leisure trips to nearby cities. Some clients even cooked for me in their own homes.

Again, due to the private nature of my research topic, I did not voice-record our conversations. Moreover, many conversations took place in shared spaces unsuitable for recording. For example, when I took a leisure trip to Hong Kong with a respondent, deep conversations emerged during our morning subway rides, over meals at noisy restaurants, and while lying in a shared hotel room together at night. Instead of recording, I jotted notes on my cellphone and wrote up a complete version from memory on the same day or the next day. My fieldnotes are written mostly in English, with key phrases noted in Chinese.

I also attended social gatherings, such as client engagement parties, weddings, group dinners, or karaoke nights. Some events were for clients only, while others included the staff as well. In addition, I visited the agencies a few times per week to observe client-staff, staff-staff, and client-client interactions on-site. When a Western man visited his prospective bride, I sometimes accompanied the couple and their translator, and sat as a fourth person at the dinner table. After leaving China in 2012, I maintained contact with my research subjects via email or online instant messaging and followed up on the marital status of all sixty-one female subjects up to 2014 or beyond. When I traveled to six different states to visit ten women whom I initially met in China but who later married and migrated to the United States, I typically lived in each woman's home for a week.

Engaging in follow-up interviews and participant observation was crucial to this study for several reasons. First, many respondents were reserved during the initial interview. For example, when asked why they sought Western husbands, many women cited only reasons they considered socially acceptable, such as their age disadvantage on the Chinese marriage market. Additional motives that involved more private aspects of their lives, such as the desire to get out of debt after a recent bankruptcy or the termination of a "mistress-paramour" relationship with a married lover in China, were more likely to surface later on, after we had spent a considerable amount of time together. Second, clients often cited multiple mate-selection criteria during the initial interviews, but it was difficult to assess which ones they prioritized until I witnessed their decision-making in real time. Finally, observing clients and staff in large group settings allowed me to see how they spoke to each other, thereby providing an additional perspective to my analysis.

MY BICULTURAL POSITIONALITY

I am a 1.5-generation Chinese immigrant, and also a Western-trained academic. My bicultural background gave me both insider and outsider advantages. My ethnicity and fluent Chinese-language skills enabled me to build excellent rapport with the women, who perceived me as a local who understood their perspective but could also provide them with valuable knowledge about life abroad, along with free translation services. Likewise, my American background helped me build rapport with the Western men. Moreover, many respondents saw me as an outsider to whom they could confide their secrets with no social consequence. Over time, I heard about issues such as extramarital liaisons, secret prenuptial agreements, sexless marriages, domestic abuse, and so on, some of which the respondents kept hidden from even their own translators, family members, and friends.

My respondents' willingness to confide certainly enabled me to collect deep data. However, serving as their go-to person for relationship advice was a major challenge, given my precarious position as a researcher. First, my access to the agencies could have been jeopardized if I accidentally divulged the couples' secrets to each other, as this could lead to breakups and subsequent loss of income for their translators. Moreover, I wanted to minimize my impact on client behavior in order to ensure data validity. Ethnographer Bruce Berg once stated that if researchers want their subjects to openly talk about their feelings and views, they must refrain from making negative judgments.[59] Similarly, sociologist Barbara Sherman Heyl suggests that researchers whose behavior is "supportive, cordial, interested, nonargumentative, courteous, understanding, and even sympathetic" will receive more information than those who act in the opposite fashion.[60] Keeping these considerations in mind, I adhered to three main principles while doing fieldwork: remain neutral, be nonjudgmental, and be supportive.

For me, being neutral meant answering client questions in a way that did not sway their decision-making. For example, when they asked me what I thought of American men or lifestyle, I often told respondents that it is difficult to generalize given America's size and diversity. When they asked me whether they should continue dating or break up with a particular partner, my strategy was to summarize the pros and cons of breaking up based on what they had previously told me. In essence, I repeated their own thoughts back to them.

In addition to being neutral, it was also important to remain nonjudgmental. Although some Chinese respondents may come across as money-grubbing and unethical from a Western view, I reminded myself to take a more culturally relativistic approach. My female respondents come from a society that recently underwent dramatic structural transformation. In contrast to the socialist era, when ownership of private property was banned, income gaps were small, and women participated in the formal labor market,[61] China's postreform era is marked by the sudden rise of a new rich capitalist class dominated by men and by a worsening of women's social position. Under these conditions, women understandably seek to cultivate and capitalize on their sexual attractiveness, including their femininity and their domestic skills, in exchange for men's money and power. In fact, their practices are part of a new strand of Chinese-style feminism.

At the agency, Ms. Fong often praised me for my cultural sensitivity. For example, she referenced a time when she reprimanded a female client for being overt with her materialistic demands. To her surprise, I commented, "You know, it's not a bad idea to be straightforward and speak your mind. Some Western women think along the same lines but just don't say it." My attitude stood in stark contrast to that of a foreign reporter who once visited her agency and asked her clients offensive questions, such as "Are you marrying for a green card?" or "Are you seeking a foreign husband because you are struggling to survive in China?"

Nevertheless, remaining nonjudgmental was not always easy. Admittedly there were moments when I felt my own tolerance being tested. The following scene, drawn from my fieldnotes, provides one such instance. The conversation takes place between Vivien, a Chinese woman, and her American fiancé, John, who was visiting her in Tunyang. Although Vivien accepted thousands of dollars from John, she refused intimate contact with him and simultaneously engaged in a secret affair with a married Chinese man named Kuan.

Vivien, John, and I are chatting while sitting in the outdoor patio of Beer Haven, a Western-style pub. Vivien tells me that she is extremely bothered by John's presence. She exclaims in Chinese, "Ahhhh, why does he have to be here right now! Why can't he just disappear?! If only he were not here, I would be out with Kuan. Kuan calls me every single day, many times a day. Oh, how I wish Kuan was not married. Then I could just marry him! My friends say Kuan is strong and healthy and has lots of sexual energy. I'm so worried I will burst into flames of passion the next time I see him."

At the end of her speech, Vivien bursts out laughing. It is that same sweet, crisp, childlike laughter that many people, including myself, find charming and irresistible. John, who is sitting opposite us, has no idea what we are discussing. He only hears her laughter and starts smiling. Turning around, he says to me, "Oh, I just love that laugh, and I love seeing her happy. It makes my day; her laugh just cracks me up."

Despite my sympathy for John at that moment, I resisted the urge to disclose Vivien's affair, and I continued acting as Vivien's good friend and confidante.

Finally, I tried to assist my respondents in the small ways that I could. For example, I provided free translation for couples during their courtship in China. After they moved abroad, I helped some women without health insurance find medical centers for low-income residents. Moreover, I frequently chatted with them and sometimes visited their homes, which many of them appreciated, particularly during moments of depression and loneliness.

Over the years, I have witnessed my respondents leave behind their families and careers, sell homes, deplete their savings, or even attempt suicide. While it often felt like watching a soap opera, for them, it was the reality that they had to confront, day in and day out. By comparison, I felt extremely privileged. I was highly educated and had a promising career, while my youth shielded me from concerns of marital infidelity, divorce, or retirement planning. In my fieldnotes from 2008, I wrote: "I have only been here for two weeks, but I feel as if I have been here for a decade. The life I once lived in a land called the United States of America feels so far removed. The women here live such different lives and hold such different values. I suddenly realize I have so much going for me which some people here could never even dream of."

My research journey has been a humbling experience. Perhaps more so than any textbook, this experience has strengthened my understanding of the intricate ways that sociological forces shape human behavior. It is my hope that the stories and insights from this book will benefit readers. Moreover, I cherish the deep friendships I built with my respondents, many of whom I am still in touch with to this day.

ORGANIZATION OF THE BOOK

This book explores how transformations in political economy reshape transnational marriage migration and the global internet dating industry. While most previous scholars examined the lives of marriage migrants either before or after they moved, I follow the same subjects from their communities of origin to their receiving countries over a span of eleven years. Examining both their pre- and postmigration experiences allows me to track how their power and agency shift throughout various phases of courtship and marriage, and this in turn allows me to assess whether such marriages ultimately empower migrant women.

My female respondents include multimillionaire entrepreneurs, ex-wives and mistresses of rich businessmen, as well as contingent-sector workers and struggling single mothers. In chapter 1, I explore their different motives in seeking Western husbands. I discuss how China's revival of traditional gender ideology emphasizing feminine youth displaced women across all class sectors on their local marriage markets. Moreover, I discuss how age discrimination subjects working-class women to additional disadvantages on the labor market, exacerbating their desire to leave China. In summary, this chapter explores the disempowering effect of globalization on middle-aged Chinese women and chronicles how it motivated them to seek marriage migration. By examining their motives for seeking cross-border marriage, this chapter sheds light on various social problems in contemporary China, such as rising rates of divorce, soaring costs of higher education, or a strained social security system.

The dating agencies in my study portray Western men as devoted, family-oriented, and hence marriage-worthy despite their lack of wealth. This image appeals to both the financially flexible women, whose nouveau riche ex-husbands divorced them for younger women, as well as the financially burdened women, whose ex-husbands lost their jobs in the postreform era and ended up drinking, gambling, and shirking familial responsibilities. While many female clients initially joined the agencies with idealized images of Western men in mind, I explore their actual marital decision-making patterns after they meet the men face to face. Chapters 2 and 3 focus exclusively on women who are financially flexible. My results show that these women rarely found their Western suitors to be desirable enough to marry, in spite of their geopolitical status as white men from the Global North, and despite being caring "family men."

In particular, chapter 2 highlights the women's desire for men who practice "provider love," or love expressed through men's provision of material goods. Coming from a society where masculinity is tied to breadwinning, particularly among the middle and upper classes, many financially flexible women lost interest in their Western suitors after seeing their "gender egalitarian" spending styles. While equal sharing of fiscal responsibility between heterosexual men and women is associated with progressiveness and modernity in the West, my respondents viewed men who embrace this doctrine as effeminate and undesirable. Rejecting Western masculinity in its existing form, my respondents sought a new, hybrid masculine ideal that combines traits from the Western family man and the wealthy Chinese entrepreneur. This chapter reveals that, contrary to the assumption of some gender scholars, Western masculinity practices do not always have a strong global influence.

Chapter 3 examines relationship conflicts that emerge from a disconnect between the Chinese women's sexual desires and their Western suitors' socioeconomic status. Specifically, many financially flexible women found their suitors sexually unappealing because those men did not embody the elite masculine traits that are characteristic of men in positions of leadership and power. I chronicle the process through which these women pursued wealthy Chinese businessmen, even if some of those men were married and unavailable, while they simultaneously rejected average-earning, unmarried Western suitors as well as average-earning, unmarried local Chinese pursuers because those men lacked the mannerisms, lifestyles, and sexual know-how of their rich local lovers. Examples from this chapter show that men who do not exhibit traits of elite masculinity are deemed unsexy and get rejected regardless of their race, ethnicity, and nationality, thereby illuminating the increasing significance of class distinction and the declining significance of race, ethnicity, and nationality as an affluent capitalist class emerges in both Western and non-Western countries.

Chapters 4 and 5 focus on the postmarital lives of the financially burdened women, who were much less choosy and who married Western men at significantly higher rates than the financially flexible women. In both chapters, I challenge the Eurocentric, middle-class feminist assumption that marriages built on a "traditional" domestic/public division of labor lead to less satisfaction than ones where women participate in the paid labor force.

Chapter 4 explores the lives of brides who became homemakers and relied on their husbands for financial support. My results show that their exchange of conventional femininity for material gain did not automatically preclude them from having a satisfying marriage. As readers will see, it is not the separation of spheres—the hallmark ideology behind patriarchal bargains—that makes or breaks these marriages, but rather the specific terms and conditions of the bargain. To have a functioning bargain, both parties must view their costs and rewards as equitable and worthy of pursuing. Nevertheless, I also argue that we must not discredit the Western feminist critique of gendered patriarchal bargains in its entirety. When we consider women as a *group* rather than as *individuals*, patriarchal bargains still put women at a structural disadvantage. My examples show that, for a subset of unlucky brides who end up in conflict-ridden marriages for reasons beyond their control, their financial dependence on their husbands rendered them powerless to fight back.

While chapter 4 focuses on the lives of homemakers, chapter 5 examines brides who chose to work outside the home. Comparing their postmarital lives to those of the homemakers, I did not see a major divide in marital happiness and perceived agency based on whether the wives worked. This finding again challenges the Western-centric assumption that women who work for pay experience greater marital satisfaction than those who stay at home. Interestingly, I show that the women's ability to work outside the home often opened more avenues over which the couple's differing gender ideologies could prove problematic in these transnational relationships. Identifying with a new strand of Chinese-style feminism called entrepreneurial C-feminism, many of my respondents expected to keep any earnings as their private money, while their Western husbands demanded that they chip in on household expenses. By exploring the role of entrepreneurial C-feminism in shaping these women's tumultuous relationships with their husbands, I highlight how endogenous changes within China's local gender order impact new marriages formed in the West.

After discussing the impact of China's economic reform on marriage migrants, I end this book by examining its effect on the global dating industry. Specifically, chapter 6 explores the livelihoods of the industry staff, the majority of whom are rural-to-urban migrants, highlighting the challenges and rewards of their job. I begin by discussing the various forms of insecurity that the translators face, including the precarious legality of their industry, their reliance on their clients' marital success for profit, and their own disadvantaged position as rural migrants working in urban centers. I proceed to analyze how these competing interests incentivize them to police the morality of their clients. Moreover, I identify the complexities of their work as emotional labor that is driven not only by profit but also by their moral and personal investment in their clients' relationships. This chapter sheds light on the struggle translators face in balancing their profit-making goals with their conscience while living through a chaotic period of social transition in China, when many traditional norms, regulations, and morals have been upturned. Moving beyond their struggles, I end this chapter by examining the rewards that they reap from working in this industry, particularly their new opportunities for upward mobility.

This book strives to unite the personal with the cultural and socioeconomic. I take seriously the concerns of my respondents and the gravity of the decisions they were making about love and marriage. Many of these women became my friends, and I analyzed their cases through an intersectional lens, viewing them as individuals and also as products of the historical and cultural factors that shaped them. Yet I also wanted to put their stories—whispered in shared beds, in the confines of their homes, in a language their partners didn't understand—into a larger global context. I hope readers will balance the endearing, fraught, and complicated relationships described with the bigger picture of gender relations and economic aspirations that bring Chinese women and Western men together time and time again.

1 | WHY DO CHINESE WOMEN SEEK WESTERN MEN?

I HAD ONLY BEEN IN Tunyang for a few weeks by that hot, humid day in July 2008, just beginning pilot research on this project, when a vivacious woman at Ms. Mei's agency again caught my eye. I had noticed her before, as she often came in during the afternoons and stayed for hours on end, chatting with the staff and other clients. A voluptuous woman in her mid-forties, she wore glittery, form-fitting tops that looked Japanese or Korean in style, and her shoulder-length hair was loosely permed and streaked with fashionable honey-colored highlights. Whenever she walked by, I picked up the faint scent of Chanel perfume. I couldn't imagine what she did for a living, until one translator whispered to me, "That's Ruby. She's a rich lady who doesn't need to work and comes here to kill time." Ruby had been divorced for several years and received generous alimony from her ex-husband, a nouveau-riche Chinese businessman. She spent leisurely days at the beauty parlor, managed her stocks online, and cooked for her twenty-something daughter, who still lived at home.

Contrary to the stereotypical Western media image of a so-called mail-order bride as young and never married, the majority of my respondents were, like Ruby, middle-aged (over forty) and divorced. Financially, they fell into two major groups: those who are financially well-off, and those who are financially struggling. Ruby is one of several women we'll meet in this chapter whose personal story falls into the former category.

Let's compare Ruby's story to that of Daisy, another divorced female client in her forties. With gleaming round eyes, raven-colored hair, and red lips, Daisy was considered very attractive by local standards. In contrast to Ruby, who retired on her ex-husband's wealth, Daisy worked as a department store salesclerk and struggled to make ends meet. While Ruby lived in a marble-lined, two-story home with the latest amenities, Daisy lived on the seventh floor of an old concrete building with no elevator, no bathroom sink, and no flushing toilet (she used a squatting toilet that she flushed with giant buckets of water). Her living room was filled with furniture from the 1980s, cardboard boxes stacked up to the ceiling, and a small CRT television. By the time I met Daisy, she had been divorced from her Chinese ex-husband for years. Despite this, they still shared an apartment because he had been jobless since the 1990s as his industry became increasingly competitive in China's postreform era.

Interestingly, both Daisy and Ruby started life on similar economic grounds. Neither attended college, and both worked as clerks at state-owned factories in the 1980s, earning roughly US$10.00 per month. However, Ruby later quit her state job and achieved financial success in the private sector, while her husband became a multimillionaire entrepreneur. Like Ruby, Daisy also dabbled in business, after she got laid off from her factory job during the 1990s, but the business failed, and she went on to struggle in the contingent employment sector. (The "contingent employment sector" refers to contractual or temporary jobs that do not provide employees with medical insurance, retirement, or other social benefits.)

Ruby's and Daisy's divergent life paths illustrate China's dramatic structural transformation over the past few decades, from a relatively egalitarian socialist state into one of the most unequal countries in the world.[1] While both Ruby and Daisy earned around US$10.00 per month back in the 1980s, today Ruby has become far wealthier than most of the Western male clients at the dating agency she's enrolled in, while Daisy has much less financial power than her Western suitors. Given this new disparity in women's economic power, in light of China's fiercely rapid but greatly uneven development, class stratification serves as a primary point of analysis. Drawing on the life histories of sixty-one Chinese female clients, we will see how their vastly different social positions and access to economic resources shape their divergent marital aspirations and mate-selection strategies.

This comparative, class-based approach to analyzing marriage migration challenges readers to think beyond the confinement of national boundaries, as wealth decenters across continents but becomes increasingly polarized within each nation. Today, Western countries are no longer the world's sole epicenter of wealth and modernity. The global integration of financial markets has led to the emergence of an affluent capitalist class in both Western and non-Western countries.[2] At the same time, increasing wealth polarization within countries has led to the emergence of haves and have-nots in every nation. Thus, moving away from a binary construction of the rich West and poor Global South, geographer David Harvey urges us to reenvision the world system as one defined not only by nationality but also by access to wealth.[3]

Take immigration, for example. Today, those who migrate to the West via immigrant investor programs are often far wealthier than most local citizens in their receiving countries.[4] In fact, public concern for this group centers not on their financial well-being, as they already stand at the top of the global economic hierarchy, but rather on the social problems they create for local Westerners, who often get priced out of their local real estate market as a result.[5] Still, poor, undocumented workers who leave their homeland in pursuit of a better financial future also constitute a portion of the immigrant population.[6]

Likewise, in the context of marriage migration, the "mail-order bride" label gives us little information about these women's motives and aspirations. Hence, I shift our discussion away from commonly asked questions such as, "Are marriage migrants poverty-stricken victims who marry Western men for a green card?" In light of a new global economic order, I no longer envision these migrant women as one uniform entity, but instead treat "wealthy migrants" and "poor migrants" as separate social groups, whose distinctly different positions within the global economic hierarchy give them dramatically different levels of power and agency.

DIVERGENT TRAJECTORIES OF CHINESE EMAIL-ORDER BRIDES
Between 2008 and 2014, I interviewed and observed 61 female clients. Among them, 52 were divorced and 50 were above the age of forty. Altogether, there were 1,740 female clients enrolled across the three agencies I studied, and just like the women in this sample, the majority of them were

middle-aged (over forty) and divorced.[7] To analyze how economic disparities affected their motives in seeking marriage migration, I divided my 61
respondents into two main groups based on their class position in China.

The first group consists of 30 women I describe as "financially flexible"
because they have access to medical insurance and guaranteed retirement
funds in China; they are not burdened by the costs of child-rearing; and
they are not in debt. Hence, their primary motive in seeking Western men
is not rooted in a desire to resolve an imminent financial problem. The remaining 31 women fall into what I call the "financially burdened" group because they all view marriage migration as a path toward financial freedom.
This group includes working-class women in the contingent employment
sector who seek access to better social services as they approach retirement
age in China. The group also includes women who may or may not be in
the contingent employment sector, but who have other imminent financial
needs due to circumstances, such as debt incurred from business failure
or a desire to send their children abroad for college but a lack of financial
resources to do so. Drawing on my interviews with the 61 women, I found
five primary reasons cited for seeking Western husbands. Here I list them
in order of frequency, beginning with the most cited:

- Difficulty finding a suitable partner in China due to older age
- Concern over Chinese men's infidelity
- Belief that Western men are more fiscally responsible than Chinese
  men
- Desire for access to better social services in the West
- Desire for children from previous marriages to study overseas

Note that these reasons are not mutually exclusive, and most women stated
more than one reason. In table 2, I compare the financially flexible vs. financially burdened women by their self-reported motives for seeking Western
men.

Among women in both groups, concern about age was the most frequently mentioned reason for seeking Western husbands. It was the only
factor cited at similar rates by both groups. For the financially flexible
women, remarriage can be challenging because Chinese men tend to seek
second marriages with women significantly younger than themselves. For

TABLE 2. Female clients' self-reported motives for seeking Western men. *Source:* Author created.

	Financially Flexible (30 women)	Financially Burdened (31 women)
Difficulty finding a suitable Chinese partner due to older age*	69% (18/26 women)	60% (18/30 women)
Concern over Chinese men's infidelity	53%	35%
Belief that Western men are more fiscally responsible	20%	45%
Desire for better social services in the West	10%	48%
Desire for Chinese children from previous marriages to study or immigrate overseas**	11% (2/18 women)	43% (13/30 women)

*This category applies only to women above age 30.
**This category applies only to women with children.

example, Ruby said, "I decided to pursue cross-border marriage because it was hard for me to find a good match in China. Here, rich men want a young girl who is eighteen or twenty to show off." Similarly, the financially burdened women also experienced an age-related "marriage squeeze." Tess, a divorced salesclerk in her mid-forties, expressed what many working-class clients feel: "In China, older women are left with few options because middle-aged men are so picky. All the ones who are financially well-off or even just financially stable want young, never-married women. If they cannot get someone young, at the very least, they want someone without children from a previous marriage to ease their financial burden."

This middle-aged marriage squeeze is not unique to China. In fact, it is commonly observed across many cultures and societies. In the United States, one in five men who remarry will wed a woman at least ten years younger than themselves.[8] Nevertheless, this phenomenon appears to be more pronounced in postreform China, where women are considered past their prime for marriage and therefore "left over," as early as age twenty-seven.[9] Moreover, it has become increasingly difficult for young Chinese men to out-earn women of their own age, given China's decreasing male–

female education gap.[10] Consequently, many young, never-married women who want a breadwinner husband now seek men significantly older than themselves, which makes the marriage market even more competitive for older, divorced women.[11]

Beyond shared concern over their older age, the two groups of women seem to diverge substantially in their other self-reported motives for seeking Western men. For example, the financially flexible women were more likely to cite Chinese men's infidelity, while the financially burdened women were more likely to cite Chinese men's lack of fiscal responsibility. Moreover, the financially burdened women were significantly more likely to cite reasons irrelevant to the conjugal relationship itself, such as desire for children from previous marriages to study overseas and access to better social services in the West. Clearly, *differences* in these women's socioeconomic background and personal life—brought on by sociostructural transformations during China's postreform era—contributed to their *divergent* motives for marriage migration, and thus are worth exploring in detail.

FINANCIALLY FLEXIBLE WOMEN
The Rich Ladies

Among the 61 women I interviewed, 6 had a net worth between US$300,000 and US$1 million or more, making them wealthy by both local and global standards.[12] Some relied solely on large divorce settlements, while others were also successful in their own careers. To explore how these women's privileged social positions in China shaped their marital aspirations, I begin with more of Ruby's story.

Through six face-to-face meetups over afternoon tea and dinner during the summers of 2008 and 2009, I learned more about Ruby's life and why she chose to date Larry, a modest-earning American factory technician. Born in the 1960s, Ruby grew up in an average-earning urban Chinese family. After graduating from high school, she started working at a state-owned factory and remained there until the early 1990s, when she left that job for a lucrative marketing position at a semi-privatized state company. She began traveling to various cities for business, and she was handsomely compensated with a much higher bonus than that of her peers at the old factory. Moreover, Ruby used her business connections to help her then-husband establish his own private company, which later expanded into a multimillion-dollar business. Although they both achieved great financial success during the reform era, it came at a cost. Ruby's frequent business travels took her away from home, and her husband started having affairs. Once Ruby realized that her marriage was in shambles, she quit her job and returned home to salvage the relationship. However, her husband refused to end his affairs and said, "Men are like teapots; each teapot should be matched with multiple teacups." They ended up getting divorced.

Ruby associates her husband's behavior with China's economic reform. On one breezy summer evening around dusk, as we walked out of Ms. Mei's office together and took a stroll toward Ruby's car, she said to me, "Little Liu [a common way to address a younger acquaintance in China], you are simply too young to understand what women like me have gone through!" She proceeded to explain how China's new entrepreneurial class got rich too quickly and too suddenly, while their *suzhi* (inner qualities) lagged behind. The men began cheating while married and showed off their youthful paramours to their friends. Ruby says her ex-husband was one of those nouveau-riche men who achieved extraordinary financial success but lost his family life. She also blames his behavior on the postreform revival of China's pre-1950s gender practices, such as mistress-keeping. Before our parting, under a skybridge, Ruby looked into the setting sun, gave a deep sigh, and said, "You see, it's old, ugly, and shameful . . . it is almost as if China never went through the socialist revolution."

Ruby's experience reflects China's shifting gender landscape. In contrast to the socialist era, when women were encouraged to seek employment outside the household and to compete in traditionally male-dominated fields, in postreform China, femininity is increasingly associated with domesticity and youth, while masculinity is centered on financial success.[13] Today, the ideal male is an entrepreneur whose financial success entitles him to attractive young women.[14] These shifting ideologies are rooted in sociostructural changes, in particular, the emergence of a new capitalist class dominated by men.

Today, male business elites are reputed for their consumption of female youth and sexuality as part of their business socializing.[15] At the same time, in light of rising labor market competition, increasing gender discrimination in the workplace, and booming desires for mass consumption, many young women now view their bodies as valuable commodities to be exchanged for income and security, reflecting a return to antiquated conceptions of gender that can leave women vulnerable.[16] Moreover, extramarital affairs and divorces are also becoming more socially acceptable, as the state loosens its grip over people's private lives and no longer requires divorces to be approved by state-owned work units. As a result, divorce rates in urban China rose from 2 percent in 1970 to 27 percent in 2013.[17] Among the new rich, divorce rates are even higher,[18] and extramarital affairs are cited as a major reason behind divorce.[19] These economic and cultural changes have left many middle-aged women like Ruby abandoned by their nouveau-riche husbands.

Ruby stayed single for many years following her divorce. She received a generous alimony, and her child was set to inherit the family business. Although she was financially well-off, looking back at her years of singlehood, she said she felt "heartache" for having missed sex between the ages of thirty-five and forty-five, the period in which, she believed, women had "the strongest physical desire." Ruby was also lonely. She said the final trigger motivating her to seek remarriage came after she experienced a severe physical injury. Lying in the hospital bed, she realized how much she wanted a partner by her side.

Ruby distinguished herself from many other female clients who were hoping to improve their material conditions through marriage. One afternoon in summer 2009, as we drank fruit tea and munched on pumpkin fries cooked in Chinese peppercorn at a local eatery, she commented, "There are two types of women at the agency. One type is struggling financially. They just want to improve their material conditions. But for women like me who are well-off, we are looking to satisfy emotional needs." While Ruby was not seeking to improve her material conditions, I observed that financial concerns still played a central role in her search for a new husband. Although most local men of her age and economic standing opted for younger women, Ruby had a substantial number of less well-off pursuers, including men in their thirties and even twenties. Yet, when I asked her why she never dated any of them, she shook her head and lamented:

If I date someone less well-off than myself, I would not be able to tell if he was going after my money. In China, a lot of average-earning men start dates with questions such as: "How many kids do you have? Do you still support your children financially? Do you have a job and a house?" I do not want someone who is going to trick me for my money. You see, if I correspond with a foreign man online, it would be much harder for him to discover my real background.

Ruby's dilemma in China is typical among the six wealthy women I interviewed. They wanted to date Chinese men of similar socioeconomic standing, but those men typically reject them because of their older age. While they have many opportunities to date lesser-earning men, they reject those men for various reasons, including lack of trust. Grace, a wealthy, divorced actress in her mid-forties, found herself in a similar predicament. When I first spotted Grace at Mr. Li's agency in spring 2011, I could immediately tell that she came from a privileged background. Slim and fit, she wore a white Lacoste tennis dress, used the latest iPhone, and spoke perfect Mandarin with no regional accent, which is a linguistic status marker in China. Grace wanted to date Chinese men with a minimum annual salary of US$18,000, which was a middle-class income by local standards but still significantly less than the US$45,000 she received each year from her wealthy ex-husband in child support alone. After joining a local dating agency, she was disappointed to find that Chinese men of this income level were primarily interested in women in their twenties. Nevertheless, Grace still had many suitors.

When I met Grace in May 2012, she spoke with three different Chinese men on a daily basis. The first man was a thirty-two-year-old security guard who worked at the gated community she lived in. Grace believed he lusted for her money after he saw her in her white Mercedes. He called her incessantly and boasted in defense, "I am not after you for your money. My parents own several apartments in the city, too." Grace shook her head, laughed, and said to me, "I cannot accept this kind of romance. It's a joke." The second man was a tall, handsome teacher in his late forties. Grace appreciated his good looks and dated him despite his significantly lower income relative to hers, only to break up with him when she saw him pick up phone calls from other, younger women. Finally, there was a nouveau-riche real estate developer, whose socioeconomic status matched well with hers, but she found him physically repulsive: he had dark, dirty nails and made lots of noise when he ate. Despite having options, Grace remained unsatisfied with the Chinese dating scene available to her.

As of 2014, two of the six wealthy women remained single and in China; of the other four, one married a British businessman of similar economic standing to herself, while three married "up" geopolitically by moving to a more developed country but "down" in terms of socioeconomic class.[20] For example, Ruby drove a Lexus and wore a Burberry coat in China, while Larry, the American factory technician she married, drove a pickup truck and bought his clothes at Walmart. Similarly, Barbara, a divorced entrepreneur in her fifties who married an American construction manager, left her posh Chinese condo in the heart of downtown to motel-hop in rural America with her husband, who moved to a different construction site every few months.

On the whole, the wealthy clients in my study did not pursue marriage migration to achieve upward economic mobility. Although these women come from China, which is considered a developing country based on its GDP per capita, they occupy the upper echelon of the global economic hierarchy. Hence, they understand that achieving upward mobility through marriage may not be a realistic or meaningful goal. While Western men's earning capacity still mattered to them, it did so more in the context of achieving a status match or asset protection.

The Middle-Class Professionals

While 6 out of the 30 financially flexible clients were wealthy, 20 were middle-class by local standards. These are working professionals who earn well above the average salary in their cities. Like the wealthy women, many middle-income professionals sought Western men because their Chinese ex-husbands and lovers cheated on them. However, unlike the wealthy clients, many of whom are retired, like Ruby, or working out of personal interest rather than financial necessity, the middle-class clients must continue working to maintain their lifestyle. Moreover, they do not have the same flexibility to relocate because their job skills are typically not globally transferrable, and they do not have the capital to invest in businesses abroad to create an alternate income stream. Thus, these middle-class clients tend to view immigration as a significant sacrifice made in order to be with the right partner. The case of Vivien further illustrates this point.

When I first met Vivien, at her engagement party to an American man named John in spring 2011, she struck me as a confident woman who spoke and moved with an engaging and sultry style. While not strikingly beautiful by conventional Chinese standards, she possessed a warm, open, inviting face and she laughed easily, wordlessly conveying emotion. Her prompt responses and brisk movements made clear that she was a polished professional with excellent interpersonal skills. In fact, socializing was part of her job as a marketing and public relations specialist at a large state-owned enterprise in China. Divorced and childless in her thirties, she was eager to marry and start a family. After experiencing several failed relationships with affluent Chinese men, she turned to Western men.

Vivien's first marriage ended when her then-husband developed a new career in business and started seeing other women. "He brought home STDs [sexually transmitted diseases]," she recalled. Her warm brown eyes suddenly turned ice cold as she continued: "I ended up at the hospital all the time. I knew I was clean, so I confronted him." Nevertheless, it was not her ex-husband's infidelity that motivated her to seek Western men, but rather her experiences with Qin, a handsome Chinese media mogul. Vivien liked Qin not only for his good looks and successful career, but also because he was cultured and charismatic. "He was an amateur calligrapher and spoke fluent English. He was always calm and knew how to handle my temper," Vivien shared.

Throughout the two years they dated, Vivien never knew Qin was married because he owned multiple homes and never lived with his wife. Eventually, when one of Qin's coworkers broke the news to her, she hired a private detective to investigate his personal life. She discovered that his true love was in fact not his wife but rather his ex-girlfriend, an actress who left him because she could not tolerate his wandering eye. When Vivien finally confronted Qin about his married status, he blocked her online and changed his phone number. "He disappeared from my life, just like that," said Vivien, "and left me with insurmountable pain . . . so I joined the agency out of impulse, because I wanted to show Qin that I could live better, be better off without him. You see, he looked down on me because, unlike him and his ex-girlfriend, I don't speak English. I wanted to make him regret not marrying me, by moving to the United States."

Beyond just her desire to upset Qin, on a deeper level, Vivien wanted to leave China because she had become highly distrustful of local men. At work, Vivien acted as a liaison between the government and businesses. Since entrepreneurs in China rely on the state for business opportunities, they intertwine closely with government officials.[21] Vivien's friend Robyn told me that many businessmen pursued Vivien partly because they wanted to use her connections with the government. Following her divorce, Vivien engaged in romantic relations with several wealthy businessmen, including Qin, who ultimately refused to marry her and left her brokenhearted. Right around the time she broke up with Qin, a friend introduced Vivien to the overseas dating agency. Vivien wrote the following statement on her membership registration form, reflecting her disappointment with Chinese men:

> China went through dramatic reform and opening up under Deng Xiao-Ping's leadership. China developed at an unprecedented pace in every sector, including the economic, educational, medical, and construction sectors. Alongside these economic changes, people also have increased desires. People's private desire—their sexual desire in particular—is growing out of control. Today, Chinese men like to have many women outside of marriage. This trend is particular to China's current phase of transition. There is nothing I can do to change it. Thus, I give up on Chinese men and take my search for true love to a global level.

Although Vivien did not own multiple homes or a car like the six wealthy clients, her salary still allowed her to dine out in trendy restaurants and to purchase designer cosmetics. Moreover, employment with her company was highly sought after by many Chinese locals for the numerous perks it offered, such as full medical reimbursement and mortgage assistance. For these reasons, Vivien viewed migration as a risky financial move. Vivien's perception of China was colored by her experience socializing with local government officials and businessmen, who took her to luxurious venues. One time, while we were enjoying a fine steak dinner together at an upscale Belgian restaurant in Tunyang, I casually mentioned that the United States offered a higher quality of life than China. Vivien immediately refuted me: "China has so many rich people and the hottest bars and nightclubs in the world! I cannot imagine what the United States could possibly offer that China could not. The only problem with China is that the men are womanizers."

Never having traveled outside of China, Vivien was actually worried that moving abroad would lead to a lifestyle downgrade for her. Throughout our meetups in the summer of 2011, Vivien frequently asked me if her American boyfriend's US$80,000 annual salary in Cleveland would be sufficient to support the standard of living she was used to. "I don't need a Louis Vuitton handbag," said Vivien, "but I am wearing a US$276 Satchi handbag and I own many purses and shoes that I have worn only once. John needs to show that he can support my lifestyle."

One evening in August 2011, I sat alongside Vivien and her translator for four hours and watched their online videoconferencing session with John. Vivien had compiled a long list of potential household expenses, such as gas, food, internet, rent, medical insurance, and so on, and she asked her translator to inquire of John the cost of each item, because she worried that his remaining salary would be insufficient to cover her personal expenses if she left China. She was even concerned about the prospect of wearing "grandmother-style" underwear, after she heard stories from other female clients who moved to remote, rural parts of the United States and found they had to shop at Walmart.

Clearly, Vivien valued her career and lifestyle in China. She considered giving it up only because she could not meet a suitable marital partner locally. Her experience shows how and why some women view migration as a potential sacrifice made in order to have a committed family. Her attitude was quite typical among the middle-income professionals I interviewed. In fact, a few women even preferred that their men relocate to China. For example, Lucy, a divorced magazine editor, distinguished herself from clients in other occupations, such as domestic work. Lucy believed they sought cross-border marriages to avoid working because their jobs were so undesirable. Looking into my face with her large, sparkling eyes, she said, "Those women feel they have worked so hard for so long, they just want to be supported by their husbands so they can live an easy life. I'm the opposite . . . I love my job and I think it is awkward, embarrassing, and ultimately risky to rely on someone else." Lucy's words reveal her privileged-class position as an editor, which gave her much higher status, autonomy, and compensation than the domestic workers. Thus, Lucy viewed quitting her job as a loss rather than a boon.

Rich Men's Mistresses

While many of my interviewees who earn a "middle income" were working professionals, such as Vivien and Lucy, a few were "kept mistresses." In China, "mistresses" refers to women involved in relationships with married men whom they rely on financially.[22] Mistress-keeping can be traced back to China's history of concubinage, which was outlawed in 1950 but reemerged in the postreform era as an informal practice,[23] particularly among business and political elites. At the agency, mistresses account for a significant subset of female clients. In fact, one translator told me that around 20–30 percent of his clients have once been involved in such an arrangement. These women seek marriage migration as an exit option as they age and see no hope of marrying their Chinese lovers. Jennifer, a divorced, childless woman in her forties, serves as an example.

Before meeting Jennifer at another client's engagement party in May 2011, my knowledge of kept mistresses came from the popular media. Contrary to my imagination of a mistress as a carefully made-up woman dressed in the latest fashion, Jennifer showed up in a white T-shirt, khakis, and sneakers. She wore no makeup, and her shoulder-length black hair was tied back in a simple ponytail. Her features were rather plain, just like her style of dress. Throughout dinner, Jennifer ate quietly in a corner, and I barely noticed her. We did not start talking until we both set out to walk home, as it turned out she lived only a few blocks away from me. Soon, Jennifer latched onto my arm as if we were old friends and started speaking to me in her deep, expressive voice. What stood out to me most about this woman was not her physical attributes but rather her pleasant, amiable personality.

Jennifer was surprisingly open about her personal life. Although we had only met minutes ago, she already started telling me about her involvement with a Chinese businessman, whom she had been seeing for the past twelve years. Despite his denial, she suspected that he was married, as he resided in the United States with another woman and their children for part of the year but traveled to China regularly for work. Eagerly pulling out her iPhone and showing me a photo of a distinguished-looking, middle-aged man dressed in a business suit, she said, "See how handsome my *lao gong* [euphemism for husband] is?" Our friendship seemed immediate, and I was invited for tea at her place a few evenings later.

Jennifer's apartment complex was located on Hundred Flowers Street, a long, narrow road leading to the downtown area. Many massage parlors, shops, and restaurants lined the street. My aunt told me that, many years ago, before all the malls and skyscrapers were built in the city, this street was once the go-to spot for high-end clothing. Aside from the shops and restaurants, there were also a number of government agencies and institutions, including a film production company, a foreign language school, a police department, and so on. Covered in shade by tall trees on both sides, the street gave a sense of peace and seclusion to pedestrians. At the same time, it was only a short walk from the biggest shopping centers and hottest nightclubs in town. Hence, although the area appeared somewhat rundown and unkempt, it was still one of the most expensive and most highly sought-after neighborhoods in Tunyang.

Jennifer's studio apartment was more luxurious than the average Chinese residence and one of the most beautiful client homes I had seen thus far. Her giant flat-screen television, piano, and treadmill all looked brand new, while the incandescent lighting inside gave the entire place a warm, sensuous feel. This stood in striking contrast to the pale coolness of the energy-saving fluorescent bulbs that most Chinese households used. "I use only incandescent lighting because I like the mood it gives off," said Jennifer. She made some herbal tea for me, served in beautiful china cups decorated with fuchsia-colored peonies and gold rims, and asked me whether I wanted dumplings or a sandwich for my evening snack. I was surprised to learn that every morning Jennifer made herself a sandwich of Spam, egg, mayonnaise, and bread, alongside a cup of coffee. Later, I found out that this Western influence came from her *lao gong*.

Born in the early 1970s, Jennifer was raised in a working-class family. Growing up under financial strain certainly affected her life trajectory; she started working full-time as a clerk at a state-owned enterprise (SOE) right out of middle school. When Jennifer got laid off in the 1990s, she decided to be a homemaker because her then-husband earned enough money to support her. However, like many businessmen of the early reform era, he eventually had an extramarital affair, and they divorced. Soon after, Jennifer met a much wealthier but married man and became his kept mistress. Looking back at that period of her life, Jennifer said, "Every day I visited high-end spas, swam at the most expensive hotels in town, and spent thousands of dollars on clothes. I ate out all the time, never cooked, and played cards with a bunch of girlfriends."

It was not until several years later, after they broke up, that Jennifer, then twenty-eight, met her current *lao gong*. Although he only saw Jennifer several times a year, he helped her purchase her condo and sent her a stipend that was equivalent to the salary of a white-collar professional in her city. Jennifer's lifestyle stood in stark contrast to many of her former colleagues, who also got laid off and later took on much less desirable, lower-paying jobs in the informal sector, such as milk delivery or door-to-door telemarketing. One afternoon, as we hung out in her home and tried out the new Lancôme makeup kit that her *lao gong* had bought for her, Jennifer said, "I really appreciate the men who supported me all these years so I never had to go out and suffer. I never had to get up early and walk to work in the rainy winter or sweltering summer." Sometimes she jokingly called herself a "lazy parasite." Candidly, she added, "I don't have the pedigree to make big money, but I want to live the high-end lifestyle. It is part of China today, you know. Everybody is *xiang qian kan* [putting money first]."

Unlike Ruby, Vivien, or Lucy, Jennifer had no marketable job skills and only a modest divorce settlement. Hence, she relied solely on her "erotic capital" to sustain her lifestyle. Defined as a form of personal asset that makes people attractive to others, especially to the opposite sex, erotic capital encompasses not only facial beauty or bodily sex appeal, but also liveliness, social presentation, and sexual competence.[24] In Jennifer's case, she excelled in both liveliness and sexual competence. A talented singer, Jennifer took voice lessons at a local music conservatory and even won several national contests. At bars and nightclubs, she always attracted admirers with her magnetic voice, while her outstanding sexual ability further cemented her appeal to men. Jennifer took great pride in her erotic capital. One evening, while we were hanging out together at her apartment and engaging in girl talk about our respective boyfriends, she smirked and said:

> Men are generous with me because they become sexually addicted to me. All the men I dated tell me our sex is the best they ever had . . . My *lao gong* has had many women. He says I have the best, most luscious pussy. I can have five orgasms in one sitting, he counted . . . You see, he used to be *feng liu* [womanizing], but since he met me, he stopped seeing other women, besides the one who gave him a son.

Since mistresses rely on married men for financial support, they are much more tolerant of infidelity than women like Ruby, Vivien, or Lucy, who sought Western men as a tonic against Chinese men's infidelity. In contrast, Jennifer said, "I believe in patriarchy. I think it's only natural for successful men to have multiple women." In fact, Jennifer even said she preferred rich men with multiple partners over lesser-earning men who were faithful to her. Back when Jennifer was married, she secretly cheated on her husband first, when she met a politician who offered to buy her a home in exchange for becoming his mistress. After spending a month out of town in an affair with the politician, Jennifer came home to her then-husband with a suitcase full of cash and a truckload of embezzled cigarettes given to her by her lover. She seriously considered leaving her husband for the politician, and later gave up on that idea only because the politician lost interest in her. Eventually, when she discovered that her husband was also having an affair, she did not hesitate to divorce him, as she felt she could easily replace him with someone financially better off, like the politician.

If fidelity was not a primary reason for mistresses to seek Western men, then what motivated them? I suggest that the vulnerability of the kept-mistress arrangement played an important role. Jennifer's *lao gong* promised her he would eventually bring her to the United States to live with his other partner and their children in one household, and even arranged for Jennifer to exchange regular phone calls with the other woman. Yet, after spending many years with him without the union he promised to deliver, Jennifer lamented, "I have been living in a lie, a beautiful lie and dream that he weaved for me." By the time I met Jennifer in 2011, her *lao gong*'s visits had waned in frequency and he started sending her less and less money each month. Although their relationship involved the exchange of sex for money, it was also built on romantic attraction and emotional attachment. Jennifer appreciated her *lao gong*'s "handsome looks," "refined taste," and "gentle, caring temperament." She found it particularly painful to experience their once-passionate relationship withering away.

When I asked Jennifer if she would consider marrying a different Chinese man, she said, "In China, rich men who are single won't come to me. It is only the ones with bad *tiao jian* [material conditions] who seek me out." Jennifer used a classic Chinese idiom to describe her situation: *gao bu cheng di bu jiu* (unfit for a higher post and unwilling to take a lower one). This sentiment was common among the mistresses I interviewed. Their lack of earning capacity, alongside their advancing age, made it particularly difficult for them to marry high-earning, high-status men. Yet, having dated men of that caliber for years, they found it psychologically difficult to settle for someone less successful. Moreover, years of unemployment made them weak candidates on the labor market, which completely mismatched the lavish consumption habits they developed while dating wealthier men. Thus, aging mistresses looked to marriage migration as a potential exit option.

Nevertheless, mistresses were not financially desperate. They accrued some economic capital through their patrons, and this gave them a basic safety net. For example, Jennifer owned two condos. Moreover, she did not need to worry about financing her retirement or health care: her *lao gong* paid her monthly contributions throughout the years she was out of work, so she expects to collect a monthly retirement check from the state as soon as she turns fifty. Jennifer continued to spend lavishly by local standards, even when her *lao gong*'s payments diminished. She always used the latest iPhone, installed a reverse-osmosis water filtration system at home, and bought a US$430 supersonic hair-dryer. Because of her relative financial stability, Jennifer could afford to date selectively. She said, "If I marry a Westerner, it would have to be someone I feel *gan jue* [passion] for. And I don't like doing heavy housework, such as mowing the grass or plowing the snow, which I hear many women who marry Western men end up doing since manual labor is so expensive abroad."

On the whole, mistresses sought marriage migration not out of financial desperation or to escape Chinese men's promiscuity, but rather out of emotional despair as they aged and lost their appeal for their wealthy lovers. This emotional despair is particularly strong because their sense of self-esteem is largely rooted in their erotic capital, which declines with age. Whenever we got together, Jennifer often recounted her most "glorious and happy days," back when she was youthful, attractive, and sought after. For example, she told me that her first husband wanted her back so badly that he continued giving her money for months after they divorced. When she first dated her *lao gong*, he flew her all over China to meet him in the various cities where he was conducting business and put her up in five-star hotels for months on end. Jennifer often expressed disdain for women who had to work for a living, as it revealed their inability to attract rich men, hence implying their failure as "real women." Jennifer said, "I really enjoy being supported by men . . . to be honest, if I had to work for money, it would take away from my intrinsic value as a woman."

Here, we can see that Jennifer takes on a gender strategy of emphasized femininity, where she offers her feminized traits to high-status men in exchange for their financial support.[25] More important, Jennifer takes pride in her emphasized femininity and views it as a significant part of her identity. As we will see, this mindset comes back to haunt her later in life as she ages and loses her ability to perform emphasized femininity.

Over the years, Jennifer's luxurious lifestyle and lavish consumption habits garnered her admiration from family and friends. At home, her parents favored her for being their most financially successful child, while her nieces and nephews looked up to her for her exquisite taste in fashion. Back in the late 1990s, when her friends were buying three-bedroom apartments for RMB30,000 (US$4,600), her holiday allowance alone was RMB50,000 (US$7,600). Yet by the late 2000s, her self-esteem plummeted as her disposable income decreased. By the time I met Jennifer in 2012, she told me she barely went out to socialize anymore because she felt embarrassed next to some of her old friends, who were once much poorer but had now caught up with or even surpassed her.

Not only was Jennifer distressed over her economic situation, but she also worried about her declining health and fading looks. After many years of dining out, Jennifer developed a number of health conditions including high cholesterol. In 2015 and 2016, she suffered several bouts of illness. Lying in bed alone, she could rely only on her seventy-year-old mother to bring food and water. During those times she often called to tell me how depressed she felt looking back at her life, one in which she ended up with nothing—no child, no husband, no marriage, and no significant wealth. Over the years I had known Jennifer, her desire for Western men waxed and waned. She expressed more indifference toward them when her relationship with her *lao gong* was stable, and more excitement when he was uninterested.

In summer 2017, I revisited Jennifer in her home after I'd been away from Tunyang for five years. When I showed up at her door, we both jumped and squealed in excitement. Up close, I was surprised to see how much weight Jennifer had gained, with her protruding tummy, thick arms, and round face. That day, Jennifer took me to a newly opened Korean restaurant in her neighborhood for lunch. Sipping on kimchee stew, she said of her *lao gong*:

> He doesn't really visit much anymore and only gives me money sporadically now. Even when he is already in China, he doesn't always stop by my city, and he doesn't pay for my flight to visit him either. He says he is short on money. We still call each other every day, usually once a day if he's in the United States and twice a day if he's in China. But it's just to say hello. We have nothing more to talk about, really. I feel his heart is no longer with me.

As Jennifer spoke, her eyes became red. Eventually she started weeping and wiping tears off her face, while she lamented over and over again, "I am so *ke lian* [pitiful]. I feel so lonely. I feel that nobody in this world cares about me . . . nobody . . . I'm all alone."

Jennifer's ultimately disappointing experience with Chinese men was not unique. Kristin, another former mistress, also claimed she would only be interested in marriage migration if she could find someone as wealthy, generous, and sexually exciting as her former Chinese lovers. When I first met Kristin at Ms. Mei's office back in 2008, she was in her mid-forties, yet she dressed much younger, in six-inch platform sandals and spaghetti straps. She had the slim body of a teenage girl, while her lazy, distracted gaze gave her a sexy, rebellious look that I often saw in high-end fashion magazines. Kristin took pride in her sex appeal and easygoing personality, which she believed made her a favorite of the opposite sex. Throughout 2008 and 2009, I witnessed Kristin reject numerous Western suitors after they flew to China to see her. Yet when we met up in the summer of 2011, the first thing Kristin said to me was, "I look so old. I cannot stand to see myself in the mirror." Kristin broke down, cried, and told me that her Chinese lover at the time, a CEO, kicked her out of his home after she shared his money with her grown daughter from her previous marriage and let her daughter drive his BMW without permission. That summer, Kristin renewed her expired membership at Ms. Mei's dating agency and promised Ms. Mei that she would start taking marriage migration more seriously instead of dating around for fun.

With women returning to conceptions of gender that place a great deal of value on their ability to perform femininity, erotic capital becomes an essential resource for sustaining their often-lavish lifestyles in postreform China. However, as they inevitably age and are seen as less attractive, their social and financial standing becomes increasingly precarious. As seen in the cases of Jennifer and Kristin, this structure is driving women to seek Western men as an alternative to their declining options on China's dating scene.

The Young Girls

While 26 of the 30 financially flexible women I followed were older and divorced, 4 were under the age of thirty and never married. Unlike the older women who were, for the most part, financially well-off, these four women came from diverse socioeconomic backgrounds: one was from a privileged family, one came from an average-earning family, and two came from disadvantaged upbringings. Despite these class differences, I consider them financially flexible because they were too young to worry about illness, retirement, or children's education. Even for those from economically disadvantaged backgrounds, their youth still gave them much better job prospects than middle-aged, working-class women had, since Chinese retail and service sectors usually hire women under the age of thirty.[26] Angel's story offers an example.

Angel was a pretty, dark-skinned, voluptuous nineteen-year-old. Born into a poor rural family, she traveled a thousand miles from her hometown to Lingshan as a migrant worker at age fifteen. In Lingshan, she worked a variety of odd jobs, from dishwashing to waitressing to retail sales before landing a medical assistant position at an acupuncture clinic. Despite her financial struggles, Angel remained optimistic and believed that opportunities were boundless in China as long as one was willing to work hard.

When it came to men, Angel was quite confident in her ability to attract them. Over dinner at a small, hole-in-the wall eatery with her translator, Angel told us about the numerous Chinese ex-boyfriends she had. One was financially stable and mild-tempered, but not handsome enough for her. The one she wanted to marry was a wealthy, middle-aged entrepreneur, but he ended up rejecting her. Later on, Angel's translator told me she was not very serious about marriage migration, rarely visited the agency, and took no interest in learning English. Unlike the older female clients, who took the Western men's occupation and income into serious consideration, Angel was more concerned over whether they shared her interests in art and music. While she sought Western men through Ms. Fong's agency, she also dated local Chinese men on her own. Fast-forward five years, and Angel is now married to an average-earning Chinese man of her own age. Although he was far less wealthy than some of her ex-boyfriends, Angel believed he had good earning potential and called him a "diamond in the rough." At the same time, she also worked hard toward her goal of opening her own acupuncture clinic in China.

Compared to the older clients, younger women appeared uniformly less enthusiastic about cross-border marriage. Including Angel, three of the four younger women I followed said they initially joined their agency as a courtesy to their friends, who worked as translators; the fourth was a college student brought to the agency by her mother, a struggling domestic worker. The girl once protested, "You are trying to sell your daughter!" and later joined reluctantly. The other three also emphasized that they had many pursuers in China. They described their correspondence with the Western men as "complete happenstance" and only "one of many options under consideration."

In Eastern Europe, Latin America, and Southeast Asia, the majority of female clients enrolled at global dating agencies are young and never married.[27] In contrast, middle-aged women dominate the Chinese agencies I study. Since I did not interview young women across Chinese society at large, I do not know if they would be interested in pursuing marriage migration through other venues besides translator-assisted dating agencies. Nevertheless, the translators believe that younger women in China today are generally uninterested in migrating for marriage, regardless of the venue through which they meet foreign men, because China is on the global rise and they have good employment and marriage prospects locally.

HOW CLASS INTERSECTS WITH AGE AND GENDER

The case studies I have presented thus far show that financially flexible women are rather choosy on the dating market because they occupy advantaged social positions in China. The middle-aged women are all relatively financially successful, so they don't feel pressured to marry in order to improve their economic well-being. Perhaps mistresses stand out as an exception, since they did seek Western men, at least in part, to recapture the luxurious lifestyle they lost as they aged. Nevertheless, these women were not financially desperate. With a safety net in place, they dated selectively and only wanted to marry Western men who were as wealthy and sexually exciting as their former lovers. Finally, while not all the young women were financially well-off, their youth expanded their local dating options, thereby contributing to their general lack of interest in pursuing marriage migration via commercial dating agencies.

In their search for new husbands, most of the women in my study, with the exception of a few particularly wealthy ones, wanted someone of equal or higher socioeconomic standing than themselves, while they saw "marrying down" as taboo. Although the desire to "marry up" is prevalent across many cultures,[28] it is particularly strong in postreform China for both cultural and structural reasons. Culturally, China has been moving away from a socialist era that "rejected displays of gender difference" to one that embraces gender differences and posits that women should remain in the domestic sphere while men tackle the economic sphere.[29] After having experienced the "double burden"[30] of having to work both inside and outside the home during the height of state socialism, many women now view homemaking as a symbol of wealth and privilege rather than one of inequality and deprivation. Structurally, wealth is increasingly concentrated in the hands of a minority group of elite men, while women are experiencing increased discrimination in the workplace after antidiscriminatory regulations from the socialist era gave way to the logistics of capitalism during the 1990s and beyond.[31] Thus, more women are seeking marriage as an alternative path to achieve upward social mobility.

Since the financially flexible women tend to be well-off already, marrying up or marrying someone of equal status often means tapping into China's economic elite. Yet, these women's older age generally makes them undesirable marital partners to men of that class stratum. The majority of the thirty financially flexible respondents told me they once passed up local pursuers either because they were unwilling to "marry down" or because they were determined to "marry up." Perhaps the Chinese idiom Jennifer used to describe her situation: *gao bu cheng di bu jiu* (unfit for a higher post and unwilling to take a lower one) best describes their situation. On the whole, these women are "migrating to marry,"[32] meaning that they seek Western men in order to have a family, while money or a green card alone is not sufficient incentive to motivate their move. I suggest that their plight is that of China's "leftover" women—which refers to never-married, well-educated urban women past the age of twenty-seven with promising careers[33]—rather than the stereotypical Western media depiction of mail-order brides as desperate young women seeking a ticket out of financial hell.

FINANCIALLY BURDENED WOMEN
Salesclerks, Nannies, and Women in Debt

I now turn to the remaining thirty-one women, who fall into what I call the financially burdened group. This group includes women in the contingent employment sector, who work on a contractual basis and do not receive benefits from their employer. These women seek to leave China as they approach retirement age because they don't have access to pension funds, medical insurance, or social security. It also includes women who may or may not be in the contingent employment sector but who have other, imminent financial needs, such as debt incurred from business failure or a desire to send their children abroad for college but lack of financial resources to do so. Nevertheless, these women were not living in extreme poverty. In fact, the agencies have tried, unsuccessfully, to expand their business to smaller, less economically developed cities or even rural areas. They found that women in those areas were too risk-averse, too "easily contented with life," and too "sexually conservative" to pursue cross-border marriage.

In my research, many financially burdened women were worried about their declining socioeconomic status in the postreform era. Hence, I suggest that their desires to out-migrate are partially rooted in a sense of "relative deprivation,"[34] emerging from the gap between their current earning capacity and their desired lifestyle. According to this theory, citizens from developing countries who are "fully exposed to modern goods and modern consumption" but cannot afford them are the ones with the strongest motivation to move.[35] We will see how the reform exposed some women to the double whammy of inequalities in both the marriage and labor markets, and how these disadvantages shape their mate-selection strategies differently from those of the financially flexible women.

Of the thirty-one financially burdened women, half were former state factory employees who experienced downward social mobility following their layoffs from SOEs. During the 1990s, when SOEs were dismantled across China and more than 30 million workers were laid off, middle-aged women bore the brunt of the impact.[36] They were laid off at much higher rates than men, and they had more difficulty finding reemployment.[37] While a minority of women, like Ruby or Jennifer, later achieved economic success through other means, such as becoming an entrepreneur or a rich man's mistress, the majority experienced downward social mobility[38] as they took on low-paying jobs in the contingent sector to make ends meet.

As an example, let's return to Daisy, whom I introduced at the start of this chapter alongside Ruby. Daisy's ex-husband was a disco singer in the 1980s, during the early stages of China's reform, when discos and night-clubs had just been introduced into the country. Women, including Daisy, swooned over his voice. He earned a lot of quick cash and always shared it with Daisy to support her shopping and gambling habits. When Daisy lost her factory job during the widespread SOE layoffs, he helped her open her own internet cafe. Even today, Daisy looks back at that time period with pride. She recounts: "It cost 240,000 yuan [US$29,000]. Back then, you could buy an entire apartment for 20,000 yuan [US$2,418]. Think about how much money I had!" Unfortunately, the business failed.

Later on, Daisy's husband lost his job as well, when the music industry became more competitive, as professionally credentialed artists entered in large numbers. For many years, he sat at home, jobless and unable to cope with his loss of status, while Daisy worked as a clerk to support him and their teenage daughter. As he lost confidence, he began to suspect Daisy of infidelity. In response, he demanded sex every day and accused her of cheating when she refused to comply. Daisy said, "He argued with me so much. It was unbearable. Can you imagine it? Every day, I would read the newspaper in bed while he had sex with me . . . and I would be completely dry, you know, because I was not aroused. It hurt so much!"

Eventually, they divorced but still lived in the same apartment because he had nowhere else to go. When I asked Daisy why she continued to support him, she said, "I look back on all those happy days we once had . . . I was so happy because he made so much money and shared it with me. Moreover, he had been so loyal to me. He never had an affair during all our years together, even though so many women wanted him." She called him the love of her life and blamed his bad luck in the postreform labor market, alongside his "deep, obsessive love" for her, for destroying their marriage.

As we can see, not all Chinese female clients had ex-husbands or lovers who climbed to the top of the socioeconomic ladder. In fact, a large number of women in the financially burdened sector had ex-husbands who fell to the bottom. Since those women's marriages did not always end with betrayal, their search for Western men was not always motivated by resentment over Chinese men.

Even in cases where their financially failing ex-husbands did cheat, sometimes the financially burdened women took pity on them. For example, Susan, a laid-off factory worker who later opened her own small business, believed her Chinese ex-husband sought out sex workers due to the trouble the couple had had at home following his job loss. She said, "I hurt his self-esteem . . . I became the breadwinner and started looking down on him for never seeking a new job after he got laid off from the SOE."

Women like Susan were less resentful of their cheating husbands, because they recognized that the men might have cheated in an attempt to soothe their hurt egos—a result of failing to act as breadwinners in a patriarchal society that expected them to perform as such. In fact, Susan even blamed herself for being the dominant wife who bruised her husband's ego and drove him away. Her apologetic attitude stood in striking contrast to the resentment we see in the wives of successful businessmen who betrayed their wives and family values simply because their status and wealth afforded them the opportunity.

In Daisy's case, her motive for marriage migration was grounded in the pragmatic desire to resolve an imminent financial problem: as a modest-earning salesclerk, she needed someone to provide long-term financial stability, particularly because she was still struggling to conquer her addictions to shopping and gambling. In China today, middle-aged women without a college degree are particularly disadvantaged in the labor market. Age discrimination is paramount in China's service sector, which engages "beauty economy" market practices,[39] where only young, attractive women get hired to promote commercial products. As a result, women over the age of thirty have great difficulty securing more desirable service sector jobs, such as those in high-end department stores, real estate agencies, or public relations companies.[40] In Daisy's case, she considered herself lucky to be working at a luxury department store at the age of forty-three, given that most of her colleagues were much younger. Her youthful, doll-like appearance certainly helped. However, as each year passed, she grew more distressed about her future job prospects.

While Daisy's attractive appearance helped her secure a department store job, many other laid-off state employees who did not have the same "bodily capital"[41] worked in less desirable service sectors. This made them even more eager to leave China. For example, Olivia, a care worker in her mid-forties, approached me one day after I had taught my usual Sunday afternoon English class for the agency and said:

> I bet you do not know too many people like me. Most of your friends at the agency are probably middle-class. Not me. I'm at the bottom of Chinese society. I work at a nursing home. I work sixteen hours a day. Life is very difficult for me. People look down on me, and I feel very repressed. I want to leave China because I want to improve my current living condition.

Unlike Daisy, who often bought new clothes and frequented beauty salons for eyelash implants and hair coloring, Olivia tied her black hair in a simple ponytail and wore clothes that looked like they were purchased in the 1990s. Olivia says people like herself, who made less than RMB 3,000 (US$375) per month, could not afford to go to beauty parlors.

Olivia's desire to leave China was somewhat typical of many lesser-earning women I met. In particular, the middle-aged *yue sao* (nursemaids) in my study, who worked long shifts—up to twenty hours per day—helping mothers take care of newborns, echoed Olivia's desire. At Ms. Mei's agency, a large number of clients worked at the same nursemaid company. In the summer of 2009, I visited their dormitories, which were bare-shell two-bedroom apartments shared by several women. While the *yue sao* stayed with their host families most of the time, they returned to those shared dormitories, paid for by their company, in order to save on rent when they were between jobs. These *yue sao* expressed distress at their loss of status, financial security, and access to social services after losing their state jobs in the postreform era. In particular, they were concerned about financing their retirement.

For exampole, Margot, a *yue sao* in her fifties, was so desperate to leave China that she even put up with painful sex with her American boyfriend during his visits to China. She said, "I could barely stand the sex. He was so big down there and he wanted it all the time . . . Oh my god, it hurt so much! After he left, I was so bruised I had to see a doctor." A few months later, he went back to the United States and started taking medication for his diabetes. When Margot saw that he could no longer sustain an erection when they tried having cam sex online, she expressed relief. When I asked Margot why she continued the relationship despite their obvious sexual incompatibility, she said, "I really need to leave China and nobody else is writing me."

Unlike wealthier clients, whose shoes and purses cost far more than the US$1,000 membership fee they paid to join the agency, many lower-earning clients could barely afford the fee. However, they still chose to migrate abroad because they viewed it as a path toward upward socioeconomic mobility. For example, Zeena said:

I recently got divorced and I am currently selling bottled water at a grocery shop. I still have a mortgage to pay off, and I do not have the money to pay for the membership fee right now, so I borrowed money from six friends. I have been educating other clients around me. I tell them that even though they are paying a lot of money up front, it is an investment. It is like paying a high price for a plane ticket so you can fly there to earn 10,000 yuan instead of walking somewhere to earn only 1,000 yuan.

Accordingly, Zeena viewed joining the dating service as a business investment. Unlike white-collar professionals, women who occupy low-skilled service sectors in China can continue working overseas, even without command of English. Since physical labor is more expensive in Western countries, many working-class women envision marriage migration as a lucrative opportunity rather than a career sacrifice, particularly when they see other clients boost their income substantially by working at restaurants and massage parlors after moving abroad.

Financial distress was prevalent not only among women who worked low-wage jobs in the contingent sector, but also among women who were strained by other circumstances, such as having debt due to previous business failure. Unlike Daisy, who took pity on her Chinese husband's failure on the postreform labor market, women whose husbands disappeared in the face of debt often saw the men as "financially irresponsible cowards." For example, Lindsay, a divorced college lecturer in her forties with rosy skin and bright eyes, described her decision to seek marriage migration after her then-husband's business venture failed:

> He owed RMB 800,000 [US$96,618]. This was back in the early 2000s. It was an astronomical number [to] me. I was so distressed, I felt like I was going to die. And when he couldn't pay it back, he just disappeared for a few months, leaving me all alone to face the lenders who knocked on our door. The most disturbing part of the situation was the fact that I borrowed much of that money from my own siblings in an effort to support his business . . . Many people tell me I'm lucky because even though I got divorced, my husband never betrayed me, so I was never hurt. I don't buy that. I was much worse off than those women with cheating husbands.

While a minority of financially flexible women also had fiscally irresponsible ex-husbands and later achieved success through their own careers, the majority had wealthy ex-husbands. In contrast, a much larger percentage of financially burdened women had married men who could not overcome adverse economic situations through their own efforts, as in the case of Lindsay. Hence, financially burdened women cited Chinese men's financial irresponsibility as motivation to seek Western husbands at a much higher rate than did the financially flexible women.

Struggling Single Mothers

Finally, 11 out of 31 financially burdened women sought Western men partly because they wanted their children to study overseas but could not afford it. I suggest that their desires are rooted in a sense of relative deprivation, partially stemming from China's shifting education system. China's exam-driven education system has long been criticized for burdening youth with excessive schoolwork and no playtime.[42] Moreover, since the statewide expansion of college admissions during the late 1990s, graduates from second- and third-tier colleges have faced high rates of unemployment.[43] In light of this, many parents now choose to send their children overseas, and today China is the world's leading country for enrolling students abroad.[44] Nevertheless, overseas study remains a middle-class aspiration in China,[45] as the lack of loans for international students makes it virtually impossible for anyone below the middle class to pursue this option. Many of the financially burdened mothers I interviewed were downwardly mobile in the postreform era and therefore viewed marriage migration as a means to help their children achieve the middle-class lifestyle they themselves were no longer capable of providing. The case of Joanne offers an example.

Joanne never attended college, and started working at a factory right out of high school. Although she came from an economically disadvantaged family, Joanne's stunning, model-like good looks and witty personality won her lots of attention from the opposite sex. She always dressed nicely, in either a business suit or skirt and boots to show off her long, shapely legs. In her friend Kristin's words, Joanne "grew up poor but always had high expectations for life, perhaps setting the bar higher than what she could realistically get." In her younger days, Joanne rejected many pursuers whom she considered financially well-off but not good-looking enough. Eventually, a tall, handsome police officer who pursued her madly won her heart. Although he loved her very much and pampered her, he had a gambling addiction, which she did not discover until after they were married.

Like many other factory workers, Joanne got laid off during the early 1990s and was forced to find work on her own. When we chatted over a lunch of crispy chicken sandwiches and French fries at a McDonald's downstairs from Ms. Mei's agency in summer 2008, Joanne told me that she started in hospitality management during the early 1990s and eventually worked her way up to opening her own karaoke bar. "I'm ambitious; I always believe you must keep moving up in life," she said. A few years later, she opened an even bigger, two-story karaoke bar. By the mid-1990s, she became one of the first people in China to own a cellphone. Joanne admitted that she was a perfectionist. She said, "I always want to be better than others around me. When it comes to work, I want to be [at the] top of my industry. At home, I want my kid to be better than other kids and my marriage to be better than other people's marriages."

Unfortunately, her husband's gambling addiction destroyed her dreams. As his debt piled up, lenders came knocking on her door. When she refused to pay, they smashed her karaoke bar and broke into her home, stealing her cash, clothing, and jewelry. Eventually Joanne was forced to sell off both karaoke bars, as well as her apartment. At this time, her husband also started abusing drugs and seeing sex workers, so she filed for divorce. After experiencing the vandalism, Joanne vowed never to own a business again, and took on lesser-paying jobs in retail management to make ends meet.

As a middle-aged woman with no college degree, and with her path to entrepreneurship compromised, Joanne struggled to support her teenage son. She moved into a small apartment with no heat and relied on a married man for financial assistance. "He was kind to me and supported my son," Joanne said, "but he could not leave his wife." Even under the most difficult conditions, Joanne strove for the best. She wore the most expensive clothing she could afford, enrolled her son at a top school, and paid for his various extracurricular activities. "I don't have much left in life," Joanne said, "no husband, no money, no career, so I put all my hopes into my child." She thought a Western college degree would be particularly useful for her son. She wanted him to achieve great career success, but felt that the Chinese job market was too competitive for youth from underprivileged families, even if they had good grades. With that consideration in mind, Joanne joined Ms. Mei's overseas dating agency.

Like Joanne, Beth was an ambitious female client who had been born into a poor family. Although Beth became a medical practitioner through her own hard work, her husband's business failed in the postreform era. At the time of their divorce, he could not even pay child support. Beth had a brief second marriage with a Chinese man, which she later broke off when he refused to support her son. At this time, friends suggested that Beth join an overseas dating agency, assuring her that Western couples were much less likely to quarrel over stepchildren because child-rearing expenses were much lower abroad: unlike in China, student loans were much more widely available in the West, and there was no social expectation for parents to purchase homes for their grown sons. Accordingly, Beth decided to give Western men a try.

By the time Beth joined the overseas dating agency, her son was close to finishing middle school. Thus, she told me, she was determined to marry quickly, as she could not afford private school tuition in China if her son did not test into a renowned public school. As a result, her perception of marriage migration was rather pragmatic. While walking down a narrow wooden staircase to exit the small restaurant where her engagement party to an American firefighter had just been held, she turned to me and said: "For me, *chu qu* [leaving China] means making one million yuan [US$150,000]. That is how much I would otherwise have to pay to send my son abroad for college. I could work in China for another twenty years and not make that kind of money." In contrast, few of the financially flexible mothers treated their marriage as a means to bring their children abroad. This is because some of their children were already studying abroad with all expenses paid in full by their wealthy ex-husbands, while others were happy to let their children stay in China because they had social networks to help their children secure desirable jobs locally.

CONCLUSION

The stories in this chapter certainly do not represent an "average" or "typical" Chinese woman's life experience. Instead, my research draws from a unique segment of the population: women whose life trajectories have been dramatically altered by China's social, cultural, and economic transformations during the past forty years, prompting them to join overseas dating agencies. Their desires to seek marriage migration are deeply rooted in their discontent over inequalities of age, gender, and class, emerging from China's reform and opening up. These women's life histories and future marital aspirations provide a unique glimpse into various social problems in contemporary China.

Digging deeper, we see that China's postreform era is marked by the smashing of the "iron rice bowl"—the end of state-guaranteed social services, employment, and housing.[46] Its entrance into the global market economy created new opportunities for individuals to dramatically alter their wealth and social status. Today, China's uneven development has fractured the marriage migration market into different niche sectors, where each sector is occupied by women with vastly different access to financial resources. For example, the financially flexible clients are clearly economic winners of China's reform and opening up. Wealthy women like Ruby climbed to the upper echelon of the global economic hierarchy, white-collar professionals like Vivien reside comfortably in China as part of the nation's "emerging middle class," while mistresses like Jennifer enjoy a middle-class lifestyle despite being unemployed.[47] As such, these women do not seek Western men out of financial desperation. Instead, I interpret their pursuit of marriage migration as a means of coping with gender inequality.

In China today, wealth and power are increasingly concentrated among a small subset of elite men, while the dominant gender ideology embraces the male breadwinner/female homemaker model. Many of the financially flexible women possessed the appropriate capital to engage in romantic encounters or fleeting marriages with wealthy men. For example, public relations manager Vivien had a career that put her in contact with those men, while mistress Jennifer relied on her erotic capital. Yet, those men eventually rejected them: Vivien's ex-husband and lovers cheated on her, while Jennifer's *lao gong* never delivered on his promise to let her join his family in the United States. Ultimately, these women were left in an awkward position where they were too old to marry rich men but unwilling to consider lesser-earning men. Despite their economic status, these women chose not to capitalize on that and date lesser-earning local men, as this strategy mismatched with the dominant gender ideology in contemporary China that equates masculine desirability with financial success. Instead, they perceive the Chinese marriage market to be dismal for women their age and seek marriage migration as a potential exit option.

In contrast, the financially burdened women pursue marriage migration in response to both gender and labor market inequality. Compared with the financially flexible women, a larger portion of financially burdened women had ex-husbands who fell to the bottom of China's socioeconomic ladder, either by losing their jobs when SOEs shut down during the reform or by failing in their new business ventures. Unable or unwilling to find new work, some husbands even resorted to drinking, gambling, and extramarital sex. Today, newly empowered businessmen represent a new ideal of China's market era,[48] while men "lacking the resources to enter the ranks of the new rich (or even a vaguely defined car- and house-owning middle class)" experience a form of emasculation that includes difficulty finding a spouse, loss of status and prestige, as well as a dwindling social network.[49] For women who cited Chinese men's lack of fiscal responsibility as a primary factor for seeking Western men, their desires also represent their rejection of a failed Chinese masculinity that emerged as a by-product of the postreform era.

Most financially burdened women, unlike their financially flexible counterparts, don't lament their loss in the competition for China's most elite men, because most of them never possessed the appropriate social, economic, or erotic capital to date those men in the first place. Instead, their desire for marriage migration is informed by their ex-husbands' financial failures, alongside their own disadvantaged positions in the postreform labor market, which led to their overall downward social mobility. The plight of these financially burdened women is much closer to the stereotypical Western media image of a so-called mail-order bride seeking a ticket out of financial hell. In fact, women like Margot, the domestic worker, were so desperate to leave China in favor of financial stability with a Western husband, they were willing to put up with painful sex or give up on a sex life altogether.

Given these dramatically different marital aspirations, we clearly cannot make generalized assumptions about marriage migrants on the basis of their nationality alone. Instead, I argue that we must examine the intersectionality of many factors in order to understand their unique positions on the global marriage market. For example, in this chapter, I examined age as a prominent source of inequality for women and explored how age can sometimes override class in shaping their desire to marry Western men. Specifically, I discussed why older Chinese women from both upper- and lower-class sectors seek Western husbands, while women in their twenties were generally uninterested, irrespective of their own class background.

At the same time, I also explored how class impacts marital trajectories among older women interested in Western men. Comparing the aspirations of the financially flexible women with those of the financially burdened women, I discussed how their vastly different social positions and access to economic resources in China shaped their motives. In addition, I looked at alternative forms of capital that determine Chinese women's class position beyond occupation and educational credentials. I showed how bodily capital[50] and erotic capital[51] affected women's access to resources in the unique context of postreform China, where practices such as "beauty economy" and "mistress-keeping" have emerged.

Finally, this chapter has important implications for how we understand and theorize globalization, and, in particular, the way we think about new differences of wealth among nations. Today, China occupies a unique position on the world stage. On one hand, it is an emerging world superpower projected to overtake the United States as the world's largest economy by 2028.[52] On the other hand, China's growth has been uneven, and the nation is still considered a developing country based on its GDP per capita. As wealth distribution decenters across continents but polarizes within individual countries, we can no longer make generalized predictions about migrants on the basis of their nationality alone. Instead, we must take a class-based approach. Thus, the stereotypical image of a marriage migrant as someone financially desperate and seeking a green card is not necessarily an inaccurate depiction or a myth, as some previous literature has asserted, but rather characteristic of migrants from one particular class sector within their native country.

Having learned about the life histories and motives of Chinese women seeking Western husbands, we start to wonder about the men they connect with through the dating agencies. Unlike the Chinese women, who come from diverse socioeconomic backgrounds, the Western men come from more homogeneous backgrounds. The majority are lower-middle-class or working-class men who feel left behind by globalization in light of the decline of agriculture, manufacturing, and small businesses in the West over the past forty years. How do the dating agencies market these men to their female clients? And how do the female clients respond to them during the next phase of the dating process, when couples meet face to face? We will explore these questions in the chapters that follow.

2 | PROVIDER LOVE

IN CHAPTER 1, I INTRODUCED Ruby, a divorced lady in her mid-forties, whose wealthy Chinese ex-husband left her for a younger woman. Tall and voluptuous, Ruby liked to wear form-fitting dresses, while her loosely permed, long hair was streaked with golden highlights. Ruby believed that women must look good in order to feel confident. Although not as youthful as some of the other female clients at the agency, she had a special kind of maturity and sophistication. In particular, she was good at finding colorful images to describe things, and she always put others in a relaxed state of mind through her vivacious laugh. Perhaps these are the qualities that emanate after many years of experience as a businesswoman. By the time Ruby turned forty, she had retired in wealth. She spent leisurely days walking her collies, visiting beauty parlors, managing her stocks online, and cooking for her twenty-something daughter who still lived at home.

Ruby was first introduced to Ms. Mei's agency by a friend who was already a client there. This friend told Ruby to give up on wealthy Chinese businessmen and look instead to modest-earning Western men, who she believed made better husbands because they were more loyal, family oriented, and willing to date women their own age. Hence, their "richness" comes not from their material possessions but rather their moral purity, which stands in striking contrast to the materially "rich" but spiritually "poor" Chinese businessmen like Ruby's ex-husband. Interestingly, the friend's condemnation of Chinese men as more likely to be unfaithful and prone to seek out younger women is not necessarily a belief she would have come to on her own. Rather, the denigration of Chinese men is often a direct by-product of the agency's business model. The agencies juxtapose a seemingly backward Chinese masculinity against an idealized Western masculinity, thus creating a market among their Chinese female clientele for Western men. This teaching supports the necessity of their services and unwittingly reinforces the manufactured supremacy of Western culture. When Ruby visited Ms. Mei's agency for further consultation, the translators, unsurprisingly, reaffirmed these ideas to her.

The agencies aggressively promoted this image of Western men as ideal family men. For example, they frequently portrayed Western men as such in their company blog, which they used to market their services and attract potential female clients. Written by the managers and translators, articles in the blog described how couples met and married, while some entries also followed up on the women's postmarital lives abroad. I reviewed 154 articles published between 2007 and 2014, and compiled a list of traits that described the Western men. Unsurprisingly, from this list, six of the most frequently appearing and most strongly emphasized traits were: (1) willing to date older women; (2) devoted; (3) family-oriented; (4) responsible; (5) hopeless romantics; and (6) caring as stepfathers.

Although Ruby joined Ms. Mei's agency with this idealized image of a Western family man in mind, she still did not have high hopes for marriage. Instead, she envisioned the email exchange process as a "fun endeavor" that could provide her with a way to "feel loved," as well as a way to occupy her free time. One day, however, when she came into the office to chat, she saw her translator writing to an American man whose profile photo caught her attention: he stood six feet, two inches tall, and had deep blue eyes, well-defined features, and a toned body. He was also a few years younger than Ruby. The translators all agreed that Larry had the "aura of a movie star." Despite his handsome looks, however, Larry was not well-off financially. As a factory technician in Vermont, he earned a modest income and, to make matters worse, he had nearly lost his home during the 2008 financial crisis.

When Ruby first saw Larry, he had been writing to another female client who rarely visited the agency and never responded to his letters. Because of this, the translator asked Ms. Mei, the agency manager, if she could simply reject Larry on that woman's behalf. Hoping to seize an opportunity that might not have arisen again, Ruby stepped in after overhearing their conversation. She asked Ms. Mei if they could put *her* in touch with Larry instead, and even went so far as to say, "If someone in this office could connect me with this stunning man, I will reward the entire company with big, big *hong bao* [cash bonus]!"

By the time I met Ruby in summer 2008, she had been exchanging emails with Larry for more than two months, and he planned on visiting her in person that fall. Interestingly, throughout the email exchange process, Larry was the perfect embodiment of the agency's portrayal of an ideal Western family man. For example, on several occasions when Ruby and I read Larry's letters together on-site, she exclaimed to her translator, "You see, I told him not to burden you with such long letters, but he still insists, and even gets mad when my letters are not long enough!" before breaking out in doting laughter. Ruby could sense Larry's dedication to her in the lengthy emails he wrote each day for months on end, even though he received much shorter replies, drafted by Ruby's translator. Moreover, Larry was completely different from Ruby's nouveau-riche Chinese ex-husband who, as described in chapter 1, had cheated on her and attempted to justify his unfaithfulness by saying, "Men are like teapots; each pot should be paired with multiple teacups." Instead, Larry expressed his belief in marital fidelity, which Ruby valued. Thus, when I asked her about Larry's best quality, she said:

> I like his *renpin* [moral character]. He respects women. He does not believe it is right to have two women at the same time. He told me one of his friends suggested that he find a sex partner in the United States while I wait in China. He told me he rejected his friend's suggestion and said to his friend, "I cannot be disloyal to my future wife."

When I revisited China a year later, in summer 2009, the couple had already married, but Ruby still faced months of waiting for her visa to the

United States. One hot day, when we met up for afternoon tea, I congratulated Ruby on landing the handsome beau she had paid a big *hong bao* for. She laughed, shook her head, and exclaimed, "You know, now I realize, being too handsome is just useless!" To my surprise, Ruby expressed regret over marrying Larry. As she spoke of Larry, I realized that the excitement and joy she once exuded had all but disappeared. So, I wondered, what was Ruby's impression of Larry when she met him in person? Why did she regret the marriage? And what would her future life abroad look like, given her newfound reservations?

FROM INTERNET ROMANCE TO REALITY

While the image of a devoted, caring, Western family man had enticed many Chinese women to pay an annual membership fee of US$1,000 for a service that put them in contact with those men, this did not necessarily mean these women would proceed to marry those men, nor did it imply they would remain happily married after moving abroad. After several months of email exchange, how would the women respond during the next phase of the dating process, when the Western men traveled to China to meet them in person? This is the primary question we will explore in this chapter and the next. These chapters focus exclusively on the dating experiences of financially flexible women like Ruby. As defined in chapter 1, the term "financially flexible" refers to women who have access to medical insurance and guaranteed retirement funds in China, who are not burdened by the costs of child-rearing, and who are not in debt, thereby indicating that their primary motive in seeking Western men is not rooted in a desire to resolve an imminent financial problem. By contrast, women who are "financially burdened" view marriage migration as a ticket toward financial freedom.

By 2014, only 12 of the 30 financially flexible women in my research group had married Western men, while 26 of the 31 financially burdened women had married Western men. Why were the financially flexible women so much less likely to marry their Western suitors? While many factors, such as language barriers, cultural differences, or age gaps, influenced the relationship outcomes of couples across both groups equally, the analysis in this chapter centers on socioeconomic class, which is the most salient factor distinguishing the financially flexible women from the financially burdened women.

Financially flexible women like Ruby occupied privileged social positions in China. As such, they often engaged in romantic relationships with wealthy Chinese men who ran in their social circles. Yet many of the Western male clients enrolled at the agencies in this study were unlike the Chinese men in that they came from the lower or working classes in their native countries. Although Ruby said, upon first joining the agency, that she preferred modest-earning Western "family men" over womanizing Chinese businessmen, her preferences were largely built upon her own imaginings of what a Western "family man" looked like. It was not until she met Larry in person that this image became more concrete. The mismatch between the men's and women's class positions became increasingly apparent as they went offline and met in person—ultimately, drastically affecting their relationship dynamics and marital outcomes.

To understand how class operated within these relationships once they became actualized in person, we first have to understand the factors that shaped the women's gender ideologies and expectations for their future husbands. These ideas were largely formed through the mainstream dating culture that existed in a newly consumerist China. As discussed in the introduction, China's postreform era has been marked by a revival of a traditional patriarchal ideology in which femininity became increasingly associated with domesticity and youth, while masculinity became centered on financial success. This revival stemmed partially from a backlash against the socialist era, during which women were forced by the state to take on the "double burden"[1] of working both outside and inside the home. It was not until the postreform era that a small group of elite men gained enough financial power to support a stay-at-home wife. Thus, unlike in the West, where shared breadwinning is often associated with gender progressiveness and modernity that are part of the post-1970s feminist movement,[2] some people in China today perceive homemaking to be a newfound privilege for women,[3] as well as a sign of wealth and status. At the same time, the ability to serve as the sole household provider became a symbol of modern masculine expression and a highly revered lifestyle for men.[4]

Alongside the revival of patriarchal gender ideologies in postreform China, the rate of infidelity also rose, particularly among wealthy men. While many single women express the desire to find a man with "good economic conditions," they also complain that men at this level cannot be

trusted to be faithful.[5] Hence, alternative masculine ideal types that emphasize men's emotional engagement and devotion to family have also emerged
in the Chinese popular media. For example, terms such as *beita nan* (beta
male), *zhunan* (cooking man), or *jing ji shi yong nan* (economic and practical man) describe local men who are not necessarily tall, handsome, or
wealthy but who have other redeeming qualities that make them ideal candidates for marriage.[6] It is these ideals that agency managers attempt to
project when writing blog posts about the Western men using their sites,
particularly when many of these men are not considered wealthy.

While female Chinese clients vary from the financially flexible to the
financially burdened, the Western men are a much more homogeneous
sample with more uniform, modest incomes. As noted in the introduction,
in a random sample of male client profiles, the majority of the men's self-
reported salaries were modest, with 50 percent earning less than the 2013
US median household income of US$50,000.[7] In order to foster a sense of
desire for these men, agency managers must stress the pitfalls of elite Chinese masculinity and present Western masculinity as a moral ideal. Thus,
Ms. Fong wrote in a blog post:

> Western men differ quite a bit from Chinese men in their attitude toward
> love and marriage. In China, we often see men showing off their young,
> beautiful wives to their friends. Everyone is comparing their wives' youth
> and beauty. Yet, foreign men rarely pay attention to their wife's age or
> physical appearance. The primary focus is on whether their spouse is
> the right fit for them, while physical attractiveness is outside the realm
> of consideration. This is the kind of respect Western men pay toward
> women, and this respect is extremely important for women seeking a
> happy marriage life.

While the managers' marketing tactics may successfully appeal to the gendered imaginations[8] of their clients, they cannot fake the lived realities of
these unions once couples move their courtships off the internet. Coming
from a society where male sex appeal is so closely linked to financial prowess, and where shared breadwinning between the sexes is considered less
than ideal, how do Chinese women reconcile with modest-earning Western
male suitors, who may expect them to take on fiscal responsibilities? This

is a prominent issue for the financially flexible women, many of whom are used to dating wealthy Chinese men.

In this chapter and the next, we will explore how economically privileged women come to terms with their own gendered imaginations when they meet their suitors face to face and discover that, in fact, the Western family man of their dreams does not truly exist. To this end, I will use case studies from each of the financially flexible subcategories defined in chapter 1: "wealthy women," "rich men's mistresses," and "middle-income professionals." First, let us return to Ruby, the middle-aged divorcée from the "wealthy" category.

WEALTHY WOMEN: RUBY'S DILEMMA

In the summer of 2009, Ruby and I met over tea and fruit at Bund Café, an upscale chain restaurant in Tunyang. Michael Jackson's sudden death had just shocked the world, and some of his soothing tunes, such as "Heal the World" or "You Are Not Alone," played softly in the background as we chatted. "I married in a rush," Ruby said, "because he insisted on registering for marriage right away." The previous fall, when Larry made his initial visit to China, he proposed to Ruby only two days after they met. He was determined to settle his marriage on that visit, and even told Ruby he would go meet other female clients if she rejected him, as he could not afford multiple trips to China to find a wife. A year later, after having had more time to think through the practicalities of their marriage, Ruby was increasingly worried that Larry would not be able to support her on his hourly wage of US$20. After observing Larry shop during his visit to China, Ruby became even more concerned. She said:

> He always thinks about whether the product is cheap or expensive, and whether he really needs it or not, etc. He always has to plan in advance, even if it's just a tiny amount of money. That's not me. When I see something I like, I just buy it, you know. I'm really worried about this dramatic difference in our spending habits.

Ruby's comment certainly reflected a big disparity in their earning capacity and lifestyle; yet, on a deeper level, she was also concerned about their vastly different gender role expectations. Although Ruby chose a modest-earning man, she still expected him to provide for her. While Ruby was willing to "compromise some materialistic enjoyment" in her marriage, to her, that simply meant downgrading her lavish lifestyle to match her poorer husband's, rather than taking over the breadwinner role herself. At the end of the day, Ruby still wanted "provider love" from Larry,—that is, love based on the provision of material goods.[9] In a newly consumerist China, money and gift-giving have become important channels through which men express their feelings for women, and through which women evaluate men's love and commitment.[10] Thus, it is normative for men to buy their girlfriends expensive presents, pick up all dating-related expenses, and possibly even give them a monthly stipend if the relationship is serious. In fact, a popular adage in China goes: "If a woman loves a man, she would try to save money for him; if a man loves a woman, he would spend lavishly on her, even if it's borrowed money." The implication here is that women show their love by not asking for expensive presents in order to ease men's earning pressure. Men, in contrast, prove their love by spending above their means on women. As we can see here, there is no expectation for women to provide because they are on the receiving end. Women's way of helping out is by asking for less, thus implying that breadwinning is a masculine expression of love, not a feminine one.

Having internalized these ideologies, Ruby became increasingly dissatisfied with Larry's failure to provide, particularly after her initial feelings of novelty and romance faded. The more time that passed, the more issues she found with the fundamental financial practices of their relationship. To give an example, among many other things, she was bothered by the fact that Larry never sent her a monthly allowance during the twelve-month period after they married and while she awaited her visa in China. At the agency, it was common practice for men to send women money—ranging from as little as US$200 to as much as US$2,000 per month—as a symbolic gesture of commitment. Not receiving an allowance, Ruby felt as if Larry "did not really love her." Not only did Larry fail to provide a monthly allowance, but he sometimes even relied on Ruby to pay when they dined out during his visit to China. This certainly embarrassed Ruby in front of her friends, who watched in dismay as Ruby picked up the tab.

Nevertheless, Ruby appreciated Larry's gender egalitarian attitude in other respects. For example, unlike her Chinese ex-husband, who left his socks all over the house, Larry always cleaned up after himself when he visited Ruby in China. In the bedroom, Larry cared about her sexual pleasure. While Chinese men "only want women to massage them," Larry offered to give her a massage instead. Despite these benefits of a home less divided by traditional gender roles, the discrepancy between Larry's financial abilities and Ruby's expectations for him to serve as a breadwinner remained an unignorable issue in their marriage.

After getting to know Larry better, Ruby anticipated a lifestyle downgrade in the United States, but she still overestimated Larry's ability to handle what she considered "normal living expenses." When she finally moved to Vermont in the fall of 2009, after two months of email exchange and twelve months of waiting for her visa, Ruby was shocked to discover that Larry lived paycheck to paycheck. During one of our Skype calls, she vented her frustration to me:

> He always says he has no money. He is scared to even go to the supermarket. After paying for child support, household expenses, and [his] mortgage, there is only money left for food. Sometimes when we are out of a small, inexpensive household item, he would say, let's go out and get it next week after I get paid. I never thought life in the United States would be this difficult. Even during the prereform era in China, most people I knew did not have to skimp on food. He lives in a two-story house, but it's in the middle of nowhere and there is not a damn piece of anything valuable in it.

During my Skype meetings with Ruby, Larry was never shy in showering her with physical displays of affection. As we conversed in Chinese, he would often come over to give her a peck on the cheek or a massage on the shoulders. Thus, Ruby said:

> He places so much importance on physical and verbal expressions of "love," which I think is naïve, like someone who is eighteen years old. Western men say "I love you" all the time, but, unlike Chinese men, they don't feel any fiscal responsibility for their wives. In China, if a man loves a woman, he would not only want to give her emotional support but he would also want to make money so that she could live comfortably.

> Here, even if your husband loves you, you are still expected to take financial responsibility for yourself. This is not my understanding of "true love."

Moreover, Ruby felt that her assets from her previous marriage, which she acquired through her ex-husband, were unrelated to Larry. Currently unemployed, she did not feel she should be expected to pay for household expenses. Larry, in contrast, wanted Ruby to pitch in some of her assets from China, and he was unwilling and unable to offer her anything beyond food and shelter.

Larry's failure to provide led Ruby to question his masculinity. When we first met in China, Ruby criticized newly rich Chinese entrepreneurs like her ex-husband for working too much. She said, "They are just *pin bo* [fighting for their career] and constantly stressed," and she expressed disdain for their lifestyle by calling them "workaholics" who achieved financial success but lost their family life as a result. Yet, after moving abroad, Ruby thought Larry was too extreme in the opposite direction. To give an example, one of her greatest frustrations was the fact that Larry would not agree to work overtime on Sundays. Even though he would be paid one and a half times his normal wage, he refused. In return, Ruby thought Larry was "lazy" and "unambitious."

Moreover, she looked down on Larry for wanting to *chi ruan fan* (eat soft rice)—a derogatory term that describes the act of living off women—when he suggested that they relocate to China in order to move into Ruby's luxury condo together. At this time, Ruby began to call Chinese men like her ex-husband "real men," for, despite being shorter and less physically appealing, they were ultimately "more masculine deep down inside" than Western men like Larry. Their lust for money and sense of responsibility to provide for women contrasted with Larry's low earning capacity and lack of career ambition, both of which, in the eyes of Ruby, effeminized him. Thus, coming from a society where masculinity is closely tied to provider love, Ruby grew increasingly dissatisfied with Larry, whose internal qualities weakened his masculine appeal, despite her initial attraction to his good looks.

In addition to Larry's perceived financial shortcomings, Ruby also began to find him annoyingly clingy and intensely insecure. For example, Larry would put up a big struggle every time she went back to China to visit her family, as he worried that she would stay there forever and never come back. After observing these less-than-desirable traits, Ruby attributed Larry's insecurity to his reclusive Western lifestyle and lack of earning power. Unlike her ex-husband, who had a robust social network in China and spent much of his time with business partners, Larry rarely socialized outside of work and often played video games at home. For this reason, Ruby believed her presence was much needed to help him combat his loneliness. Ruby even joked to Larry that he had found himself a "free nanny" who did all the housework in exchange for only basic living necessities. Although Ruby had taken on many household chores in her previous marriage, she was at least rewarded for her labors with a life of luxury. Ruby believed no Western woman would accept the lifestyle Larry offered his wife. While Ruby had once thought Chinese men were more superficial than Western men for wanting younger women, she now began to speculate that Larry chose her over younger women because they would have been much more financially demanding.

Ruby was used to driving a Lexus, enjoying redwood furniture, and buying high-end designer clothing, while Larry drove a pickup truck, had Ikea furniture, and went clothes shopping at Walmart once a year. To compensate for his frugal lifestyle, Ruby took trips to China twice a year and bought US$5,000 worth of clothes for herself each time with her own money. After living in Vermont for several months, Ruby summed up her situation in her own words as follows: "God's eyes are extremely bright. He will not let you have everything. If you are happy in one respect, you will be lacking something in another. When I was in China, I had everything—money, family, friends—the only thing missing in my life was a man. Now I have a man, but I lost everything else."

Instead of walking away, however, Ruby decided to work on her marriage. After all, Larry's loyalty and dedication satisfied her desire for a faithful partner. Over time, Ruby convinced Larry to compromise in certain respects. When we met up in China during the summer of 2011, Ruby told me that he had begun to change, and now did things such as taking on more overtime shifts to increase their household income. He also sold his house at her suggestion and replaced it with two condos, one of which they rented out to generate more cash flow.

Ruby's story shows that although some Chinese women could now afford to marry lesser-earning men and possibly even take on the provider role, they were not mentally prepared to do so. Although a minority of Chinese women like Ruby benefited immensely from China's economic reform and achieved financial success at an individual level—either by developing successful careers[11] or by marrying wealthy men—women as a group still experienced declining economic status, as wealth became concentrated within the hands of a small subset of elite men. These macro-level structural changes contributed to a new society-wide cultural emphasis on the separation of spheres, alongside the association of masculinity with an ability and willingness to financially provide. Having internalized such ideologies, wealthy women like Ruby felt uncomfortable with gender role reversals, despite their own newfound economic power.

The type of clash in gender ideology seen in Ruby's marriage was actually a significant source of conflict for many couples at the agency. It was particularly prominent among the financially flexible women, many of whom were used to dating nouveau-riche Chinese men. Grace's story serves as an additional example to illustrate this point. As described in chapter 1, Grace was a divorced actress in her mid-forties. By the time we met in 2011, she had mostly retired from acting, but she still taught part-time at a local film academy and occasionally hosted television programs. Slim, poised, and exquisitely dressed in designer clothing, Grace was considered very attractive by local standards.

Having received a divorce settlement of more than US$1 million, plus US$45,000 per year in child support, Grace was financially well-off. Yet, she still expected her future husband to be the sole household provider because her frame of reference was her Chinese ex-husband, who practiced provider love to the extreme. To put Grace's previous lifestyle in perspective, while she and her Chinese husband were traveling together in Hong Kong, he bought her the first Louis Vuitton handbag she set her hands on. Moreover, when he saw her glance at the same bag in a different color, he immediately purchased that one as well. Throughout their four-year marriage, Grace quit her acting job at his request but was compensated handsomely with lavish presents and several condos.

Aware of Grace's lifestyle and expectations, the translators thought she would be extremely difficult to marry off. Among other issues, there were few wealthy Western male clients to begin with, and not many practiced "provider masculinity" to the same extent as Grace's ex-husband. Moreover, some wealthy Western men who were willing to spend lavishly on women preferred that they were (1) childless, and (2) still in their twenties—a profile Grace most certainly did not fit. Thus, many of her relationships faltered during the negotiation process. It was not until two years after joining the agency that Grace finally met a generous ranch owner. Their financial negotiation went smoothly, so she eagerly traveled to meet him in the United States. Yet, upon arrival in his central Oklahoma home, Grace knew rural American life was not for her. Moreover she worried about her daughter, still in grade school, joining his family when she learned that his teenage sons were both in rehabilitation for substance abuse. Sensing a grim outlook for her future, Grace canceled her membership at the agency. Her path was the one that the majority of financially flexible clients took when they realized that their Western suitors could not meet their expectations in the way of socioeconomic class, while Ruby's marriage to Larry was an exception rather than the norm.

RICH MEN'S MISTRESSES: JENNIFER'S PLIGHT

While Ruby and Grace were both ex-wives of wealthy men, Jennifer was a rich man's mistress. As related in chapter 1, Jennifer and I met back in 2011, at another client's engagement party. Although Jennifer would be considered average looking by local Chinese standards, her melodic voice and amiable personality gave her a unique appeal. At the time, Jennifer was dating a Chinese businessman who resided with his family in the United States for much of the year but who visited Jennifer whenever he traveled in China for work. He helped Jennifer purchase a condo and sent her a monthly stipend that was equivalent to the salary of a white-collar professional in her city.

Ms. Mei told me that mistresses were the most difficult clients to marry off. These women had been pampered for years by wealthy Chinese patrons who would not marry them and who in lieu of a marriage proposal showered them with lavish presents, generous stipends, and surprise romantic getaways. Thus, the mistresses often viewed average-earning Western men—particularly those who expected women to make financial contributions within a relationship—to be stingy and unromantic.

In her early forties, Jennifer was still dating her Chinese patron upon entering Ms. Mei's agency, seemingly never having fully made up her mind about marriage migration. In fact, Jennifer even declined to meet the Western men she conversed with online, thus illustrating her general lack of interest in seriously considering these Western partners. Nevertheless, she still ended up engaging in a brief romantic liaison with Jason, a British language instructor living in Tunyang, whom she met while drinking with me at a local pub.

Jennifer said she dated Jason both out of sexual curiosity about white men and because of her frustration with her Chinse *lao gong* (euphemism for "husband"). Although Jennifer preferred "rich men with multiple women" over "poor men who were loyal to her," she still could not hold back her frustration whenever her *lao gong* spoke of his special fantasy, in which he would wake up with Jennifer in one arm and his other "wife" in the other. In retaliation, she decided to engage in a secret, short-term affair with Jason while still maintaining relations with her *lao gong*. However, when Jason offered to give her RMB 5,000 (US$760) per month in exchange for moving in together, she rejected him. Laughing, Jennifer said to me, "This offer is probably a huge sacrifice for Western men who are not used to providing for women ... I'm flattered to see Jason bend his so-called 'gender egalitarian' ways for me, but I would not seriously consider his offer because this money simply does not match what my *lao gong* gives me."

To explore Jason as a romantic prospect for Jennifer outside of his unsatisfactory financial contribution, I asked her about his bedroom performance. She smiled and said, "In terms of size, he is indeed much bigger than my *lao gong*." Yet she also exclaimed, "It was so big, it looked kind of scary when he first took it out, you know! I still think Asian bodies are better sized for each other." Apparently, to Jennifer, bigger did not mean better. She added, "I am also worried—if he's so big, will he stretch me out? What if I'm not as tight as I used to be and my *lao gong* could tell when he came back?" One morning, around a month after she first met Jason, Jennifer called me. Sobbing, she said Jason's condom fell off the prior evening and she was now paranoid about catching HIV (human immunodeficiency virus). After getting an STD check—which came back clear—Jennifer broke up with Jason.

Through Jennifer's example, we can see that even if a Western man agrees to give provider love, a relationship can still falter if the amount

offered is too low. Given Jason's relative lack of wealth as a language instructor, as compared to wealthy businessmen like her *lao gong*, Jennifer
decided to treat Jason as only a short-term partner and an "exotic sexual
conquest."[12] After a brief romantic liaison, she quickly returned to her *lao
gong*, who was able to give her enough provider love despite engaging in
multiple relationships.

At the agency, conflicts over gender role expectations often surfaced
during the face-to-face meetup stage, when decisions involving money,
such as who pays for dinner, what gifts the man is expected to bring, and
various other financial negotiations, took place. In particular, negotiations
over bride price and home purchases were common sources of contention.
Historically, Chinese grooms were expected to pay a bride price, which
is a large sum of money, to a bride's family.[13] During the socialist era, the
custom was modified such that only small items, such as Thermos flasks or
bedding, were given. In light of the market reform, today's bride price in
China has returned to large sums of cash.[14] Moreover, after housing became
privatized in the postreform era, many women and their natal families now
expect men to buy a home, or at least put forth a down payment, as a precondition for marriage.[15]

Because of these norms, many female clients request monetary compensation from their Western suitors. Some ask the men to purchase an
apartment in China in the woman's name, while others insist upon their
suitor paying off their parents' or their grown children's mortgages. I witnessed several relationships falter when the Western men rejected such requests. For example, Lily, a woman in her forties, moved to Canada on a
fiancée visa, only to return to China three months later because her fiancé
did not agree to purchase an apartment for her daughter in China. From his
perspective, not only was the amount of money she requested beyond his
financial capacity, but he also did not agree with the bride price practice,
which was not normative in Canada.

These conflicts were so prominent that Ms. Fong, one of the agency
owners, dedicated several blog entries to addressing these financial issues.
One of the common complaints Ms. Fong heard from her female clients
was that Western men were "stingy." Ms. Fong thought that while some
of those complaints signaled a genuine character flaw in the men, many

others simply reflected an East-West cultural clash, in which the women embraced a Chinese-style "provider masculinity" that many of the Western men rejected. For example, Ms. Fong noted that one of her female clients felt women should never share fiscal responsibilities with men. She believed that since women were already giving away their bodies—the greatest gift women could ever give men—during marriage, they should not be obligated to make any further sacrifices in the name of the household. Thus, even if a woman worked, her earnings should be kept separately as her own pocket money. This client even went so far as to claim that men and women should identify in completely separate spheres, where men are solely responsible for fiscal matters while women work exclusively within the household. This mentality often didn't align with that of her male suitors.

Just like the women featured in Ms. Fong's blog, Jennifer agreed that it was natural for men to spend money on women, but not vice versa, since women are born "the weaker sex." Moreover, Jennifer believed a woman's feminine value was best reflected through the amount of financial support she could garner from men. Thus, Jennifer could not understand why I continued to date my American boyfriend of five years—a relationship that didn't subscribe to the provider love mentality. Once, when I fell ill in China and stayed for a series of doctor's visits, she made the following comment: "You say that he loves you, but what does that mean? He doesn't send you a monthly stipend. This time you got sick, he didn't mail you any money. And you said he doesn't buy you expensive presents either. So he gives you nothing. If I were you, I would feel very *chi kui* [taken advantage of]." When I challenged Jennifer's view by stating that her lifestyle puts women in an objectified, powerless position, she rebutted: "I'm not convinced by your Western perspective. Today Chinese women have much higher status than they did during the socialist era. Women no longer need to earn money. They can just get it by controlling men. Isn't that power? I think women who can get money without having to work have much higher status and power than women who must go to work every day."

These women's ideologies certainly reflect gender norms in contemporary China, which hinge on a revival of traditional values emphasizing a separation of spheres.[16] For example, consider an adage that emerged during the 1990s: "Women conquer the world through conquering men." The implication here is that, rather than gaining direct access to power, women should derive power indirectly from men. The popular media framed this motto as a new way to think about femininity in the postsocialist era, when a capitalist class dominated by men came to power. This view resonated strongly with the former mistresses of rich men.

Many mistresses experienced an extreme version of "provider masculinity" during the 1990s, which they knew to be a time of decadence. During this early reform era, corruption was rampant, as newly rich businessmen colluded with government officials for profit and then used their embezzled money and goods to support mistresses.[17] For example, Emma, another former mistress, went out to gamble every night and could afford to lose as much as US$35,000 in one sitting because her then-lover, a married Chinese businessman who smuggled electronics, would place a new bundle of cash on her dresser the next day. When Emma told an American suitor over dinner that she once lost a Rolex watch worth US$8,000, he gasped. Turning to me (I was serving as their translator that evening), Emma smiled, shook her head, and whispered in Chinese: "He thinks it's awfully expensive, but I did not think it was a big deal back then. In fact, I never even bothered looking for that watch. You know, these American men have no idea how much I have been pampered in my former life." Interestingly, Emma later told me that it was normative for men in her boyfriend's social circle to compete among themselves to see who spent more on their mistress. For these wealthy businessmen, giving provider love is a performance they put on not only for women, but also for *other men* in order to boost their own masculinity.

Mr. Li, the other agency manager, told me that in contrast to these Chinese women, many Western male clients held a different view on gendered division of labor. In line with the decline of men's provider role in the West, alongside women's increased labor force participation and new gender egalitarian dating norms in recent years, many male clients believed that expenses should be shared between men and women.[18] Some Western suitors even felt taken advantage of when they ended up paying for everything during their China visit. In fact, Mr. Li told me that sharing dating expenses, such as the cost of dinner or taxi rides, boosted the women's chances of marriage. Despite knowing that making financial contributions could make them a more appealing match, many female clients still refused to do so because they saw it as an insult to their femininity.

In response, the agencies generally tried to persuade both sides to compromise. To the Western men, they explained the prevalence of "provider masculinity" in China today and asked them to make small compromises, such as bringing pricier gifts to China or always picking up the tab when dining out. On the women's end, they sometimes criticized the female clients' expectations of lavishness in hopes that they would self-reflect. This strategy is seen in the following blog excerpt, which illustrates Ms. Fong's attempt to persuade her female clients to lower their financial expectations:

> I often hear from my female clients that they want men to give them money, to buy them a condo in China, to be financially supported by men, if the men don't give them presents, then the men are stingy, if he really loved me, he would help me pay for this and that . . . and at first I tried to change their view by telling them that you are no longer young, and if your understanding of marriage is still so warped, then don't come to my agency, we are not a company set out to satisfy your materialistic desires, we are launching a platform where you can seek a partner and find happiness in life and end your loneliness. If you believe that only men who give you lots of money qualify as good men, then your view of marriage is wrong, especially given that you are middle-aged!

As we can see, Ms. Fong criticized these women for equating love with financial support, and for defining "good men" as those who gave them a lot of money. She recognized that wealthy, high-status Chinese men aimed to offer their financial support in exchange for women's youth, beauty, and domesticity. Since beautiful faces and bodies decline with age, Ms. Fong did not think her middle-aged female clients could expect to strike the same patriarchal bargain as young women. Thus, she criticized them for having unrealistic expectations.

Yet, these persuasion tactics *don't* always work. The agencies are powerless to improve the Western men's financial condition, and many translators have difficulty persuading them to embrace a Chinese version of "provider masculinity" that may not be normative in their country. On the women's end, the translators find it difficult to persuade them to give up the "provider masculinity" expectation that is integral to contemporary Chinese dating culture, particularly among women in elite social circles. Hence, in some blog articles, the agencies frame the men's perceived stinginess as a "shortcoming" that the Chinese women must "endure" if they choose to marry Westerners. However, since the financially flexible women are not under economic pressure to marry or leave China quickly, they do not always tolerate such shortcomings and often end up rejecting their suitors entirely.

THE HAPPILY MARRIED MINORITY

Despite reservations about the Western men's financial and gender expectations, three of the financially flexible women I followed ended up happily married to Western men. Interestingly, all three marriages operated on a hybrid model that included gendered division of labor as well as a more egalitarian balance of sharing fiscal responsibilities. Unlike some of the other financially flexible clients who acquired their wealth from their Chinese ex-husbands, Anna was a self-made woman whose Chinese former husband earned a modest income. Over the years, Anna worked her way up from secretary to business manager and bought several homes. After the death of her husband, she joined Ms. Fong's agency, met a business owner from Kentucky named Wayne, and moved abroad. Although this new marriage meant quitting her job and taking a financial hit, Anna was happy to do so as she felt she deserved a break from having worked much too hard in her younger years. Both in their sixties now, Anna and Wayne spent half of each year living in the United States and the other half in China.

In the United States, their marriage was based on very clear gendered divisions of labor. Anna became a stay-at-home wife who took over all the cooking and cleaning while Wayne paid for her personal expenses. Both parties appeared to be very content with this arrangement. Having been the primary household breadwinner for the past thirty-five years, Anna felt exhausted in China and was ready to try out a more traditionally feminine role in her new marriage. For his part, Wayne appreciated Anne's domestic contributions and called her a "kind, loving, generous lady" who agreed to give him all her love. Here are some anecdotal examples he gave:

If I do not get up in the morning when she does, I later find a plate on the bed for me to eat, that wakes me up with the beautiful smell of well-prepared food . . . when I come home and my shoes have some type of soils on them, she cleans them and makes sure they are polished. I have tried to do this myself, but she always insists that this is her job . . . the clothes are always washed, all spots removed, and neatly hung and folded for my use. After I put my clothes on, if a collar is out of place or if she sees a spot on my shirts or pants, she runs to get something to remove the spot.

Wayne viewed the meticulous care Anna took in housework as her way of expressing love to him. For her part, Anna enjoyed the provider love Wayne gave her. "Money is not everything," Anna said, "but it's an important criterion through which to judge how good someone is to you." Anna said Wayne bought her anything and everything she laid her eyes or hands on, thereby making her feel deeply loved in a way that her modest-earning Chinese husband never did. When we met up for lunch in the summer of 2018, Anna proudly pointed to her Louis Vuitton handbag and necklace, telling me that they were both gifts from Wayne.

Although this provider love may seem one-sided, I also witnessed Anna reciprocate Wayne's efforts to provide. Pointing to the Gucci pants, Louis Vuitton belt, Lacoste shirt, and jade ring Wayne wore, Anna told me she had bought them all. In fact, when Anna first moved to Wayne's Kentucky home, she threw away at least ten suitcases of what she called "no-name, rural-style clothing" and replaced them with designer items. Even during Wayne's first visit to China, long before they were married, Anna bought him a US$700 coat when she saw that the jacket he wore was much too thin for the local weather. When reporting on their love story in her blog, Ms. Fong attributed Anna's successful marriage to her generosity and gender egalitarian spending habits, which, Ms. Fong noted, were rather atypical for female clients at the agency.

Like Anna, Ms. Mei, the manager, eventually married a Western man of similar age and socioeconomic standing as herself. Following their 2017 wedding, Ms. Mei resigned and moved to Switzerland with him. When Jennifer saw photos of his beautifully manicured home in Switzerland, she asked Ms. Mei whether he had added her name to the property. Shaking her head, Ms. Mei said, "I'm not so concerned with that. I'm also not interested in finding out how much savings he had before we met or how much of it he would share with me. I live in the moment and try to enjoy what is in front of me. Even if I don't own the place, I am happy to just live there." Later on, Ms. Mei told me in private that if Chinese women wanted to marry foreign men, they would have to learn to be more financially independent, as Western men would not spoil women in the same manner as Chinese men. Although most would likely pay for women's basic living necessities, Westerners would often scoff at the idea of giving their partners large sums of pocket money. Thus, with unrealistic expectations of what their foreign partners were willing to offer them, many women experienced miserable failure at the agency. They were unwilling to compromise on a more fiscally egalitarian relationship, like that which succeeded in the marriages of Anna and Ms. Mei.

CONCLUSION

Sociologist Michael Kimmel once stated that the masculinity practices of elite Western men have a strong global influence, as Western hegemonic masculinity is often deemed the most developmentally advanced form of masculinity, superior to all others.[19] Yet, the examples from this chapter show that this is not always the case. While the gender egalitarian sharing of fiscal responsibility is associated with progressiveness and modernity in the West—particularly among the upper middle class[20]—the women in my study view men who embrace this doctrine as effeminate and undesirable. Unable to persuade a majority of their clients to accept this aspect of Western masculinity, the agencies chose to frame it as a shortcoming that Chinese women must endure if they want to pursue a successful marriage migration.

It appears that most Chinese women in this study do not accept Western masculinity in its existing form. Instead, they desire a hybrid masculine ideal that combines traits from both the Western family man and the wealthy Chinese entrepreneur: they want their future husband to be devoted, caring, faithful, and accepting of a woman's older age; yet, at the same time, they also want him to be a generous provider. Some women even expect their future husband to give them exorbitant amounts of money whenever they deem it necessary. Unwilling to compromise in the absence of this ideal man, many financially flexible women opt out of marriage migration halfway through the courtship process and remain single.

It is worthwhile to note that, from a Western perspective, the Chinese women featured in this chapter may come across as lazy, greedy gold diggers. Nevertheless, I encourage readers to take a more culturally relativistic perspective and consider the sociocultural context in which these women exist. They live in a society that has experienced dramatic structural transformation. In contrast to the socialist era, when ownership of private property was banned, income gaps were small, and women participated in the formal labor market,[21] the postreform era was marked by the sudden rise of a newly rich capitalist class dominated by men and a worsening of women's social position. Given this, the women's expectations reflect the most revered model of marriage in China today—that is, marriage based on the exchange of women's beauty and domesticity for men's money and power. Yet, this patriarchal bargain poses risks for women in the long run. As Ms. Fong noted, middle-aged women cannot expect to strike the same bargain as young women, since beautiful faces and bodies decline with age. As these women's first marriages to wealthy Chinese men falter, they look to Western men in hopes of striking the same patriarchal bargain.

Ultimately, I suggest that these women's gender strategies are still byproducts of structural inequality in postreform China. Their ideologies work in favor of the most socially advantaged group in China—that is, wealthy, heterosexual, capitalist men—while putting women and lesser-earning men, including white men, at a disadvantage. While some women may benefit from the patriarchal bargain in the short run, the stories in this book show that many end up single and unhappy in the long run. The inevitable aging process costs them their youth and beauty, thereby also costing them their best bargaining token on the Chinese marriage market. At the same time, their resistance to more gender egalitarian marital practices—as informed by their belief in China's reemerging patriarchal ideologies—also hinders their path to successful marriage with Western men.

3 | TRANSNATIONAL BUSINESS MASCULINITY

IN THE SPRING OF 2011, I had just moved to China for my yearlong fieldwork after completing preliminary research there during the previous three summers. One cold, rainy day, while I was chatting with translators at Ms. Mei's office, they invited me to attend a client's engagement party, to be held that evening. The engagement was between Vivien, a divorced public relations executive in her thirties, and her American fiancé, John, a business manager in his early forties. The ceremony, held at a luxurious lakeside hotel, was rather small: there were only three tables, one for the bride's family, one for the bride's friends, and one for staff and clients. Although I had never met the couple, I was able to spot them immediately, dressed in matching Chinese silk gowns. John had strawberry-blond hair and appeared somewhat overweight, while Vivien was a shapely woman who smiled and giggled much of the time. As soon as Ms. Mei saw me walk in, she introduced me to everyone as a PhD student looking to recruit new subjects for a study on cross-border marriage.

That evening, there were lots of tears and hugs. The agency managers and translators, as well as Vivien's friends and family members, all got up in front of the room to give the couple their blessing one by one. At one point, Vivien's mother, an elderly widow, embraced John and said, "I want to thank this gentleman for marrying my daughter. I sincerely hope he will treat my daughter magnanimously when she moves to his country, because her safety and livelihood will rest with him." At this point, Vivien started weeping, while John blushed. Nervously wiping sweat off his forehead, he turned to Vivien's mother and said in an earnest voice, "She is becoming my . . . my whole world; I am going to protect that with everything I can." The three of them stood before the room with their hands tightly clasped together. That evening, Vivien and I were among the last to leave. She approached me and shook my hand firmly before slipping me her business card. In all seriousness she said, "I have many, many important things to ask you, please, I hope we can get together soon."

A week later, Vivien invited me to dinner. Since I didn't know her well, I was quite curious to find out if there were hidden grievances behind her seemingly successful engagement. Since she worked across town, she took a forty-minute cab ride just to pick me up. As her taxi pulled up in front of my hotel, I could sense she was different from many of the agency's working-class clients, who could not afford to commute such long distances by taxi. Vivien's long, silky hair was tied into a ponytail, while her perky hips swayed as she walked toward me. Although her facial features were not considered strikingly beautiful by conventional Chinese standards, she was pleasing to look at because she put on a variety of expressions and laughed often, thereby conveying her emotions even when not speaking.

Vivien wanted to treat me to a pricy seafood buffet across town but changed her plan in light of the rush-hour traffic. Instead, she opted for Bund Café, an upscale chain restaurant that served both Chinese and Western-style food. With dim lighting, plush velvet couches, and Kenny G's "Going Home" playing softly in the background, the ambiance here clearly differed from many other, more rowdy and affordable eateries. As we walked in, Vivien laughed and said, "Bund Café was literally my canteen before my office got relocated to a different part of town! You see, I used to come here for lunch every single day."

Just as we sat down, she looked me straight in the eye and blurted out, "You know, I don't love him." I was astounded by her bluntness, given that we hardly knew each other. "I feel extremely conflicted," continued Vivien, "because I finally met a nice guy, but the problem is, I'm not attracted to him. I *just* don't feel the passion." First, she told me that the disparity between John's American "pounds" and the metric "kilograms" that she had been accustomed to caused her to overlook the weight that was listed on John's dating profile. Since John only sent her headshots, it was not until she saw him at the airport that she realized he weighed more than two hundred pounds. Beyond his physical appearance, Vivien found his introverted, slow-paced personality unappealing. Yet, just a few days after his arrival in China, John proposed. When I asked Vivien why she accepted the proposal, given all the flaws she saw in John, she laughed bitterly and whispered, "You see all the men eating here at this Western café tonight? I bet eighty percent of them have been in an extramarital affair before."

Compared with the numerous Chinese playboys Vivien had previously dated, John was a "nice guy." In an email to Vivien, John described himself as follows: "I know I am not the most attractive man, but you should know what I lack in looks I make up for in affection, devotion, and respect for my love." The striking difference in personality between Vivien's previous beaus and John was made obvious when they met in person. John never pushed Vivien for sex, unlike her Chinese lovers, or even some of her other Western suitors. While John was not initially interested in having children, he agreed to try when he learned that Vivien wanted a baby, and even completed fertility testing at her request. It seems that John genuinely prioritized Vivien's comfort and happiness, as he promised to lose thirty pounds and even underwent intimate plastic surgery when Vivien told him that his obesity made their sex life very difficult.

Vivien found herself in a bind. On one hand, her ticking biological clock, distrust of Chinese men, lack of better options among other Western suitors, and John's unrelenting devotion motivated her to continue dating him. On the other hand, she was at a loss as to how she would overcome her lack of attraction to John. Finally, after a few months of contemplation following their engagement, Vivien asked her translators to start writing to other men again. She decided that John was her "bottom priority," and she would drop him immediately if a better catch appeared.

TRANSNATIONAL BUSINESS MASCULINITY

While we saw in chapter 2 that conflicts over expectations regarding provider love doomed the relationships of many of our financially flexible women, these women faced other conflicts, too, often generated by the disconnect between the Chinese women's sexual expectations and the Western men's socioeconomic status. For example, many financially flexible women are attracted to men who exhibit "transnational business masculinity"—a particular masculine ideal embodied by wealthy, powerful business executives who control the global market.[1] This type of masculinity, characteristic of the wealthy Chinese entrepreneurs these women once dated or married, represents a new ideal of China's market era.[2] Interestingly, despite being Western and white, most of the men enrolled at Ms. Mei's and Ms. Ding's agencies do not come from the upper echelon of the global economic hierarchy, and therefore do not exhibit traits of transnational business masculinity.

Historically, Asian men have been stereotyped in both China and the United States as weaker and less sexually desirable than white men.[3] These stereotypes originated with Western imperialism, which defined Asians as inherently effeminized relative to their Western aggressors.[4] Throughout China's socialist era, from 1949 to 1979, when ownership of private property was banned, most local men were also significantly poorer than Western men. But today, China's marketization has produced a new group of local business elites who are just as economically powerful as their Western counterparts and far richer than the average Westerner.[5] Their new command of economic resources has allowed them to develop tastes, lifestyles, and sexual know-how that Westerners once seemingly monopolized.[6]

Nevertheless, in China today, Western men, and white men in particular, still enjoy some degree of racial sexual capital,[7] meaning that their whiteness and foreign status alone can give them increased access to sexual resources. However, this race-based privilege might not be enough to overcome other, class-based disadvantages if they were to compete with local Chinese men of higher socioeconomic status than themselves. For example, as we saw in chapter 2, Jennifer initially dated Jason out of a sexual curiosity about white men. Yet, in light of Jason's relative poverty as a language instructor next to her businessman *lao gong*, Jennifer ultimately rejected Jason's proposal to move in together.

The concept of transnational business masculinity[8] is a crucial component of sexual attraction for many financially flexible women. Interestingly, this masculine ideal type is largely dependent on class instead of race, as Asian men who had it were much more desirable to the female clients than white men who did not have it. To explore this, I will continue with the case of Vivien.

MEETING KUAN

One sunny October afternoon, about three months after Vivien started writing to other men following her disappointment with John, I received a phone call from her inviting me out for dinner. That night, she came by in a black Lexus, and as I slipped into the car, I immediately recognized the driver sitting next to her. A few nights earlier, while I was drinking at a local pub with several Western expatriates, Vivien dropped by with a youthful-looking Chinese businessman, whom she introduced to me as her cousin Kuan. Short and dark-skinned, Kuan was certainly not considered handsome by conventional Chinese standards. Nevertheless, he had panache. From the way he flashed the bills in his Louis Vuitton wallet to the perfectly pressed Burberry shirt he wore, it was obvious that he was part of China's nouveau-riche class. Every little thing he did radiated wealthy, successful energy. He spoke fluent English and engaged in long conversations with the other men at our table. He told us about his new work projects and exchanged business cards with the expats. Before leaving, he generously picked up the tab for all our drinks. After their departure that night, the expats asked me about this "boyfriend" of Vivien's. At the time, I blurted, "They are not a couple, you know, he's her cousin!"

Somehow, upon meeting Kuan again, I had a feeling that I was wrong. When Kuan walked ahead of us to get seating at the restaurant, I prodded Vivien on who he really was. Smiling, she simply whispered, "He is one of the contenders for a project I manage at work." In his mid-thirties, Kuan owned a business worth US$1 million. Although not extremely wealthy, his income of US$80,000–$160,000 was high for Tuyang, where the average annual salary was US$8,000. "I really like being around him because he has the drive, ambition, and persistence with his career that I don't have," said Vivien. At one point, she blushed and asked me, "Have you discovered that he sort of likes me?" to which I replied, "Yes, I could tell from the way he looked at you and the way he brushed his elbow against yours in the car that something was going on."

Upstairs, we converged at the restaurant on the top floor of a Sheraton hotel—where Kuan was a VIP member. "He volunteered to treat us tonight," said Vivien, smiling at the thought of Kuan's princely generosity. At the dinner, there was a sushi station, a hot bar serving both Western and Chinese cuisine, and a salad bar with imported brie and baguettes.

Unlike many crowded and noisy local restaurants, only a handful of people occupied this large open space, all of them dressed in formal evening wear and conversing quietly while looking at the city skyline. Through casual conversation, I learned more about Kuan's life as a grassroots entrepreneur. Born and raised in a poor mountain village, Kuan dropped out of middle school to work in the city, doing everything from working construction to cleaning homes to fixing cars. Then, he was lucky enough to join his uncle's company, where he was promoted to manager by the age of twenty-three. By the time he was thirty, he had started his own business. Although Kuan had little formal schooling, he took English classes evenings and weekends. His experience hanging out with American, British, and German expats, coupled with his own business travels to Europe and the Middle East, gave him a global outlook. Because of this, his mannerisms were somewhat Westernized. He was always opening doors for us and saying, "Ladies first."

Kuan started telling us funny stories about his interactions with foreign business clients. Vivien, who got one plate of roasted seafood after another, clearly enjoyed his company. At one point, she laughed hard enough to choke on a sip of water, and after regaining her composure, she looked at me, grinned, pointed to Kuan, and said, "Okay, [Monica], aren't you a sociologist wanting to learn more about Chinese society? Well, here is the typical *cheng gong ren shi* [man of great success]! He's rich, accomplished, and has a stay-at-home wife and baby son. In China, only successful and accomplished men can have stay-at-home wives!"

After dinner, Kuan took us to a bar, then proceeded to start a game of dice with Vivien in which the losing party was penalized by having to take a drink. After they finished an entire bottle of champagne, Vivien switched to pinching Kuan's nose whenever he lost, and I awkwardly watched their flirting from a distance. Unsurprisingly, the next day Vivien called to tell me they were dating. Sounding very giddy and excited, she said, "We do it anywhere and everywhere, in the car, by the lake, at his place, my place . . . and it is as intense as in the X-rated movies!"

Over the next few weeks, Kuan took Vivien to all the hotspots in town, while I sometimes tagged along as a third wheel. (In China, men often treat their girlfriend's friends, as a way to impress the girlfriend.) Together, we went club-hopping and wine-tasting, toured farmer's markets, and ate freshly roasted fish by the river. Vivien assured me it was just a fling, given that neither of their significant others were sexually available: Kuan's wife had just given birth, while John visited China only once every two or three months. Meanwhile, Vivien continued corresponding with John while secretly dating Kuan on the side.

While many couples broke up over the Western man's inability or unwillingness to give provider love, as we saw in chapter 2, this was not a source of conflict between John and Vivien. John sent Vivien all the money she requested, including a US$1,500 monthly stipend, US$50,000 as compensation for her future resignation from her high-paying job in China, and an additional US$5,000 each month in order to cover the fees for her studies in English. On top of all this cash, John bought Vivien lavish presents and took her on exciting and exotic trips abroad. Some of the more notable purchases included a US$4,000 camera, a US$2,000 designer coat, and US$5,000 diamond earrings. To afford it all, John took on side gigs and dipped into his savings. His generosity took even Vivien by surprise. She said, "I was hoping that he would give up on me once he saw my shopping habits, but to my surprise, the more I wanted to buy, the merrier he was!"

Despite his generosity, however, John remained insecure in their relationship. During the months of July and August alone, I received sixty pages of instant-messaging chat records and emails from John, who had no one else to turn to in order to vent his frustrations. He wrote me: "[Vivien] put some requests (AKA demands) out . . . I must do these things—'or else'—[she] leaves me . . . I often feel as if she has all these standards she expects, and I do not meet any of them. Like more of applying for a job than just being in love and wanting to get married . . . My biggest fear is that if I fail in any way, she will be disappointed and will decide not to marry me." In those emails, John would also add follow-up questions: "Do you think I am what she is really looking for, or just that I had the interest in her and I meet enough of her 'checklist criteria' for her to say, 'Yeah, okay, I guess he'll do'?" Since I did not want to meddle in their relationship, I offered John a few words of sympathy with his frustration, but no further insights.

The new financial burden that Vivien placed upon John did cause him to hesitate; after experiencing her "shop 'til he drops" attitude in Singapore, John actually considered holding off on their marriage. However, nothing ever came of his concerns, as John's strong infatuation seemed to overtake his reason and caused him to ignore the multitude of red flags that continued popping up over the course of their relationship. For example, when he tried introducing her to some of his Chinese friends who worked as waitstaff at a restaurant in his hometown, Vivien said, "Please don't force me to befriend waitresses; we are simply not in the same socioeconomic stratum and have nothing in common." John realized Vivien was "really materialistic and into social status"—something he did not appreciate. However, in a self-rationalizing manner, he thought of her as an "angel and devil in one," so that even when her "devil" side appeared, he would see it as "edginess" or a "no-bullshit approach" to life, while attributing the rest to a language and cultural barrier. Because of his strong infatuation, John chose to ignore many apparent problems in their relationship, including his numerous sacrifices, which amounted to an extremely unequal exchange, as he received neither physical nor emotional intimacy from the woman for whom he was willing to change so drastically. Despite John's suffering, I sometimes felt that he had no one to blame but himself. As far as I could see, he chose to prioritize Vivien's physical attractiveness and charisma, while he knowingly ignored all her character flaws and their incompatible worldviews.

In contrast to John, Kuan had none of the same financial commitments to Vivien, and also none of the same anxieties. By comparison, Kuan spent much less money than John. Although Kuan's own marriage was modeled on provider love and he spent lavishly on his stay-at-home wife, he never gave Vivien cash or expensive presents. Throughout their courtship, he only paid for food and entertainment. In a private interview with me, Kuan admitted that he never imagined becoming Vivien's lover, as she was "not pretty at all" compared to his wife and other girlfriends. In fact, he said, he initially pursued Vivien only to get access to her government connections. Despite the flashy dinners and elaborate daytrips, Vivien's affair with Kuan was *not* an exchange of her beauty and sexuality for his wealth, as he actually spent significantly *less* money on her compared to her American fiancé, to whom she was not sexually attracted.

Interestingly, Vivien did not find Kuan to be physically attractive either. While John was the "fattest guy" she ever dated, she called Kuan "the worst-looking Chinese guy" compared to her exes. Pulling out photos of them to show me, she said, "You see, all my previous partners were tall and hand-some." In China, height is of crucial importance to male attractiveness, and dark skin is associated with signs of physical labor, rural origin, and low status. Kuan, who was dark-skinned and well below five feet seven, cer-tainly did not fit the local aesthetic taste. Yet, Vivien seemed quite taken with him.

So, if their affair was not an exchange of his wealth for her sexuality, and if she also did not find him physically attractive, then what motivated Vivien to have sex with Kuan? As we have seen in chapter 1, according to sociologist Catherine Hakim, "erotic capital" is a form of personal asset that makes people attractive to others.[9] It encompasses not only facial beauty or bodily appeal, but also personality and behavioral traits such as liveliness, social presentation, style of dress, and sexual competence. I suggest that Vivien found Kuan more appealing than John because he had much higher erotic capital in regard to social attractiveness.

Unlike John, who often appeared nervous and self-conscious, Kuan was relaxed and confident. While Vivien initially thought John appeared quiet and uptight due to their language barrier, after observing John at a social gathering with other Western male clients, she concluded that he was so-cially awkward. Even Vivien's translator once asked me, "Is John like the loser type in the United States? You know, we can kind of tell." This stood in striking contrast to the outgoing and gregarious Kuan, whose brisk movements highlighted John's slow way of walking and speaking, which was "much like an old lady," according to Vivien, and in response to which she exclaimed, "I can't stand it!" She also found John's personality to be passive and thus effeminate. For example, while traveling with John in Sin-gapore, Vivien called me to complain. Treating me like a close girlfriend, she vented: "He is a man, but he is worse with directions than I am. Even though there are English signs everywhere, I had to figure everything out while he just followed me around . . . I feel like he is the woman in this rela-tionship!" Upon their return, Vivien even asked her translator to tell John, "I want someone who can take charge, a real man who can lead a woman, not a 'yes-man' like you who is always nodding and saying 'I understand.'" In contrast, Kuan exhibited masculine dominance without being overly domineering. He did many things that Vivien appreciated. For example, when making plans for the evening, Kuan would decide on two or three options and then allow her to choose one. In contrast, John rarely voiced his opinion, even when a translator was present, and instead relied on Vivien to take charge.

Through Vivien's interactions with Kuan and John, we can see that both men embodied a type of masculinity that was commensurate with their social status in their respective home countries.[10] In America, John was middle-class; he drove an Acura and lived in a safe suburban neighborhood. Although he sold his house following his divorce, he had enough savings to make a new purchase. Compared with other Western men at the agencies I studied, John's US$80,000 annual salary stood at the higher end of the spectrum.[11] However, compared with Kuan, who made US$80,000–$160,000 a year, John made significantly less in both absolute and relative terms. Perhaps more important than income, however, was the type of masculinity each man embodied, which corresponded to their respective social positions. Individuals who occupy the highest positions in their workplace, such as heads of corporations or senior management, often exhibit confidence and leadership.[12] Kuan, who owned and managed a company of five hundred people, certainly had those traits. In contrast, John, who held a technical job and managed only a small team at work, was much more passive. While not all men who exhibit confidence and leadership reach high positions at work, those who get promoted to the top are not usually passive and introverted.

In some ways, the masculinity Kuan exhibited resembled transnational business masculinity,[13] which describes corporate executives who control the global market. One version of transnational business masculinity is the "impeccably and smartly dressed" Wall Street investment banker, who shows "confidence," "mental and physical quickness," and "aggressiveness."[14] Kuan seemed to be the physical embodiment of this definition, especially in comparison to the middle-class, introverted John. Kuan was also talented at hosting and entertaining, which is characteristic of Chinese entrepreneurs, who must spend an exorbitant amount of time courting government officials and other potential business partners at restaurants, karaoke clubs, and massage parlors.[15] Indeed, Kuan once told me he spent four to five nights a week at entertainment venues, in great contrast to John, who rarely engaged in relationship-building out-side of the office and thus did not have the same opportunities to hone his hosting skills.

Kuan also exhibited higher erotic capital than John in the way of sexual competence. Throughout their courtship, Vivien had sex with John only once, which is rather infrequent by comparison to other female clients. She had to fantasize about other men to get aroused, and just as she finally got into the mood, John killed her desire with his performance. She said, "He moved so slowly, treating it as if . . . as if he were sipping his morn-ing latté . . . I nearly fell asleep! Halfway through, I lost my patience and kicked him off the bed." Interestingly, Vivien even saw a personality flaw behind John's bedroom performance. She said, "I just hate making love to fat people. Why are fat people fat? Because they are lazy. Lazy people don't like to move. It's the same thing in bed. They either don't move or move very slowly. In my eyes, this type of slow-moving man is simply not a 'real man.'" As we can see, John's lackadaisical bedroom performance, which Vivien associated with his slow-paced personality, effeminized him. Having imag-ined Western men to be "better in bed" than Chinese men before joining the agency, Vivien told the managers and other clients about John's disap-pointing performance.

By comparison, she found her Chinese lovers to be more sexually skilled. In particular, Vivien believed Kuan was good in bed because he *wan de duo* (screwed around with many women). As part of his business socializing, Kuan visited high-end sexual entertainment venues every week. Thus, his career and command of economic resources enabled him to have sex with many different women, improving his bedroom skills.

Before dating John, Vivien rejected an American firefighter named Edmond. She flagged Edmond as provincial as soon as she saw him and ended their relationship after sharing a cup of afternoon tea. "He brought lots of luggage," she said, "including a bunch of batteries. This shows he is not well traveled, because people who travel regularly would know you can get batteries anywhere." In contrast, the suitor she most wanted to marry was a British business executive of Pakistani descent. "He was high-class, well traveled, cosmopolitan, and handsome—a great catch overall," said Vivien reflectively, "but I was too financially demanding and that turned him off." Vivien's translator later told me that, to Vivien's disappointment, the suitor rejected her after they spent a weekend together.

As we can see, Vivien liked both Kuan and the Pakistani suitor even though they were men of color, while she found John and Edmond to be much less appealing, despite being white. Vivien's preferences illuminate the increasing significance of class distinction and the declining privilege associated with race, ethnicity, and nationality as an affluent capitalist class emerges in both Western and non-Western countries. Women who are used to dating wealthy Chinese entrepreneurs expect their Western suitors to also exhibit traits such as confidence, leadership, assertiveness, and extroversion, which is often characteristic of men who occupy the upper echelons of their society. They find men who do not embody this type of elite masculinity to be unattractive, even if they are white.

VIVIEN'S RESIGNATION

Although Vivien and Kuan initially agreed their relationship would be nothing more than a short-lived sex affair, over time she inadvertently fell in love. One chilly November evening, I received a phone call from her begging to meet up. "Come help me, please," Vivien said. "I have not slept for a few days and I have not been eating . . . I think I could eat a bit more if you joined me." I agreed, and thirty minutes later I arrived at our usual meeting place: the Bund Café. When I saw Vivien, I immediately felt sorry for her. She looked frail and thin, as if she had lost a significant amount of weight. Her eyes were puffy from crying, her skin sallow, and her face spiritless.

That night, we had a long conversation about her recent struggle to break up with Kuan after he rejected her proposal to divorce his wife and marry her, and after she discovered he had been seeing sex workers during his business trips out of town. Vivien said she had successfully resisted seeing Kuan for the past week, but all of her defenses crumbled again when she ran into him at a bar the previous night. At the bar, Kuan sent Vivien mixed signals by flirting with her but also with other women. He forced Vivien to dance with him but quickly moved on to other women, thereby causing Vivien to leave the bar angered and heartbroken. It didn't stop there, however. Kuan called Vivien later that night, saying that he accidentally left his wallet in her purse and insisting on fetching it from her home.

When he arrived, an explosive argument broke out. Vivien screamed and cried, shouting about the fleetingness of their relationship, about the ways in which he flaunted other women in front of her, and about how those indiscretions cruelly emphasized her insignificance to him. He merely retorted, "Darling, you are so stupid. That's all just for fun. I'm not serious about those women." To make matters worse, Kuan's phone began to ring. In a fit of rage, Vivien slammed it against the floor, then picked it up and answered: "Hello, I'm his wife. Who are you? Why are you calling? If he is abusing you, let me know, I will beat him for you!"

After a brief exchange with the woman on the other end, the phone call ended. Vivien continued to scream and cry, demanding to know about the other women in Kuan's life. To this, he said, "I'm so drunk. I have such a horrible headache, and I have no idea what you are talking about! I don't know any of these women!" "He got so mad, his lips turned purple, and he started shaking all over," Vivien said, "then he pushed me onto the bed and ripped off my clothes . . ." Promptly at four a.m., Kuan left to catch the train for his next business trip.

Looking back at the situation, Vivien added, "I had no sensation from the sex. It was practically rape. I was numb from all the emotional pain and damage he brought onto me." Despite Kuan's sexual assault, Vivien still pined for him. Her interactions with Kuan clearly revealed the gender privilege that wealthy entrepreneurs enjoy in China. Kuan was sought after by young, attractive women like the girls at the bar, as well as older, financially successful professionals like Vivien. Unlike with John, Vivien's conflict with Kuan stemmed not from a lack of attraction, but rather from her immense attraction to him, which brought about her jealousy, anger, and frustration over his womanizing ways.

Following dinner, I went to Vivien's apartment to keep her company. When we sat down on her couch, she clutched the giant teddy bear Kuan had bought for her and took out a laptop to show me some blog entries she had written about him. She soon paused, though, and instead pulled out pictures of Kuan's wife. "How did you get access to these photos?" I asked. "Are you friends with her through instant messaging?" "Yes," she said, "I made up an account just for this." When I saw his wife, a fashionable woman in her early twenties, standing next to Kuan and their baby son,

I inadvertently blurted out, "Doesn't it pain you to see him with another woman like this?" It did. A gloomy nod preceded Vivien's grabbing of a shelled walnut and a nutcracker on the coffee table, followed by her manic muttering: "Look, this is Kuan, okay?" while pointing to the walnut. Vivien found herself writhing in hysterical laughter and muttering, "I'm going to crush you, crush you, crush you . . . !" Before I was able to stop her, there were crumbs all over the floor.

That evening, I came home with a heavy heart. Clearly, Vivien was suffering as a result of her affair with Kuan. Acknowledging the bittersweet nature of their affair in her blog, she described their time together as "always sweet," and their parting as "always torturous." She knew that she was merely a "passenger in his life," and that their relationship had no prospect of ever becoming more than what it was. Vivien wanted to marry Kuan and could do nothing but fall into depression once she realized he was unattainable.

A few months later, I was shocked to learn that Vivien had resigned from her prestigious, high-paying state job that offered mortgage assistance, free health care, and guaranteed lifetime employment, in order to be with John. Even Vivien's translator commented that she would never give up a job like that just to immigrate to the United States. Vivien's decision came abruptly during the Chinese New Year holiday, which Kuan spent with his wife instead of with her. When a distraught Vivien called his home to protest, instead of comforting her, Kuan threatened to break up.

Kuan's rejection encouraged Vivien to view John's generosity and willingness to change to please her in a different light. "I was so moved and touched," said Vivien. "I felt that this was the man for me, the one who truly loved me, so I impulsively resigned. I did not want to give myself any backup options in China."

After Vivien quit her job, Kuan convinced her to join his business, as he valued her management skills and her government connections from her previous workplace. Thus, rather than studying English and preparing for her move to the United States, as she promised John, Vivien held off on her US visa application. She readily confessed that her primary motive in working with Kuan was not financial gain, but rather to give him a reason to continue their affair. This strategy might have worked, because whenever I visited Vivien at her new office, Kuan was there as well, sitting right across from her. Yet Vivien feared her plan might fail. She said: "I want *qing* [love] but he wants work. I can give him connections and management skills, but he has to reciprocate with the love I need. Otherwise, why should I continue helping him? I need more than just his presence. I want the emotional aspect."

The phenomenon Vivien experienced, in which women hold off on marrying Western men in order to continue pining for their married Chinese lovers, is not unique to her but rather characteristic of a sizable group of women. For example, let's consider Tiffany. Working as a secretary, Tiffany struggled to choose between Barry, a divorced American writer she had been dating, and Zihan, a Chinese multimillionaire she had been seeing on the side. At the tender age of twenty-two, Tiffany was not initially serious about marriage; she joined the agency to help a friend who worked there as a translator, and later fell in love with Barry unexpectedly. Blond and fit, Barry drove a Lexus, owned a two-story home, played piano in his spare time, and impressed Tiffany by showing her his books for sale on Amazon. While waiting for her US visa after they got engaged, however, Tiffany found her emotions began to wane, particularly after she met various other successful Chinese businessmen through work. Zihan, a wealthy but married entrepreneur, was one of them.

Short and overweight, Zihan was far less physically attractive than Barry. In fact, even after Tiffany and Zihan started dating, she frequently joked to him, "You are so ugly, I cannot believe I am dating you!" Despite the disparity between their physical appearances, Tiffany felt much stronger sexual chemistry with Zihan. Unlike with Barry, she was able to achieve orgasm with Zihan every time they had sex. When I asked Tiffany why she had so much passion for Zihan, she said, "I'm attracted to his power, ability, and decisiveness. For example, I was so sad I could not go home to attend my uncle's funeral, held around the Chinese New Year holiday, when all the train tickets were sold out. When Zihan heard about it, he immediately had his assistant buy two plane tickets and flew home with me, even though they cost ten times more than normal flights. To give you another example, when my friend moved away to Switzerland, I was so sad because I thought I would never see her again. Zihan said, why are you so sad? I could take you there tomorrow if you want."

Tiffany's attraction to Zihan was not confined to his money and status, however. She also admired his social and leadership skills as the former class president of his college and current CEO of a major corporation. Moreover, she liked his carefree, adventurous personality and his exquisite taste for the finer things in life. She described him as "the kind of man who can drive for several hours to buy a bottle of imported wine." As we can see, just like Kuan, Zihan embodied a form of elite masculinity that Chinese women find particularly attractive. Ultimately, however, Tiffany had to choose between Zihan and Barry. One night, Zihan showed up at Tiffany's apartment, knelt down, and begged her to stay. Although a divorce from his wife was not yet on the table, he offered to find Tiffany a high-paying office job and buy her an apartment if she agreed to stay in China for just one more year, creating a difficult choice for her. Eventually Tiffany married Barry and moved to the United States. However, her heart was still with Zihan, and her doomed marriage to Barry ended in divorce several years later.

As illustrated by both Vivien's and Tiffany's stories, the female clients' entanglement with wealthy but married Chinese men is such a prominent issue at the agency that Ms. Fong wrote several blog articles to address their plight. The excerpt below describes Veronica, a woman who was initially uninterested in her rural Australian suitor due to her involvement with a married Chinese man:

> [Veronica] cannot decide whether she should continue seeing the Chinese man with whom she has no future, or break with her past and start afresh . . . I can hear so much sadness and helplessness in her voice . . . through this job, I have met many, many single women who have a lot of love and care in China that they should leave behind. Those men who supposedly love them but cannot give them a real future probably never realized how much agony they are causing.

Through the women's agony, we can see that their wealthy Chinese lovers had a particular appeal that their Western suitors lacked, even though the Westerners were single and available, while the Chinese men were married and reluctant to leave their wives.

Unfortunately for Vivien, things did not turn out the way she had hoped. In a private interview with me, Kuan confessed that he would not leave his wife. As we spoke, he took out a photo of his six-month-old son and said,

"My son is really young, have you seen his picture? . . . Maybe I'm too selfish about this, but as much as I want to please Vivien, I want to take care of my family, too." Seven months into their affair, Kuan had lost interest in Vivien. He slut-shamed her, saying, "Why are you always thinking of having sex with me? Are you some kind of sex addict? I'm so busy with work, I have no time to see you," and eventually stopped picking up her calls.

After two years of email exchanges and John's three trips to China, Vivien finally agreed to marry him. A few days before I left Tunyang following a full year of fieldwork, Vivien and I met up with a friend of hers, a Chinese businessman at a multinational corporation in Beijing. After hearing Vivien's story, he said, "China is developing so fast, all my friends abroad are trying to move back. Why are you leaving?" He then added, "If John was handsome and you liked him like that, then I would say it's worth it. At least you are doing this for love. But now, what do you get?" When Vivien told him she needed to escape China to remedy her emotional wounds, he rebutted, "Why penalize yourself over another man's mistake? You want to marry someone you don't like just because the one you liked did not treat you right?"

After purposely holding off on her visa paperwork for more than a year, Vivien finally landed in the United States in 2014. To nobody's surprise, her marriage to John lasted only a few months. From John's perspective, Vivien had been both physically and emotionally unavailable. She insisted on sleeping in a separate bedroom and left her room only to eat or watch TV. Meanwhile, John's expenses piled up as Vivien spent thousands of dollars on furniture, clothes, health supplements, and such. From Vivien's perspective, John's low erotic capital made sex with him impossible, particularly given his failure to lose thirty pounds, while his solemn personality made their time together stilted and awkward. She says that he relied on her to cheer him up with her vivacious laugh and dance moves, but if she did not act jolly, he would have a sullen look on his face. She also feared his temper, stating that he had a habit of slamming things on the floor when he got upset.

As Vivien realized their marriage was not working out, she debated whether she should wait two years to get her permanent residency before filing for divorce. She often called to ask me, "Should I sacrifice two years of my youth for a green card? What good is a green card if I'm not happily married?" When John discovered Vivien's affair with Kuan through one of his Chinese friends, their conflict escalated further. Furious, John told Vivien that if her spending style did not change and if their intimacy did not improve, he would consider divorce. Meanwhile, Vivien's friends suggested that she hurry back to China to reconcile with Kuan, who was getting serious with yet another woman outside of his marriage. In fact, they warned her that she might lose Kuan forever if she did not return. One day, John woke up to find Vivien missing. She secretly packed her bags and flew back to China without telling anyone, including me, until she landed.

Through close examination of these women's intimate entanglements with their American fiancés and Chinese lovers, these case studies reveal the conflict that emerges from a mismatch between the type of masculinity Chinese women desired versus that which their Western suitors embodied. Financially flexible women like Vivien, who are used to dating stylishly dressed, well-mannered businessmen who exhibit an elite cosmopolitan masculinity associated with traits such as confidence, leadership, assertiveness, and sociability, have a hard time falling in love with middle- and working-class men who do not exhibit those traits, even if those men are white and from the West.

OTHER BREAKUPS

Like Vivien, Kristin, a former mistress now in her forties, also rejected Western men whose appearance and demeanor did not fit the type of elite masculinity she liked. Tim, a Canadian trucking company owner, serves as an example. Tim was actually financially better off than some of the other Western suitors who visited Kristin in China, such as the British supermarket manager who constantly ran out of money during his China trip despite Kristin having booked him the cheapest hotel in town. By contrast, Tim bought Kristin jewelry from Tunyang's most expensive department store and bragged about all the trucks and motorcycles he owned. Nevertheless, Kristin was still not impressed. Coming from a "well-educated, formerly aristocratic" family, Kristin was used to dating "clean-cut, soft-spoken" businessmen or government bureaucrats. After seeing Tim's rough, tanned skin, tattooed arms, and working-class demeanor, she could barely smile at him or hold his hand.

Lucy, a divorced magazine editor in her forties, faced the same dilemma but with a Chinese suitor. After meeting and turning down several rural Western suitors who did not embody the type of elite masculinity she sought, Lucy started dating Jin, a local Chinese man. Although not nearly as wealthy as her ex-husband, Jin was well-off by local standards. Despite being good-natured, honest, and attentive toward Lucy, Jin had some deal-breaking shortcomings. Lucy liked men with *cai hua* (talent), which she could not see in Jin. He performed simple clerical tasks at work and received high pay only because his brother owned the multimillion-dollar company he worked for, thus causing Lucy to often joke that he was a security guard on a CEO's salary.

While Jin's brother exhibited leadership qualities and adept social skills, Jin was a follower; he was socially awkward and rather blunt with his words. Moreover, unlike other smartly dressed, well-mannered Chinese business-men, Jin never ironed his shirts and ate with his face down, "as if he were washing his face in a basin," according to Lucy. She told me that Jin's short-comings killed off any feelings of attraction or romance on her end. In fact, she held off on getting married, as she was *bu gan xin* (unwilling to settle) for someone she felt no *gan jue* (passion) for. Thus, Lucy rejected not only Western men but also Chinese men who did not embody the elite mascu-linity she sought. Through this example, we can see that men who do not possess the elite masculine traits these women desire get rejected regardless of their race, ethnicity, and nationality. This sheds light on the increasing significance of class distinction in mate-selection as an affluent capitalist class emerges in both Western and non-Western countries.

While many of the Western suitors did not embody the type of elite masculinity the women had expected and were therefore rejected, this was not the case for all Western male clients. A small subset of men, such as the British man of Pakistani descent whom Vivien once dated, were upper-middle-class or upper-class in their native countries and embodied "trans-national business masculinity." Since there were so few of these men at the agencies I studied, I never had the opportunity to meet one in person while on-site in China. Nevertheless, I heard through the translators that they were highly sought after. Due to their desirability, these men were just as selective as the financially flexible women, and rejected the major-ity of potential mates they met. In fact, the translators warned everyone that well-educated, financially successful Western men, such as physicians, lawyers, and corporate managers, were the most *"nan gao ding* [difficult to captivate]."

For example, the translators told everyone about Claire's inability to secure such a desirable Western client. Claire was attractive and in her late twenties with a prestigious job in China and owned several homes. She wished to marry someone who was even more successful than herself. After turning down numerous average-earning Western suitors, Claire finally met a man she was eager to marry—a corporate executive who owned his own private jet and had numerous properties around the world. Yet, to Claire's dismay, he rejected her when he discovered that her English was not fluent enough and that she did not share his interests in bungee jumping and horseback riding.

Similarly, while Kristin turned down several working-class men, she also experienced rejection by a CFO who lived in a beachside town in Southern California, several miles away from UC San Diego, where I attended graduate school. Eager to continue dating him following their initial meeting in China, Kristin even asked me to deliver a jade bracelet she had bought for him. Yet, despite my own efforts, he never followed through on his promise to meet up with me in California, and the bracelet still sits in my home. Likewise, Lucy was rejected by the one Western man she really wanted to marry—a Canadian lawyer. While he initially considered relocating his business to China, he changed his mind and broke up with Lucy upon discovering that the move would cost him CA$300,000 in taxes.

CONCLUSION

The stories from this chapter show the extent to which masculinity is fluid and situational. In chapter 2, I described the agencies' depiction of Chinese men as unfaithful, patriarchal, and ageist. Although they may be materialistically "rich," they are spiritually "poor." In contrast, the devoted, caring Western family men supposedly rejected infidelity and looked beyond women's physical age. Even if they were modest-earning, their moral purity made them "rich." In this framework, Chinese masculinity is depicted as backward, deficient, and in need of Western liberation. By casting Western men as superior to Chinese men, the agencies create a Chinese desire for

Western masculinity, thereby reinforcing the global hegemonic power of Western culture.

However, in the next phase of the relationship, when couples go from online to real life, we see Western masculinity lose its hegemonic power. The financially flexible Chinese women, many of whom initially said they preferred modest-earning Western family men over philandering Chinese businessmen, later changed their minds after meeting their Western suitors face to face. Two main reasons for their relationship failure were, first, Western men's inability or unwillingness to practice Chinese-style provider love (see chapter 2), and, second, the fact that they did not embody the type of elite Chinese masculinity the women desired, which typically entailed leadership skills and social prowess.

The stories in this chapter certainly do not imply that all Western men are poor and undesirable to Chinese women. Instead, my research subjects draw from a unique segment of the population in both China and in the West. Most of the Western male clients are modest-earners who face diminishing wages and a drop in social status as a result of declining agriculture, manufacturing, and small business sectors in the West during the past forty years. In contrast, the financially flexible women happen to be economic winners of China's reform. Aged out of their local marriage market in the competition for high-status men, they look to Western men as an alternative. While Western men's racialized sexual capital, geopolitical status, and the translators' portrayal of them as devoted, caring husbands may have initially attracted the women to join the agencies, these factors were ultimately insufficient to entice all of the women to marry or remain happily married to these suitors. Instead, their dissatisfaction is partially rooted in a mismatch between the socioeconomic positions of their Western suitors and their own expectations. Nevertheless, financially flexible Chinese women do not look down on all Western men. In fact, well-educated, highly skilled men in finance, consulting, and medicine are highly desired. This shows that a new global hierarchy of masculinity based on economic distinction has emerged.

This chapter challenges readers to rethink the relationship between race and class outside of the American context. In the United States, ethnic minorities still hold significantly less economic, political, and social power than the white majority, despite their accomplishments at the individual level. For example, although some African American athletes and entertainers achieve fame and fortune, the average income of African Americans still lags far behind that of whites.[16] Similarly, while Asian Americans are now the best-educated and highest-income racial group in the United States, they still face a "bamboo ceiling"[17]—a term that refers to the specific obstacles Asian Americans face in reaching the upper echelons of leadership and management. In the Western popular media, films and television shows rarely feature Asian men in leading roles, while Asian sidekicks are often depicted as nerdy, unattractive, and asexual.[18]

However, the scenario is completely different outside the American context. China's recent economic ascendance has led to the emergence of a new capitalist class dominated by local business elites who are deemed as rich, powerful, and sexy as Western men in both the media and the popular imagination. Moreover, China's economic ascendance has fundamentally altered its geopolitical relationship with the West. For the first time in history, Asia is home to the largest number of billionaires in the world,[19] while China's GDP is projected to surpass that of the United States by 2028.[20] Clearly, wealth is decentering away from Europe and the United States, thereby creating a more balanced power dynamic between Asia and the West. At the same time, wealth is also becoming increasingly polarized within individual nations. In both China and the West, globalization has created economic "winners" and "losers." Against the backdrop of these macro-level structural changes, I argue that China's global rise does not signify a uniform process of racial or geopolitical disempowerment for all Western men. Instead, I show how these dynamics are now class-dependent. In a new world order, people are increasingly divided along class lines of haves versus have-nots. The stories from this chapter show that Chinese women who became economic winners of globalization ultimately desire men who are also part of the global economic elite: that is, high-earning, well-traveled cosmopolitan professionals who embody transnational business masculinity. These women are quick to reject nonelites, even if those men are whites from the Global North.

4 | EMBRACING DOMESTICITY

WHEN I FIRST MET JOANNE on-site at Ms. Mei's agency in summer 2008, she was in her forties and divorced with a teenage son. Tall and leggy, with long, silky hair and carefully manicured nails, Joanne had an elegant charm. While many other female clients were loud and loquacious, she spoke slowly, in a low-toned voice that was gentle but firm. At the time, Joanne worked in retail marketing and struggled to support her son, Kevin. In order to make ends meet, she often engaged in romantic liaisons with married Chinese men who gave her money. However, Joanne was not always poor. Years ago, she was a successful businesswoman, before her Chinese ex-husband gambled away the bars and restaurants she owned. His gambling put her in a financially burdened position, and upon their divorce, she looked to marriage migration as a pathway toward upward mobility. This stood in contrast to many of the financially flexible women described in previous chapters, who were economically well-off and could afford to send their children abroad for college without external assistance.

Upon joining Ms. Mei's agency, Joanne started dating Fredrick, an American businessman in his fifties. Among male clients enrolled at the agency, Fredrick was one of the few whose self-reported income appeared in the highest category of US$150,000+ on the dating website's drop-down menu. As the co-owner of a transnational company with satellite offices in China, he traveled there frequently for work. Divorced with two young children in grade school, Fredrick told Joanne that he wanted a wife who enjoyed doing housework, loved spending time with kids, and, most important, listened to what he said and did everything his way. Unsurprisingly, he expected her to become a full-time homemaker upon moving abroad.

Determined to *gao ding* (captivate) this rich man, Joanne played up her "emphasized femininity"[1] throughout their courtship. In the way of appearance, her shapely figure and soft, husky voice resembled the Asian baby-doll portrayal prevalent in the Western media, which mixes feminine docility with exoticism and sensuality.[2] Moreover, she made careful observance of Fredrick's habits and tried to *tou qi suo hao* (cater to his every pleasure). For example, although Joanne had always despised cooking, she experimented with various recipes during Fredrick's stay in China. She also tried to be soft-spoken, invited Fredrick's children to visit China, and showered them with presents. After seeing Fredrick and his children in Joanne's home one summer, even her translator noted: "I think he can deeply feel a Chinese woman's softness and domesticity, given the way she takes meticulous care of him and the kids."

While Joanne presented the epitome of emphasized femininity, Fredrick also bore some resemblance to a so-called hegemonic male. In sociology, this term refers to men who, in our collective imagination, embody the most positive traits on the masculine side of the gender binary.[3] Fredrick was white, tall, muscular, and Ivy League–educated. In the way of socioeconomic class, he fared much better than many of the blue-collar men enrolled at the agencies. Moreover, he was extremely generous in his gift-giving and exhibited the kind of provider masculinity[4] that many Chinese women admired. For example, he moved Joanne out of her tiny apartment without heat into a two-bedroom apartment in a luxury high-rise in China and promised to pay Kevin's future tuition bills. He also showered Joanne with Chanel dresses, Louis Vuitton necklaces, and cash cards, which she brought to her agency to show off. Soon, Joanne became the envy of the crowd at her dating agency, where other clients called her a "golden phoenix." In Chinese mythology, "phoenix" refers to a beautiful bird that rises from the ashes and becomes something new, while the saying "a golden phoenix that has flown out from the valleys" describes a person of inferior upbringing who has achieved a dramatic rise in social status.[5] When used to describe women, the term refers to those who exchange their extraordinary beauty for a life of luxury provided by wealthy men.

Since the 1970s, many Western feminists have perceived marriages built on such "traditional" domestic/public division of labor to be exploitative, while they viewed households where women also participated in the paid labor force as more equal. Yet, some scholars later critiqued this perspective for its Western-centric, white, middle-class vision of gender equality, and for failing to take into account the vastly different conditions under which women of other racial, ethnic, and class backgrounds lived.[6] For example, working for a wage might feel liberating to a middle-class American woman, but not to a woman from Vietnam who has been laboring in the fields or factory since childhood.[7]

Building on these recent critiques, this chapter will explore the lives of women like Joanne, who labored exclusively at home upon moving abroad and thus relied completely on their Western husbands for financial support. As stay-at-home wives, they struck a patriarchal bargain that involved their heavy performance of emphasized femininity,[8] meaning that they provided feminized, unpaid work at home in return for a share of their husband's income and other provisions such as housing, vacations, health insurance, and retirement benefits. Unlike the financially flexible women described in previous chapters, some of whom were independently wealthy even if they became homemakers, these financially burdened housewives were completely economically dependent on their husbands. Thus, their marriages exemplified an extreme version of a gendered patriarchal bargain.

This chapter and the next focus exclusively on financially burdened women. This chapter looks at whether the male breadwinner/female homemaker model of marriage fundamentally disempowers migrant women, by exploring the private lives of Joanne and two other brides who became full-time homemakers in the United States. The next chapter compares these homemaker case studies with the stories of several women who *did* take on jobs outside the home, to see if there is a main divide in marital happiness and perceived agency based on whether or not the wives worked.

Interestingly, both sets of respondents wanted a marriage built on gendered economic ideals. Some preferred to stay at home, while others wanted to work, but they all still expected their husband to be the sole household provider so that they could keep any earnings of their own as their private money. Their attitude stands in striking contrast to the Western feminist assumption that women who work would take pride in splitting their household bills with men and view it as a sign of empowerment.[9] Challenging this Western-centric feminist perspective, my respondents' ideology is rooted in a strand of "Made in China" feminism called entrepreneurial C-fem.[10] Before delving into their postmarital lives abroad, let us first look at how this strand of Chinese-style feminism shaped their premigration expectations.

ENTREPRENEURIAL C-FEM

In China today, two strands of local feminism have emerged in the post-reform era. The first, called noncooperative C-fem, encourages women to retain their financial independence and choose a career over marriage and childbearing when faced with conflicting obligations. This strand of feminism is more prevalent among women born after 1980, following the launch of China's modernization campaign and One-Child Policy. As a result of these policy changes, women from the post-1980s generations received an unprecedented increase in attention and investment from their families. Compared with women from older generations, this one-child-policy generation benefited from China's rapid expansion of educational resources and carried forward their parents' "expectations for them to achieve high academic and professional success."[11] As readers have probably already guessed, the women in my study, most of whom were born before 1980, do not identify with noncooperative C-fem.

Instead, my respondents identify with a second strand of Chinese-style feminism called entrepreneurial C-fem. This model encourages women to abandon traditional virtues, such as submissiveness and self-sacrifice. Even so, it does not associate female empowerment with participation in the paid labor force. Instead, women are encouraged to capitalize on and cultivate their sexual attraction, including their femininity, and domestic skills to maximize their material gain on the marriage market. While the desire to "marry up" is not new in China, what distinguishes this entrepreneurial C-fem proposition is "its emphasis on women's individual agency and its blunt utilitarian view of marriage."[12] Here the woman's ultimate goal in her pursuit of wealthy men is her personal economic security, not the economic success or respectability of her parents or any other authorities.[13]

Entrepreneurial C-fem resonated with many women in my study due to the unique social and historical context of their upbringing. For example, some viewed paid labor as a burden because they lived through the socialist Mao era, when women were forced to join the paid labor force and ended up taking on the double burden of working both inside and outside the home.[14] Moreover, during the early reform era of the 1980s and 1990s, they witnessed the emergence of a wealthy entrepreneurial class dominated by men, alongside a worsening of women's social position.[15] Many of these early-era businessmen were not well educated and made their fortune by engaging in a business culture characterized by heavy drinking and sexual entertainment,[16] which was not accessible to women. At the same time, when state-owned companies shut down, female workers were laid off at much higher rates than male workers.[17] Moreover, the state stopped sponsoring child care services and subsequently encouraged women to become homemakers in the postreform era.[18]

In essence, China became governed by a market logic that emphasized women's economic dependence on men and their sexual objectification by men.[19] Under such conditions, many women aimed to achieve leverage over men by cultivating their attractiveness to men through performing conventional femininities, rather than by competing with men directly in the labor market.[20] Behind this utilitarian approach toward marriage lay women's hidden class grievances. In subscribing to entrepreneurial C-fem, my respondents are not trying to *escape* the patriarchal bargain, but to *enter* it and begin to benefit from it alongside the men to whom it has always catered. They pursue Western men largely because they can no longer strike such a bargain in China, given their older age and subsequent loss of feminine appeal.

For these women, the sociopolitical events of their lives have intrinsically linked their perception of gender roles in marriage with economics. Thus, their marriages cannot always be about "pure love," but rather are rooted in a more entrepreneurial interpretation of the bond between man and wife.[21] A C-feminist marriage is one in which a woman has agency, where agency is defined largely as personal economic security. This is especially the case for financially burdened women like Joanne, who have few other routes to such security, for themselves or for their children. However, as with all bargains, the patriarchal agreement between financially burdened women who choose to be homemakers and their Western, breadwinning husbands is not always fair or successful. Unfortunately, these women do not always have the privilege to leave unhappy marriages, due to their financial vulnerability. Let us return now to the story of Joanne, whose financial insecurity led her to stay with Fredrick despite his inability to uphold his end of the bargain.

THE GOLDEN PHOENIX

Unlike some women who dreamed of becoming a stay-at-home wife, Joanne actually wanted to work upon moving abroad, even if she married a rich man. "I want to open a nail salon in the United States, but I am concerned about getting licensing. Can you tell me more about that?" This was the kind of question that she frequently asked while we chatted at the agency back in 2008. In the eyes of her longtime friend Kristin, Joanne was a woman with insatiable desires. She wanted not only wealth, but also power and control, both at work and at home. However, she chose to hide this dimension of her personality during her courtship with Fredrick.

Throughout their courtship, during which Joanne still lived in China, she was well aware of Fredrick's controlling personality. For example, he told her no clubbing, no skirts above the knees, and no swimming, as he did not want other men to see her in a bikini. He also demanded that she be available for webcam meetings twice a day and discouraged her from taking driving lessons. I could sense Joanne's uneasiness when she continuously asked me if all Western men were controlling like Fredrick, or if he simply loved her too much. Nevertheless, she still kept her head low and continued performing emphasized femininity in order to win Fredrick over. For example, she stopped swimming, cut back on socializing with her friends and family, reduced her shifts at work, and later even quit her job just to please him.

Their relationship was built on this illusion: Fredrick thought Joanne was a domesticated, submissive homemaker with few materialistic demands, while Joanne thought she would be living the high life abroad. Unknown to her at the time, however, was the economic reality that Fredrick's business took a big hit with the 2008 financial crisis. Ironically, her gender strategy of never asking him any income-related questions in order to appear like a perfectly earnest housewife helped Fredrick conceal his economic situation throughout their three-year, long-distance courtship.

In 2010, Fredrick finally married Joanne and brought her and Kevin to the United States. To her disappointment, Joanne feared she had landed in rural America when she first saw his suburban Washington home, located two hours away from Seattle. Moreover, she came to realize that Fredrick's financial capacity didn't match her expectations. While he claimed to be a business owner, she barely saw him working. When she asked for money and gifts, he would only give her small change of US$20 or $40 at a time, and he added: "I'm afraid I just cannot please you." One time, after he bought her the bracelet she had asked for, he told Kevin: "Your mom is very greedy; she wants many things, and she only wants expensive things."

While Fredrick could no longer fulfill the generous provider role in this patriarchal bargain, his desire to exercise control at home and adhere strictly to a gendered division of labor remained unchanged. Joanne was expected to do all the housework, which became particularly burdensome during the weeks when he had custody of his two young children. Given their language barrier, much of the care work Joanne performed involved menial tasks such as picking up toys or doing laundry. "I have never cooked so much or washed so many dishes in my life!" Joanne exclaimed. Even Kevin observed with sadness: "Mom, you are just like a maid in this house." On top of the extensive housework, Joanne was also hurt by Fredrick's condescending attitude that reinforced his dominant status at home. She said:

> He wants me to dress, eat, and act the way he likes. He does not give me any space. For example, he hates it when I go to church or speak on the phone with other people, so I try not to use my cellphone around him. In China, I always dressed formally as I do not look good in casual clothing because I'm thin. But after moving here, he wants me to wear casual clothes and tells me that I should dress the American way because I'm now in the United States. At home, I must always smile at him and flatter

him; I cannot say anything bad about him or his children. He thinks that because I live in his house, eat his food, and use his things, I must accommodate his every whim. When I do something he does not like, he puts on a poker face.

Here, we can see that this patriarchal bargain is dysfunctional because neither party really kept their promises from before marriage, while their expectations for the other party remained unchanged. Fredrick wanted dominance and a gendered division of labor, although he had trouble fulfilling the provider role he once displayed in China. Joanne, for her part, started resisting emphasized femininity, although she still expected to live a life of luxury. During her courtship with Fredrick in China, Joanne followed the tenets of entrepreneurial C-fem. She capitalized on her sexuality and femininity for material gain through careful calculation and self-discipline. Upon discovering her husband's true economic condition, however, she stopped.

Finally, conflict over stepchildren further complicated their marriage. An A-student in China, Kevin had expected to attend a good university in the United States. Yet, his dream was shattered when Fredrick said, "It's very expensive; do you have the money to pay?" When he found out that Fredrick could only enroll him in a community college, he locked himself in his room and cried. Although this was somewhat of a misunderstanding, as Fredrick wanted him to establish in-state residency first, before considering other options, he never effectively explained this to Joanne or Kevin. After spending months cooped up in his room playing video games, while having taken only one course at a community college, Kevin broke down and said to his mom, "I cannot stand this retirement-like lifestyle anymore; I feel that my future is in ruins."

Watching Kevin fall into depression deeply upset Joanne. Yet, Fredrick saw them both as demanding and ungrateful. Over time the couple spoke to each other less and less, and Fredrick started sleeping on the couch. When they did fight, it escalated from verbal to physical and ended with Joanne calling 9-1-1 after Fredrick injured her wrist. "This marriage has stressed me out so much," Joanne once sobbed during a phone call with me, "there are times when I just cry and cry and cry, until my tears run dry." Eventually came a day when Fredrick told Joanne and Kevin, "You must leave," as he wanted a break to rethink their marriage. Thus, he bought them one-way flights to China and dropped them off at an airport hotel with US$4,000.

Two months later, in April 2011, I saw Joanne in Tunyang. We met up at a restaurant upstairs from Ms. Mei's agency and ordered her favorite dishes: enoki mushroom with beef, steamed pork ribs, and stir-fry lotus bud. As we ate, Joanne lamented how much the stress of her marriage had aged her, as her hair was now falling out by the handful while new wrinkles had crept up on her face. Yet, somehow, she looked the same to me as before—youthful, elegant, and fashionably dressed. That day, she wore a white summer suit and had her long, slender nails painted emerald green. Determined to save her marriage, Joanne told me she wrote Fredrick long emails from China, starting each letter with "Dear Husband" and signing them "Love, Joanne," even though his replies were only one or two sentences long and he never acknowledged her as his wife. "I hate writing those emails," Joanne said, "it feels like *re lian dui leng pi gu* [pressing my warm face against his cold butt]."

Although Joanne called Fredrick "the one who treated me worst out of all the men I ever dated" and said he completely destroyed any feelings of love she once had for him, she still wanted to win him back. "I just want Kevin to get a US education; that's all I'm seeking," Joanne said, and she explained why this was vital: "I am not like some of the other women at this agency who do not have to worry about their children. For example, Ruby's ex-husband has a big company in China for their daughter to inherit. Kevin's father has died, so I cannot just stop helping him. If I don't, who will? In China, my salary is too low to support him through college." Here, we see Joanne attempting to salvage her marriage out of desperation due to her financially burdened status as a poor single mother.

The power dynamics in this relationship took a surprising and yet drastic shift when Joanne decided to divorce Fredrick. After several months of hopeless waiting in China without a clear response from Fredrick on the status of their marriage, Joanne wanted to leave him so that she could apply for her own green card. She even made arrangements to work as a live-in nursemaid for a Chinese family in Seattle. When her lawyer contacted Fredrick for divorce proceedings with a request for alimony, he suddenly backed down and begged to get back together. He even bought her a car and rented a place for Kevin in Seattle.

In January 2013, I visited their Seattle townhome, where Joanne lived with Kevin while Fredrick split his time between this location and his suburban Washington home. Their townhome was in a clean, upscale residential area with plenty of Asian shops and restaurants nearby. Upon my arrival, both Kevin and Fredrick came out to greet me and eagerly took my suitcase inside. Joanne was dressed much more casually than I had ever seen her, in a plain black sweatsuit, makeup-free. Fredrick looked tall and muscular, just like in his photos, and spoke in a deep voice. He drove us to dinner in his BMW, courteously dropping us off at the restaurant entrance before taking off to find parking himself. During dinner, he let Kevin pick all the dishes, while Kevin called him "Daddy" and poured green tea for all of us.

That evening, when I told Joanne that they looked like the perfect happy family, she kept shaking her head and said, "It's fake; it's all fake!" Apparently, all the same problems they struggled with before, including Fredrick's financial troubles and domineering personality, were still there, except now everything was exacerbated by a new challenge: his cancer diagnosis. Although this was a slow-growing tumor that required only a minor surgery, Fredrick still worried about the potential effects of his medication on his sexual performance. As a result, he became even more insecure than before, frequently accusing Joanne of checking out other men on the street. When he learned that Joanne was training for a massage parlor job, he told her she was not allowed to serve men and if she did, he would shoot her with a gun. He even hired a neighbor to follow her to her training location, thereby forcing Joanne to give up this job.

While Fredrick was controlling, he did not prohibit Joanne from taking all jobs. For a while Joanne worked at a coffee shop and later quit only because she found it exhausting. She also took real estate agent training courses, which Fredrick paid for, but failed the license exam due to her limited English. At the same time, Fredrick's limited financial capacity made it impossible for him to help her finance her own business. Thus, Joanne was stuck in a bind where she found blue-collar jobs physically distressing, while white-collar jobs remained unattainable. "I feel like a wilted flower at home, with nothing better to do and no money to spend," she lamented.

Joanne's pent-up frustrations caused a blowup with Fredrick during my second night staying in her home. She spent the entire duration of our hot-pot dinner yelling at Fredrick in Chinese: "Why don't you drink beer; why do you drink wine? Why are you pretending? Why are you faking? You make me want to throw up!" Even her son, who intercepted several times by saying to his mother, "Oh my god, just eat; the more upset you get, the worse it is for your own health," could not appease her. Looking embarrassed, Fredrick excused himself from the table to take out the garbage. Upon his return, I overheard a conversation he was having with someone about his company in China. At this time, Joanne started yelling again, this time in English: "Where is your factory? Where is your money? Do you have a factory?" When Fredrick exclaimed, "Oh my god, would you please just stop, we have a guest here!" I excused myself to go upstairs while they continued bickering in the kitchen. Later that night, Joanne explained what she had meant by "everything being fake":

> He wanted to make a good impression, so he drank wine instead [of beer]. In fact, he hardly drinks around you. Normally the first thing he does after coming home is drink two bottles of beer. That's how he got me! He impressed me with his gentleman-like manners. But as time went by, I started to realize that everything about him is fake. He is always putting up an image, as if he were so rich and powerful. That is why he bought a used BMW even when he could not really afford it. You know that phone call he made? It's fake. He had actually set the alarm when he took out the trash. My son had observed it a few times before: his phone screen goes black when he talks and there is no sound coming from the other side. He does that whenever something like this happens and he feels embarrassed.

Joanne's assessment reminded me of America's economic decline throughout the past two decades. On the surface everything looked good, people drove nice cars, lived in big homes, and seemed happy. Yet, in reality, many people lived crumbled lives, stressed about deep debt. In Fredrick's case, his business was suffering, and he struggled to support two residences. He held off on selling his Washington home because the housing market had barely recovered from the 2009 crash. Thus, he sometimes failed to make his Seattle rent payment. When debt collectors came, Kevin had to pay with his hard-earned money from his side job. This aggravated Joanne, whose dream to live in luxury had been shattered, and she was instead left constantly stressed about Fredrick's financial instability. Worrying about putting a roof over her head sounded like the nightmare life she had escaped from, not the one she was expecting to live in America. She lamented:

> Truth of the matter is, I don't know what the hell is going on. I have no idea how much money he has or how we will pay rent tomorrow. I don't know anything about the future. I have never seen any kind of financial record from him, whether it is his tax return, pay stub, or housing title. Nothing . . . In China, I suffered so much over the years from my ex-husband, who abused drugs and gambled away my business. After meeting Fredrick, I wanted a big, spectacular wedding to show off to the whole world my newfound happiness. But I never got that big wedding he promised me, and you know the rest of my horrendous sufferings. How can I think of what happened to me? I can only think that I was dreaming about my wonderful, amazing American life that never existed.

Later, in 2014, I visited Joanne in Fredrick's suburban Washington home during my summer break. She had moved back there to save money, while Kevin paid for his own shared apartment with his schoolmates in Seattle. Even after consolidating their living situation, their marriage was still haunted by all the same problems. For example, I saw Joanne yell at Fredrick: "You said you were going to give me a thousand dollars today, where is my thousand dollars?" or "When are you taking me to Hawaii, you liar?" By now, Joanne no longer performed any domestic duties except cooking, and even then, she only cooked for Fredrick, while his two children ordered takeout when they visited. At home, Joanne seemed perpetually bored. His large, three-bedroom house, located on one acre of land with a swimming pool and goldfish pond, could not keep her happy. She hated living there because there was no Chinese community and she did not get along with his children, who laughed and played together but became dead quiet around her and Kevin. At dinner, the six of us—Fredrick, his two children, Joanne, Kevin, and me—ate in utter silence. The kids hurriedly finished and went back to their own rooms, shutting their doors. "I hate the atmosphere here; it's stale and deadening," Joanne said. I could not agree with her more.

Joanne's unhappy marriage exemplifies a dysfunctional patriarchal bargain, in which both parties wanted to reap the rewards, but neither was willing or able to pay the price. In Fredrick's case, he wanted dominance at home alongside gendered division of labor, but he was not able to provide the luxurious lifestyle that Joanne had expected after she saw him perform provider masculinity in China. In Joanne's case, she wanted to continue living a high-end lifestyle and could not adjust her expectations once she discovered the reality of Fredrick's economic situation. Unfortunately, unlike the financially flexible women, who had the economic capital to divorce if they were truly unhappy, Joanne had few exit options. She had a son in college, and she herself was reluctant to engage in hard physical labor. She felt she had no better choice than to stay with Fredrick as a homemaker, even if their day-to-day life felt toxic and unhealthy. The only thing that kept her going was her son, who planned on transferring to a four-year university in the fall.

As much as I would have liked to stay in touch with Joanne, that opportunity was lost during my summer 2014 stay at her home. One evening, I asked to tag along with Fredrick on a ten-minute trip to the local grocery store to grab a box of pasta. As a researcher, I was hoping to have some one-on-one time to speak with Fredrick after spending all day with Joanne. To my surprise, this incited Joanne's jealousy and insecurity as his wife. In a fit of rage, she asked me to leave her home immediately and decided to sever ties with me thereafter.

In summary, the case of Joanne and Fredrick shows that the separation of spheres—a hallmark ideology behind patriarchal bargains—was not the cause of her faltering marriage. Their relationship had gone much more smoothly during the courtship phase in China, when Joanne performed emphasized femininity in exchange for Fredrick's generous financial support. Although Joanne did not like Fredrick's controlling attitude, she put up with it back then and continued to perform emphasized femininity for material gain. It was not until after she left China that things started falling apart. To have a functional patriarchal bargain, both parties must view their costs and payout to be fair and worthy of pursuing. In Joanne's case, she no longer felt that way about her gendered economic deal with Fredrick after she discovered the reality of his economic condition upon moving abroad.

While Joanne was deeply unhappy with the patriarchal bargain she had struck, not all such bargains are as dysfunctional as hers. I turn next to two cases where the women stayed at home full-time but were far more satisfied with their Western husbands. These women struck a better-functioning patriarchal bargain, one in which both parties enjoyed their gendered economic deal while they also accepted its costs. I will begin with the case of Susan.

I NEED A LITTLE HELP FROM GOD

Like Joanne, Susan was considered beautiful by Chinese standards. She had fair skin and almond-shaped eyes, and presented herself stylishly with artsy jewelry. She was divorced and had a son who was in his thirties. Susan had a pleasant personality for the most part, always smiling and laughing, although I sometimes found her shrill laughter annoying as it sounded disingenuous. Born in the 1950s, Susan grew up during China's Mao era, when women were required to work outside the home and were told they could do whatever men could. Thus, Susan always assumed she should be "at least equal to men, if not more successful," and believed it would be "utterly embarrassing" to live off men. Like Joanne, Susan ventured into business during the 1990s following her layoff from a state-owned factory. She enjoyed business success for a while, until her ex-husband gambled her store away. After that, Susan worked in marketing retail and struggled to make a living.

Susan started rethinking her Maoist gender ideology following her divorce, because she believed it had ruined her marriage. "I was a *nu qing ren* [career woman] and focused most of my energy on work," Susan recalled. "I thought I was above my husband because I was the family breadwinner." She blamed her failed marriage on her own "bad temper" and arrogance, which she believed had hurt her husband's self-esteem, thereby driving him into the arms of other women. Following her divorce, Susan joined a Christian church, where she reinvented herself to become more mild-mannered and feminine. Now identifying more with entrepreneurial C-feminism, she decided to shift gears and perform conventional femininities for her own well-being and for a better shot at financial security.

In 2014, Susan met Tony, a Californian business owner around her age. Like Fredrick, Tony resembled the hegemonic male in that he was white, college-educated, and financially better off than many other male clients enrolled at the agencies. While not particularly tall, Tony had blond hair, blue eyes, and a deep tan. He came from a traditional Irish family, and his million-dollar home was tastefully decorated with European antiques and black-and-white family photos. While Fredrick's company experienced dramatic downfall following the 2008 financial crisis, Tony's business remained profitable. Thus, he was able to offer better perquisites to his partner, including a fancier home, an exclusive country club membership, and trips to exotic locations such as Milan or Barbados.

Like Fredrick, Tony had a controlling personality and expected a gendered division of labor at home. But unlike most Western men who made multiple trips to China to visit their girlfriends, Tony arranged for Susan to visit his American home several times, staying for a few months at a time. During her stays, Susan performed the bulk of the housework, from scrubbing the floor to walking the dog to doing laundry. Like Joanne with Fredrick, Susan found Tony difficult to please, as he was "very self-centered and domineering," she recalled. For example, he often wanted to have sex on a whim, even when she was in the middle of cooking, and would sulk for days if she rejected him. He also expected Susan to watch American TV with him every night and acted displeased if she glanced at her phone.

Like Fredrick, Tony expected Susan to eat, dress, and act according to his preference. In August 2016, when the three of us sat down at a seafood diner for lunch after crabbing on Tony's private yacht, Susan whispered to me in Chinese, "He set so many hurdles for me. Take this sandwich, for example. When I first came to the United States, he complained about my table manners, about how I slurped my noodles and took huge bites out of sandwiches. Since then, I learned to take small bites and eat with my mouth closed. I really had to change myself a lot." Susan's idea of a gendered economic deal was one where she gave up some rights, sometimes even *bie* (suppressing) her own desires, in order to win financial support. Thus, not only did she alter her personality without demanding similar changes from Tony, but she also did not expect to be treated as a financial equal. For example, even though Tony used a high-end Mac computer, he bought Susan a cheap US$200 netbook, which I helped her fix numerous times because it crashed so often. Even her friend gasped when she saw Susan's low-end cellphone: "If he's such a big boss, how could he be so stingy as to get you this kind of crappy phone?" Yet, Susan told herself to remain thankful for having a free phone and computer to use.

To give another example, Tony did not buy Susan medical insurance during her visits. One time, after spraining her arm while playing tennis, he simply bought her ibuprofen and suggested that she return to China if she needed surgery. When Susan's friend suggested that she get acupuncture, Tony agreed to pay for it. However, after learning that each session cost US$40 instead of US$20, he changed his mind. Shaking her head, Susan said, "I feel sad that he can spend one hundred dollars on Christmas decorations, but he cannot spend a little bit of money to treat my illness."

Despite her misgivings, Susan never faltered in her performance of emphasized femininity. She understood that she could not command equal treatment in the relationship because she was not making comparable financial contributions to their household, unlike back in China, when she was the primary breadwinner. Thus, she told herself to "focus on his strengths, accept his flaws, and reexamine my shortcomings." During moments of anger and disappointment, she opted for self-suppression, which she felt was the most sensible tactic: "If I express unhappiness, it would make him unhappy, and that would ultimately be bad for me. Sometimes you must tolerate the little things in exchange for bigger rewards for yourself." Here we can see Susan practicing entrepreneurial C-fem by cultivating her own femininity and domesticity to advance her personal interest.

By "bigger rewards," Susan was referring to the lifestyle that Tony provided her. However unfairly Tony had treated her, Susan still looked to him with gratitude because he offered her a better life than the one she had in China, where she felt constant pressure to perform in her job as a sales manager. Collapsing in bed after coming home at midnight each day, she could feel the toll her job took on her aging body. By comparison, the light housework she performed in Tony's home felt like a walk in the park, and the stomach ulcers she developed from the stress of work in China had healed due to her more relaxed lifestyle. Moreover, living with Tony allowed Susan to support her grown son in China, who could not hold a steady job. Since

Tony paid all her living expenses in the United States, Susan used her retirement income in China to purchase insurance for her son, while she also let him live in her now-empty apartment rent-free.

Although Susan perceived her relationship with Tony to be a fair exchange in the large scheme of things, dealing with his demands was still challenging. He pushed her tolerance to the limit, and there were days when she thought she would snap. In such moments, she turned to God for help. For example, Susan hated visiting the casino, as it brought back haunting memories of her ex-husband's gambling addiction. Yet, she also felt compelled to please Tony when he asked her to go, and even pretended to enjoy the slot machines while there. Upon her return from each trip, Susan would pray for Tony to stop going. To give another example, Susan wanted to get up well before Tony each morning, but she worried that it might upset him since he liked to cuddle in bed. After praying to God for a week, Susan finally mustered up the courage to ask for permission, and thankfully Tony approved.

After two years of courtship, Tony finally decided to marry Susan. However, she found the preconditions that he laid out for her difficult to swallow. One fall morning in 2016, when I visited Susan's home, she pulled me aside and told me that she had just signed a very "unequal treaty"—referring to a prenuptial agreement Tony had given her. The document asked her to waive all claims to property and alimony in the event of a divorce or his death. Even Tony's lawyer, who presented this document to Susan, advised her against signing. Meanwhile, all Tony would give Susan was his verbal promise to take care of her upon his death.

After days of struggling to decide what to do, Susan signed the contract, as she felt she had already invested too much in the relationship. If she went back to China now, she would not only become a laughingstock among her friends and family, but she would also be jobless. Susan chose to gamble on Tony's words, believing he had reason to be cautious. In an old family photo, Susan saw that Tony had gray hair when his daughter was only five years old. Looking at it, she could imagine how difficult life must have been for a single father, and she empathized with his desire to guard this hard-earned money. Ultimately, Susan believed Tony was responsible and kindhearted. After all, he supported his adult daughter, ran a successful business, and donated to charity. She reasoned that he acted with suspicion only because of emotional baggage from his previous marriage. Finally, when those thoughts could not appease her worries, Susan turned again to God for support: "I trust God. God brought me to America, and God cannot give me a bad life here."

Before I left her home, Susan held my hands and said earnestly, "Please don't tell anyone about my prenup. It is a secret. I don't want anyone in China to know."[22] As I stepped out the door and looked behind me, I saw a beautiful mansion, with a perfectly manicured lawn and a doll-like lady living inside, with her stylish clothing, elegant makeup, and cheery laugh. Yet, behind this façade of flawlessness, anxiety seeped through every crevice. In the eyes of many women at the agency, Susan was a lottery winner. Yet up close, I saw a hidden price she paid for her marriage.

To my surprise, Susan's gamble paid off. After a dreamlike wedding in Dublin, Tony added Susan's name to his will, where he bequeathed to her one of his vacation homes, with an additional sum of US$300,000. Over the next two years, he also became less domineering and more trusting of her. Long gone were the days when she cut open the tubes of her Estee Lauder lotion to squeeze out the last bit, because he now agreed to buy more. He also bought her medical insurance and a car, and agreed to let her work outside the home part-time if she so wished. In 2017, I was surprised to see Tony show up at a New Year's gala that Susan had organized with her Chinese friends from church, particularly since Tony had initially disapproved of her socializing with them. Although Tony joked that he should have stayed home to watch football, he also noted: "To keep a marriage going, you have to do stuff like this sometimes."

Tony's transformation shows us that Susan was not passive, powerless, or genuinely submissive. She had her own strategy and plan. Instead of complaining and making demands up front, Susan chose to put on a happy face and reason with Tony slowly over time. For example, in Tony's original will, Susan shared ownership rights to the same vacation home with his daughter. Only after she reasoned with Tony numerous times as to why she deserved the home outright did he revise his will. "You should never go against him directly," Susan said, "but rather think of different strategies to persuade him to make small concessions, one at a time." Her strategy was to win his trust by appearing devoted and selfless. It is important to note that this strategy is still rooted in emphasized femininity, such that it emphasizes appearing compassionate, tolerant, self-critical, and deferential, all of which are associated with the feminine side of the gender binary.

Despite Tony's promises to reward Susan in his will, she knew that everything was still contingent upon her continued performance of this emphasized femininity. She said, "Basically, I have to serve him to his liking until he passes away; if he's unhappy, he could change the will at any time." As an example of her continued insecurity, she even asked me to visit her when Tony was not at home to review the will—written in English—and make sure he had not changed anything. Occasionally, Susan looked to her other friends, who married poorer men but wielded more power at home, with envy. When one friend complained to her, "You live in heaven and I'm in hell," Susan rebutted, "But do you clean? At home you just glare at the dirty floor, and your husband would come over to scrub it out of fear that you don't think it's clean enough." Sighing, Susan added, "My marriage takes so much mental energy. Sometimes I would rather be with someone less well-off but less demanding." Despite these occasional misgivings, most of the time Susan felt extremely lucky to have met Tony and took great pride in her lavish lifestyle by showing it off regularly on social media. Moreover, she shared her success story with other clients in China through videoconferences, during which she imparted her wisdom of how she snatched a wealthy husband who paid all her bills and remained faithful to her despite her age.

Comparing Susan and Tony's patriarchal bargain with that of Joanne and Fredrick, one is clearly more dysfunctional. While both men had similar expectations for their wives, in that they wanted dominance and control alongside a traditional gendered division of labor, the two women responded differently to their demands. Joanne performed emphasized femininity only during the courtship process and started resisting it after moving abroad. Susan, however, performed it consistently throughout her relationship with Tony, both before and after marriage. Meanwhile, Tony also did a better job providing for his wife than did Fredrick. Not only did he offer her better perquisites, such as fancy health club memberships and exotic vacations, but he was also much more financially stable. Given Tony's net worth of several million dollars, Susan never had to worry about where their next meal might come from or how they would pay rent. Their marriage functioned smoothly in that both parties enjoyed the rewards of patriarchy, while they also accepted its costs. Tony summed up the status of his marriage to Susan in a private interview with me when he said, "We never fight. You see, we fit very well together, because I'm looking for a traditional marriage and she is traditional."

While Susan's marriage with Tony has been marked by his dominance and assertiveness alongside her empathy and tolerance, this has not been the case for all marriages based on a male breadwinner/female homemaker model. The final example in this chapter features a couple whose marriage was not built on masculine dominance and the appearance of feminine submissiveness, although it was still a patriarchal bargain in that the woman focused exclusively on feminized, unpaid work at home in exchange for a share of the man's income and other material benefits.

A FAIR EXCHANGE

Lindsay, a former university lecturer whom we met in earlier chapters, was one of the first women to join Ms. Fong's agency, back in the early 2000s. At the time she was in her early fifties, recently divorced, and had one daughter. Light-skinned and petite, Lindsay had bright eyes and a warm smile. Contrary to the stereotypical Western media image of Asian women as shy and quiet, Lindsay was an extrovert who loved to speak and ended every sentence with a vivacious laugh. Soon after joining the agency, she met Henry, a retired college professor from Oregon who shared her passion for Italian opera and British literature. While Lindsay enjoyed their email exchanges and sensed a growing friendship between them, she hesitated on getting more serious with Henry because of his older age. Nevertheless, when her dates with some other Western suitors faltered, she agreed to meet Henry in China.

Upon seeing Henry, Lindsay appreciated his clean-cut, well-groomed appearance and melodic voice. However, she also noticed his many wrinkles. One evening, while they were chatting in his hotel room, Lindsay asked to see Henry's passport. When she opened the booklet, she nearly fainted. Henry was nearly twenty years her senior—much older than what she saw in his dating profile! At that moment, Lindsay felt so angry that she started packing up her bag. Before dashing out of the hotel room, she called her translator to vent. But when the translator asked her, "If it were not for his age, would you accept this person?" Lindsay admitted, "Yes." "Then why don't you just forget about his age, which is essentially just a number?" the translator suggested. Having calmed down a bit, Lindsay decided to give Henry a second chance.

As Lindsay got to know Henry better, she realized that there were many things she liked about him, such as his sense of humor and mild temper. Moreover, she was impressed by his financial stability and generosity. Henry said, "I have a stable income; I live a good life. If you are willing to share these fruits of my labor with me, I would be very proud because my happiness would be doubled." These words felt particularly endearing to a financially burdened woman like Lindsay, whose Chinese ex-husband failed in his business and then just disappeared, leaving her to face his mounting debt all alone. By comparison, Henry seemed much more responsible and reliable. Eventually, she accepted Henry's proposal.

Between 2010 and 2019, I visited Lindsay's Oregon home several times. Although her house was no mansion like Susan's, it had a beachside location and I could smell the salty ocean breeze whenever she opened her windows. While not wealthy by any means, Henry was financially comfortable. He received a monthly pension and had bought his home before the price surge in recent years. On most days, Henry sat in a sunny corner of the living room with a book in hand, sipping a cup of tea. Unlike Lindsay the chatterbox, he was rather shy and smiled often, like an endearing grandfather. At home, Lindsay enjoyed a life of leisure. She experimented with Western cooking and impressed me with her homemade tartar sauce and French onion soup. Aside from cooking and hosting dinner parties, Lindsay also went on yoga retreats and worked in her garden. Showing off the roses, peonies, and other plants in her yard, Lindsay proudly said, "When I first came, it was all barren."

On their tenth anniversary, Lindsay told me that her marriage was one of the most successful among women from Ms. Fong's agency, and then summarized several key contributing factors. First, Henry trusted her from the start. Unlike some men who worried that their brides would run away or dominate the household once they learned how to drive and developed their own social circles, Henry had none of those concerns. In fact, he was the one pushing Lindsay to taking driving lessons, as he recognized that Lindsay would ultimately be unhappy if she felt stuck at home. For the same reason, he tried to help Lindsay find new friends, sometimes even approaching other Chinese people in his neighborhood and asking them if they wanted to meet his new wife. Henry's approach stood in striking contrast to that of both Fredrick and Tony, who discouraged their wives from driving or socializing during their first days in the United States. By keeping busy with driving lessons and English classes, and meeting new friends, Lindsay's transition into her new American life was smoother than that of many other clients, who found it a particularly lonely and daunting experience.

Henry also treated Lindsay with respect, sometimes even putting her interests before his own. For example, he bought a down comforter for Lindsay but not for himself because he felt it was too expensive. It was not until several years later, when his old quilt fell apart, that Lindsay convinced him to finally buy one for himself. When he saw that Lindsay liked his new comforter, he said, "Do you want mine? I don't mind taking your old one if you like this one better." His words made Lindsay feel loved and respected. To give another example, during Lindsay's first month in the United States, Henry ate all the Chinese food she cooked, even though he did not enjoy it and even ended up losing five pounds from a loss of appetite. But Henry did not want to criticize Lindsay because he knew that in China she was an avid cook who took great pride in her dishes. Instead, he said, "Thank you so much; now would you like to try Western food? We could take turns cooking." Lindsay appreciated Henry's thoughtfulness, something she felt was lacking among many of the Western men she had met.

Moreover, Henry was sensitive to the loss Lindsay felt in the United States, after giving up her job as a teacher in China. To appease Lindsay's anxiety over her financial dependence on him, he immediately gave her a monthly allowance and a credit card. Although Lindsay took on more of the housework, Henry always insisted on washing the dishes if she cooked and would say, "You cooked, so it's my turn to help out." And although Henry preferred that she not work outside the home, he never opposed her job search openly and instead said, "First, see what you can find." Like Joanne, Lindsay quickly discovered that her English was not good enough for white-collar positions, while she had no interest in blue-collar work. Although both women eventually gave up on their job search, Lindsay and Henry never had a clash over this issue the way Joanne and Fredrick did, given Henry's more respectful approach.

Nevertheless, Lindsay understood that her marriage was still a gendered economic deal, where Henry provided for her economically in exchange for her domestic labor and companionship. Thus, Lindsay spent money with caution and was careful not to break the bargain by asking for too much. For example, although Henry paid for many of her activities, such as dinner parties, ballet shows, and occasional trips to Europe, he did not believe in providing financial support to grown children in nonemergency situations. Thus, although Lindsay sometimes wished she could share some of his money with her daughter in China, who was in graduate school at the time, she refrained from asking Henry. She said, "If we gave my daughter just a few hundred dollars each month, her life could be so much easier. But I know it is not my place to ask because, after all, it's his money."

Even with her own spending, Lindsay knew the importance of restraint. She would always consult with Henry before purchasing any item over US$100. Although Henry usually told her not to worry about the cost, she still felt self-conscious. Lindsay stopped getting facials and massages, even though she was a regular consumer of both in China. Given the higher cost of labor in the United States, she felt that many middle-class Americans deemed these services too expensive, and she did not want her spending style to be out of sync with Henry's income level.

Given the restraints Lindsay imposed on herself, she often criticized other female clients who she felt were overly "greedy." "The reason some women have failed marriages is because they did not correctly *ding wei* [position] themselves," Lindsay said. "They have overestimated their own contribution to their household." Specifically, she referred to women who expected men to shower them with lavish presents and treat their Chinese stepchildren like their biological children, even though these women were neither youthful nor beautiful themselves, and they also did a poor job cooking, cleaning, or fulfilling the men's other demands. "Why would you expect to be treated like a queen? What do you have to offer in return?" Lindsay questioned. Moreover, she believed that if a woman relied on her Western husband to finance her Chinese children's education in the United States, then she should *fang xia shen duan* [swallow her pride] and cater to her husband's other demands. "Ultimately, you must be willing to *fu chu* [give]; you cannot just take things from another person without giving them what they want," Lindsay said.

Here we can see that Lindsay's perspective on marriage corroborates the utilitarian view promoted by entrepreneurial C-feminists, where women perform conventional femininities in exchange for men's financial support. Applying this principle of gendered deal-making to her own marriage, she felt that Henry was willing to *fu chu*: he bequeathed all his property to Lindsay and her daughter in his will. In return, he got someone significantly younger to take good care of him until the end of his life, while Lindsay faced a long, lonely widowhood in the years ahead. "I will do it willingly, with all my heart," Lindsay said. She added, "That's what marriage is: a fair exchange."

Lindsay's marriage to Henry showcases yet another patriarchal bargain, where the woman focuses exclusively on domestic work, while the man acts as the sole household breadwinner. Like Susan and Tony, Lindsay and Henry reaped the rewards of their patriarchal bargain while accepting its costs. For Lindsay, this involved performing care work and taking on the risk of a long widowhood in exchange for financial security in her old age. What distinguishes Lindsay's marriage from those of the other women was that theirs had an undertone of masculine dominance and feminine submissiveness, while hers was built more on mutual respect and mutual sacrifice. Despite Lindsay's underlying financial dependence on Henry, in some ways, her marriage actually resembled a so-called American soulmate marriage,[23] commonly found among two working professionals, which emphasizes equality and deep friendship, as well as shared hobbies and interests.

From Lindsay and Henry's successful marriage, it is clear that the patriarchal bargain cannot be immediately dismissed as oppressive to women. The equity of the bargain depends on intersections of other factors, including respect, ability to sacrifice, and reasonableness within the exchange. With the right combination, both parties can feel happy and fairly treated in a marriage that ultimately expects different contributions from each gender.

CONCLUSION

The three examples in this chapter show that marriages built on an exchange of female domesticity for male financial support do not automatically preclude women from being happy. In fact, two of my three respondents felt satisfied with their husbands overall, and believed that marriage migration had been the right move for them. Thus, it is not gendered division of labor per se that makes or breaks the marriages, but rather the specific terms and conditions of the gendered economic bargain. To have a functional deal, both parties must view the costs and rewards as equitable and worthy of pursuing. Moreover, couples must represent themselves authentically during their courtship so that, once married, each party can meet the other person's expectations in their gendered economic deal.

Next, let us address the question of whether the male breadwinner/female homemaker model of marriage fundamentally disempowered women. If we were to consider marriage migrants at the *individual* level, these marriages might feel empowering to some women, depending on the specific circumstances. Among my interviewees, many judged whether their marriage had empowered them by comparing their current living situation with the life they left behind in China. In Susan's case, even though she found Fredrick's domineering personality oppressive, it still felt *less* oppressive than the pressures from her boss in China. Therefore, she experienced an overall sense of empowerment by marrying Tony. It is important to note that none of the three women in this chapter was barred from working by her husband; instead, all three *opted* not to work. Their decisions to stay home were largely based on the reality that the only type of job available to them was blue-collar work, which they were reluctant to take on. Thus, whatever oppression or inequity they experienced as homemakers, it perhaps felt *less* oppressive than what they believed they would have been subject to if they worked, either back in China or in the United States.

Moreover, the women's marital satisfaction varied greatly at the *individual level* and was determined not only by money but also by the intersectionality of other factors. For example, although Tony had more money than Henry, his wife, Susan, was not necessarily more satisfied with her marriage than Lindsay was, because Tony never gave Susan the same degree of trust, respect, and freedom that Henry gave Lindsay. Age could also have shaped the women's marital satisfaction differently. In the case of Joanne and Fredrick, their conflicts over young stepchildren who still lived at home did not apply to the other couples. Moreover, Joanne's lofty dreams to open her own business and her subsequent disappointment may also have been associated with her relative youth, while the other two women were probably more easily contented with a retirement-like lifestyle due to their older age.

Nevertheless, if we consider migrant women as a *group*, then marriages that rely on their performance of emphasized femininity in exchange for men's continued financial support would certainly have an overall harmful effect on future migrants, because such marriages reinforce Western media stereotypes of Asian women as submissive, domesticated, and erotic "China dolls."[24] While some men, like Henry, are indeed thoughtful and respectful to their wives, this is not the case for all Western husbands. As we saw, other men, such as Fredrick, turned out to be abusive. Moreover, these men's decisions to seek out a Chinese bride are often based on their perceptions of Asian women, gleaned from Western media, as domesticated and submissive.

Another reason why the patriarchal bargain disadvantaged migrant women as a *group* is that some factors that affected their marital happiness fell beyond their control. For example, Joanne had no way of discovering Fredrick's true financial condition until she moved abroad, since he deceived her while they were in a long-distance relationship. In Susan's case, she was not passive or powerless, but also not in full control of her circumstances, either. Her gender strategies, rooted in emphasized femininity, failed at times. As a result, she often described her marriage as a "gamble." During various moments when she felt powerless to take control of her own life, she turned to God for support. While some women, such as Lindsay, were fortunate in that their marriages ultimately turned out fine, others, like Joanne, were not as lucky. Women who ended up in conflict-ridden marriages found themselves in a precarious position to fight back, given their lack of language skills, social networks, and permanent citizenship status, and, most important, their financial dependence on their husbands.

This chapter contributes to the existing scholarship on marriage migration by reaffirming the importance of adopting a culturally relativistic approach, as advocated by scholars such as Nicole Constable, and acknowledging migrant women's own sense of empowerment rather than judging them solely through a Western-centric, middle-class, feminist lens. This is particularly important when we examine migrant women at the *individual* level, where their marital happiness varies greatly from person to person and is dependent on the intersectionality of many factors. Nevertheless, we must also not discredit the Western feminist critique of gendered patriarchal bargains in its entirety. When considering women as a *group*, evidence from this chapter shows that marriages built on their performance of emphasized femininity in exchange for men's financial support puts them at a structural disadvantage. For the subset of unlucky women who end up in conflict-ridden marriages for reasons beyond their control, their financial dependence on their husbands renders them powerless to fight back.

5 | BODY OF A WOMAN, FATE OF A MAN

IN LATE DECEMBER 2017, I drove toward a remote community in the Deep South. As I traveled farther, the roads narrowed and shops and restaurants started disappearing, until I was surrounded by nothing but trees, a few gas stations, and occasional fast-food joints. Several hours later, I arrived at a retirement community of mobile and manufactured homes. This was where Robert and Meredith lived. They had invited me to visit for the holidays, and as I pulled into their driveway, the couple waved and exclaimed, "We are so happy to see you; it's been too long!" Indeed, I could hardly believe eight years had passed since I had first met the couple in China. Meredith, a woman now in her fifties, wore a form-fitting, low-cut black shirt and bright red lipstick, a change from when we first met in China and she barely wore makeup. Robert was a tall, thin, silver-haired man with tattoos on both arms and wrinkles that seemed to have deepened over the years.

Their home stood on a small plot of land, and they gave me a quick tour of their back yard, which was filled with orange and banana trees. Inside their mobile home, I saw all the usual amenities that a normal house would have, such as washer, dryer, refrigerator, shower, and so on. Nevertheless, the ceilings hung low and the walls were extremely thin. In fact, one could easily overhear another person talking, watching television, or snoring next door. Before long, Meredith pulled me inside her bedroom and exclaimed: "Welcome to this humble little abode! You know, I own two apartments in China, both of which are ten times more beautiful! When I first arrived, there was nothing here—absolutely nothing, no furniture—except two bare mattresses. I wanted to cry. I wanted to leave right away. I never imagined the United States to look like this!"

It was not hard to see how much Robert struggled financially. Nearly seventy and officially retired, he still drove trucks part-time to make ends meet. During the two evenings I stayed in their home while Meredith was out working, he treated me to meals of ramen noodles and kimchee from his kitchen. Robert told me that, back when he was in a long-distance relationship with Meredith, he often ate just a few dumplings for dinner and sometimes had to skip meals. To pay for all his China trips, he went so far as to sell his car.

Although Robert's poverty was much worse than what Meredith had expected before moving abroad, she had long been aware that he was not a rich man. Throughout their courtship, during which Meredith lived in China, they fought over everything from the size of her engagement ring to his budget for their wedding banquet. Yet, Meredith still married Robert because she faced economic burdens in China. Although she made a comfortable living for herself as a small business owner, she had two teenage sons, one of whom had a minor physical disability, was out of school, and unemployed. At the same time, business at her shop was declining. Meredith wanted to help her son immigrate to the United States, where she imagined there would be better job opportunities and less discrimination against people with a disability. This was particularly important to Meredith, given that her Chinese ex-husband never paid child support. Moreover, despite her desire to marry rich, Meredith was not confident in her ability to do so, since she did not consider herself pretty, youthful, or well educated. Rather than taking her chances and waiting for a better catch, Meredith decided to jump on this opportunity to help her sons.

Unfortunately, things hardly turned out the way she had hoped. While their engagement party was held in 2009, Meredith did not move abroad until 2012. She blamed this on Robert and called him *lao jian ju hua* (crafty and deceptive) for purposely delaying her move until after her disabled son had turned twenty-one, so that he would have to submit a separate application and wait for many years before immigrating. This matter, alongside the poverty she saw in the United States, which was far worse than she expected, shattered her dreams for a happy marriage. When Meredith realized that Robert could not meet her financial expectations, she decided to seek outside employment. She first worked as a nanny for several neighborhood families with young children, and later obtained a license to become a full-time masseuse, earning up to US$5,000 per month and remitting a sizable portion of that money to her sons in China.

Meredith's decision to work stood in contrast to the brides featured in chapter 4, all of whom remained homemakers. Many Western feminists assume that women become more empowered when couples share breadwinning and domestic duties more equally.[1] However, this view does not resonate with my respondents, whose gender ideology aligns with a strand of Chinese-style feminism, described earlier, called "entrepreneurial C-fem."[2] This ideology asserts that women's empowerment is not always associated with their participation in the paid labor force. Instead, women are encouraged to take a utilitarian view of marriage and to perform conventional femininity in exchange for material gain. Entrepreneurial C-feminism emerged in response to China's changing structural conditions in the postreform era, when wealth became concentrated among a small subset of men, while women's social position worsened. As a result, Chinese society today is governed by a market logic that emphasizes women's economic dependence on men and their sexual objectification by men.[3]

This chapter will focus on the clash in gender ideology between Chinese wives who subscribe to entrepreneurial C-fem and their Western husbands who take on a more gender egalitarian perspective. Specifically, I chronicle the private lives of four different brides who chose to work outside the home, comparing their lives to the homemakers we met in chapter 4, to determine if there is a primary divide in marital happiness based on whether or not the women worked. This comparison will shed light on the Western-centric assumption that women who work for pay experience greater marital satisfaction than women who are full-time homemakers, and also examine its applicability to the Chinese brides in my study. We first return to Meredith's story.

MOBILE HOMES

Meredith's conflict with Robert stemmed not only from her disappointment with his dire financial condition, but also from their out-of-sync gender ideologies. In line with entrepreneurial C-fem, Meredith wanted a marriage built on a separation of spheres. To her, this meant that, regardless of whether she worked or not, her husband should remain the sole household provider. If she chose to work, she should keep her earnings as her private money. This attitude obviously contradicts the Western feminist assumption that women who work would take pride in splitting the household bills with their husbands and would view that equal division as a sign of empowerment.[4]

Adhering to this Chinese-style feminism, Meredith got extremely upset when Robert asked her to chip in on their household expenses after she started working as a masseuse. Since Meredith believed men should provide food and shelter for their wives, she felt that Robert had breached his duty. Robert, for his part, saw no reason to foot the household bills alone, now that Meredith was working and earning even more than he was. Moreover, he thought it was unfair for Meredith to be sending thousands of dollars to her grown sons, while he struggled to support his teenage daughter. "I'm skimping on financial duties to my own children," Robert said, "while she is treating thirty-year-old men like babies." This became a major source of conflict in their marriage and almost led to their divorce at one point.

Eventually Meredith compromised and paid Robert some money each month. However, she felt exploited and mocked Robert: "He must be so happy to have a wife like me; he is the one to profit from this relationship, by marrying a wife whom he does not need to support and instead supports him!" She added, "I compromised only because I'm not money-obsessed like him." From a Western standpoint, some readers may perceive Meredith to be the haggler in this situation, but from her perspective, any money she gave Robert reflected her *generosity* since it was *not* her responsibility to pay for household expenses in the first place.

Meredith had plenty of money left over for her sons even after paying Robert. Just because she achieved her financial goals through working, however, does not mean she felt satisfied with her marriage. Since Meredith's workplace was in a major city several hours away from Robert's remote trailer park community, she only went home once a week. During the last day of my visit, she took me to see the strip mall massage parlor where she worked, which offered a variety of services from foot-soak to full-body work. The parlor had several individual guest rooms and a full-sized kitchen in the back where employees cooked and watched television. For five nights a week, Meredith would sleep in one of the massage rooms. The shop owner, a middle-aged woman from northern China, sometimes spent the night there as well. Ironically, Meredith appeared much chattier and more relaxed at work, where she spoke Chinese with her boss all day, than she did at home with her husband. Laughing bitterly at her current situation, she said, "At my age, most people in China are enjoying their retirement, but I'm still working away alone in a foreign land. How can I think of what happened to me? I can only think of this marriage as an opportunity to earn money for my sons."

Back in China, Meredith's dream had been to marry a breadwinner. She felt disappointed by the fact that she had had to take on a provider role throughout her life, both in China and in the United States. She lamented: "I have the body of a woman, fate of a man . . . I never had the good fortune of relying on men." Here we can see that Meredith perceives her financial independence as a misfortune rather than a privilege. I suggest that her aversion to breadwinning is shaped by her previous life experiences.

Meredith called herself "a man stuck in a woman's body" because she felt just as competent as the men around her. Growing up in a family of seven, she started cooking for the entire household at age five and took on leadership roles at school and at work. After getting laid off from a state-owned factory during the 1990s, she opened a private company with some friends and made lots of money. At that time, her then-husband, who earned much less than she did, started gambling away her assets until he drove her to bankruptcy. Upon their divorce, he blamed Meredith for being overly *qiang shi* (domineering) to the point that he lost his masculine dignity, a claim she vigorously refuted:

That is a lame excuse he made up. I respected him; I never hoarded the money. In fact, I was so busy making money that I had no time to keep track of where it went. I simply tossed all the cash in a drawer that we shared. Because I was so unmindful, I did not discover his gambling addiction until it was much too late. What is worse, he used my hard-earned money to sleep with other women. I could hardly believe my ears when other people told me about this.

Following their divorce, Meredith took custody of their young children, while her ex-husband never paid a penny of child support. She never remarried, either, because she was at an extreme disadvantage on the Chinese dating market: many men have qualms about marrying women with sons, given the social norm in China in which parents are expected to help their grown sons with their mortgages.[5] In Meredith's case, having two sons, one of whom was handicapped, only exacerbated her plight.

Given her bitter experience as a single mother, Meredith did not look at her financial independence positively. In fact, she felt her provider role in her previous marriage had brought her nothing but pain and injustice: her husband freeloaded off her earnings, used her money to cheat on her, and then blamed her for being the domineering breadwinner. By comparison, she witnessed other women achieve upward mobility by capitalizing on their youth and femininity to marry wealthy men and become homemakers. Even upon divorce, some of these women received big settlements, while she was left with nothing but her ex-husband's debt. Here, Meredith's prior life experience may explain why entrepreneurial C-fem resonated with her more than the egalitarian, husband-and-wife sharing of household fiscal responsibilities. To some Western feminists, this utilitarian approach to marriage may seem disempowering to women in that it encourages them to seemingly succumb to gendered stereotypes. Yet entrepreneurial C-fems would argue that it is in women's best interest to avoid marrying for "pure love" out of "self-protection,"[6] given that contemporary Chinese society is so structurally oppressive to women. Note here that since entrepreneurial C-fem emerged in response to China's social conditions, its tenets may not fit with the structural realities in the United States.

The case of Meredith and Robert sheds light on conflicts that emerge between transnational couples when Chinese women bring their gender ideologies from their home country into their new marriage abroad. In Meredith's case, working outside of the home provided her with a sense of community and some financial security for her children. However, she was ultimately unhappy with her marriage because her gender ideology clashed with Robert's more Western beliefs, which saw both partners contributing to household income and expenses. Here, Meredith's ability to work outside the home did not innately translate to greater marital satisfaction. Instead, it opened a new avenue for conflict.

On the last day of my 2017 visit, Meredith pulled me aside and whispered, "Don't laugh at me when you hear this, but we never have sex. Our marriage is simply an arrangement of practicality." She proceeded to reassure me that money was the primary source of their conflict, not sex. Indeed, based on my observation over the years, Meredith did not seem to care about her absent sex life. In fact, at one point she even said, "Robert is not a bad guy, I'm pretty okay with everything else about him, but I just can't stand his attitude toward money." Meredith's nonchalant attitude toward sex stands in contrast to Emily and Joe, whose marriage we will examine next.

VIAGRA PILLS

Emily was once a successful small business owner in China. Starting in the 2000s, however, she saw her profits decline until she closed the business down, right before joining Ms. Mei's agency. There, Emily met Joe, an American construction manager. Although he owned a house on the West Coast, he rarely spent more than a few months at home each year and instead motel-hopped from site to site for work. In 2015, his team was stationed in a small town located near the Canadian border. Given the region's breathtaking views, the couple invited Ms. Mei and me to visit them for a week in the summer of 2015.

Upon my arrival, the chilly winds and light rain could not dampen my excitement. The landscape felt surreal, with deep fjords covered in white mist, aqua-colored ocean, and pink peonies in full bloom. I was excited to reunite with Emily, whom I had not seen since 2012, when she was still living in China and dating Joe online. Now in her fifties, Emily was still slim and energetic, just as I remembered. However, she had developed a tan, and her style of dress had changed dramatically, from long skirts and silk scarves to jeans and T-shirts. On our way back from the airport, Emily tugged my arm and pulled me away from the rest of the group. As we trotted far ahead of everyone else, she whispered, "You know, although everything between me and Joe looks okay on the surface, in reality, my marriage is in shambles."

Like Meredith, Emily had a grown child to support and cited this as a primary motive for pursuing marriage migration. Emily's daughter was in her thirties, unemployed, and married to a struggling artist. Feeling guilty for having ignored her daughter throughout her childhood years, when Emily was constantly traveling for business, she let her daughter live rent-free in her Chinese condo and spoiled her with pocket money to spend on designer shoes and handbags.

Compared to Meredith's husband, Robert, Joe was in much better financial shape. Upon their first meeting in Tunyang, Joe gifted Emily with a US$1,000 Longines watch and eagerly picked up every tab when dining out with her friends. Perhaps it was his generosity during the initial courtship that ramped up Emily's expectations, thereby causing her great disappointment when she actually moved abroad. Emily recalled the first time she stepped into Joe's home: "My heart felt cold as soon as I saw his dirty house—all empty, with no furniture. I immediately knew that he had no *sheng huo pin wei* [taste in his lifestyle]." Although Joe's tax return showed an annual income of US$100,000, his lifestyle hardly matched what she expected of such a high earner: his house was barely paid off; he did not have a car—a major status symbol for many Chinese people—and instead drove his company-owned pickup truck.

Not only was Emily disappointed by Joe's standard of living, but she also realized that she had no control over his finances. In fact, she was not even sure how he spent his monthly paycheck, and she could only guess that much of it went to his grown children, including a son who struggled with substance abuse. This was quite disappointing for Emily, whose vision of a good husband fell in line with the Chinese perception that "a man shows his love for a woman by handing her his wallet." The idea here is that although men in the postreform era have become household breadwinners, they should still let their wives be the financial managers, so that women could feel more secure in their marriages. This perception falls in line with entrepreneurial C-feminism, which encourages women to acquire wealth indirectly by controlling men's wallets through their feminine power, rather than directly competing with men on the paid labor market.

Since Emily had no control over Joe's finances, she still felt financially insecure despite his large salary. Due to her limited English and his frequent moving, which made it difficult for her to find employment elsewhere, she joined Joe's construction team, where she performed manual labor for US$250 per day. With this money, she bought herself a car and remitted the rest to her daughter in China. Despite her newfound opportunity to make money, Emily was still unhappy with Joe. Deeply offended when Joe asked her to sell off her condo in China and transfer her assets to America, she called him a "terrible man" for "wanting to take a woman's money." Moreover, she was upset that Joe drove the car she had bought with her hard-earned money. "It's my money, my car, he should not be driving it without paying me!" Emily exclaimed. Through these comments, we can see that this couple struggled over the same clash in gender ideology that plagued so many other couples, where the women wanted their husbands to be the sole household provider, while the men wanted their wives to share fiscal responsibility.

As was the case for Meredith, Emily's aversion to female breadwinning was shaped by her life experiences in China. Emily perceived herself as very smart and talented, often outcompeting the men around her. Thus, she left her job at a state-owned factory when she saw a lucrative opportunity in the jewelry business. By the mid-1980s, Emily had become a *wan yuan hu* (household with annual income of 10,000 yuan [US$28,000] or more, which was considered wealthy) who could afford mink coats and designer watches. Yet, at this time, her marriage broke down. "I took such good financial care of my ex-husband that he had too much time and money on his hands, so he started having affairs," Emily said. After catching him and his mistress naked on her own bed, she filed for divorce. Emily's second marriage followed a similar pattern. She helped her then-husband get rich by reinventing his failing business. In fact, she ended up managing his company while he partied away and eventually cheated on her. Hence, like Meredith, Emily did not look at her breadwinning in a positive light, as she felt that her provider role had brought her nothing but heartache.

Although Meredith and Emily had experienced many of the same struggles, one big difference was their desire for sex. While Meredith had no interest in having sex with Robert, for Emily, sex was the biggest source of her discontentment. "It's like I'm married to a dead person," she complained. Dragging me into her bedroom and pointing at their queen-sized bed, she said: "You see, we sleep on separate sides of this bed. You can literally fit a whole person in the middle. If I touch his arm accidentally, he will shirk away. One time I called him out on it, I said, 'I'm your wife; you are my husband! I have the right to touch you; why do you shirk away?' He apologized, but I told him this is not a matter of apology. This is a very serious problem."

Having abided by the principle of no sex before marriage, a norm that some Chinese women from older generations still followed, it was not until after Emily arrived in the United States that she noticed their sexual incompatibility. For the entire duration of their marriage, she recalled having intercourse with Joe only two or three times. Each time, Joe would get hard in the beginning but turn soft before penetration. At the same time, Emily found piles of the erectile dysfunction drug Viagra stashed in secret corners of the house. Pointing to a box she had just pulled out of the closet, Emily said to me, "A few pills would go missing each week, until they are completely gone, and then they would get replaced." She also noticed that Joe's face would turn bright red whenever pills went missing. "We never have sex," exclaimed Emily, "so where does all his pent-up desire go?"

Several times, Emily caught Joe watching gay porn on his iPad. Moreover, she noticed that he avoided picking up phone calls during the evenings and disappeared from the house in the mornings, sometimes stepping out as early as four or five a.m. One morning, she even noticed two sets of giant footprints on her bathroom floor. Emily began to suspect that Joe had been cheating on her with a man, and that their marriage was a cover-up for his bisexuality. Observing Joe every day at work, Emily suspected his lover was one of his subordinates. One afternoon, when I visited their construction site, Emily pointed to a young, tall, brown-haired man and whispered to me, "Look, look, he's the one!" At home, she was not shy about expressing her discontent in front of Ms. Mei and me. One evening, as we sat around the kitchen chatting after dinner, Joe's cellphone rang again. Pointing her finger at Joe, Emily shrieked, "Pick up! Pick up! Why don't you pick up! Huh? Huh? Why don't you? What are you hiding?"

Not only was Emily upset by Joe's probable cheating, but she also looked down on him for what she perceived as his working-class behavior. Despite

Joe's US$100,000 income, Emily thought he had poor *pinwei* (taste). Here I count *pinwei* as a part of one's cultural capital,[7] a term that refers to non-economic factors, such as one's educational credentials, family background, linguistic capability, and tastes or mannerisms, that can be converted into social or economic advantages. Joe, who had a rural upbringing, lacked the kind of cultural capital Emily found desirable. By her standards, he was too "rough," "uncouth," and "uncultured." Every night, she watched in despair as he came home from work, plopped down on the couch, and watched TV while sucking on popsicles, sometimes consuming as many as twelve in one sitting. To Emily, this behavior signified a lack of basic health awareness and self-control—a lack that characterized uncultured people. By contrast, Emily refrained from processed foods and practiced portion control. Back when she was a successful businesswoman in Tunyang, she wore designer clothing, practiced yoga, and wrote gourmet health recipes. Thus, she often claimed that women like herself who sought Western men were the cream of the crop in China, while Western men who sought Chinese brides were "the trash of the West."

Unfortunately, things had not improved much when I revisited the couple in 2016. When I asked Emily whether she would consider getting a divorce, she said, "It's not likely at this point . . . I'm too old; it's too late." Shaking her head, she commented on her bleak future: "I don't have any other hope or expectations at this point. My life now is just about money. The more I make, the happier I am." Emily had found a new job at a Chinese massage parlor, just like Meredith. On New Year's Eve, when I visited her at work, one of her coworkers offered to give me a free massage and I accepted. This massage felt rather rough, as I could tell Emily's coworker had little professional training. The employees here consisted mostly of women who had traveled to the United States on tourist visas so as to work under the table because they owed debt in China. They worked seven days a week and were paid a base wage of US$20 per hour. I felt a bit sad watching Emily, who had once been a successful business owner, now laboring away into her old age. While everyone else went out to celebrate New Year's Eve, these women brought rice and vegetables, and cooked in the back kitchen during their work breaks.

Nevertheless, Emily's life was not all bad. Each year, she took a three-month vacation to China, where she would eat, shop, travel, and have fun.

In the summer of 2018, Emily treated me and a group of her friends to a lavish dinner in Tunyang. There, I learned that she now owned a second condo in China and was back to oversee its renovation. While it is clear from her vacations and investments in China that Emily's breadwinner role empowered her in a general sense, it is important to distinguish that it was not a source of empowerment in the context of her marriage. Her financial contributions to the relationship felt like salt in the wound of what was already a sexless marriage that did not provide her with the financial security for which she thought she had bargained.

Emily's decision to stay in the United States confirms the observation that financially burdened women often endure less-than-ideal marriages out of economic need. Like Meredith, Emily felt deeply discontented despite her ability to work outside the home. In fact, her new income became a leading source of contention in her marriage and brought to light an East-West clash in gender ideology. Other factors, such as sexual incompatibility and a gap in cultural capital, further decreased Emily's marital satisfaction. Yet unlike middle-class professionals, who could return to their high-skill positions in China, or independently wealthy women who wouldn't need to work for the rest of their lives regardless of whom they married, Emily faced a different economic reality. As a middle-aged woman with no college degree and a failed business, her job prospects in China were bleak, and her daughter still needed financial support. Thus, Emily chose to stay in the United States and earn fast cash in the low-end service sector.

LIKE A ROBOT

Unfortunately, the situation of women putting up with sexless marriages because their other financial opportunities were limited is not unique to Emily, but rather a common occurrence at the agency. Mr. Li, one of the managers, told me that a substantial number of his Western male clients struggled with impotence, which often resulted in disappointment and dissatisfaction for the Chinese wives. This was certainly the case for Beth, a pretty nurse introduced in previous chapters. When Beth's American husband, Edmond, initially visited her in China in the summer of 2011, she was appalled by his relentless sex drive. One evening, when Beth stopped by my apartment with Ms. Mei to chat over tea, she told us that they had sex six times on the first day and then four times per day for the remainder of Edmond's week-long stay in China. Breaking into giggles, Beth said, "I told him twice a day, but he wanted four . . . I can't handle that; it's too much!" Then she proceeded to ask me, "Are most foreign men this horny?" Worried that she was only trying to please Edmond, I asked Beth if she also enjoyed the sex. To my surprise, she said, "Actually, I liked it. He would turn me on and make me want it." At the time, I thought perhaps the sexual chemistry played some role in keeping them together despite other problems that plagued their relationship.

Beth always felt she deserved someone wealthier than Edmond, a firefighter. To help understand her discontentment, we must return to the mentality of entrepreneurial C-feminism, which encourages women to trade their feminine sensibilities for security via male providers. In this exchange, a woman's physical appearance is deemed extremely important, and women are advised to aim for men whose financial capability matches their own physical worth. For instance, Chinese relationship consultant Ayawawa's "PU [paternal uncertainty]–MV [mating value] theory" on how to marry well has become extremely popular with her nearly 3 million followers on Weibo, a Twitter-like platform.[8] The "MV" portion of the equation refers to a woman's reproductive potential and sexual attractiveness.

Beth had always thought of herself as good-looking, and she worked hard to present herself nicely. Yet, she was never able to trade her beauty for the kind of wealth she felt she deserved. Her first marriage ended in divorce when her then-husband failed in his business endeavor. Her second marriage, to a man who treated her and her son in a miserly fashion, ended in divorce as well. Comparing herself to her friend Jennifer, a rich man's mistress, Beth lamented, "I'm ill-fated in that I never get to date men who are rich and generous." Moreover, Beth felt it was utterly unfair that Jennifer, who she thought was far less physically attractive than herself and who had only a middle-school education, got to live in luxury without ever having to work outside the home. By contrast, Beth had put herself through nursing school, worked day and night, but still struggled financially.

At one point, Beth broke off her engagement with Edmond to date other people. Yet, a few months later, Beth went back to Edmond because she felt she could not wait around any longer due to her financially burdened situation. Her son was soon to enter high school while her Chinese ex-husband could not pay child support, and she did not want to risk paying expensive tuition at a comparable private school in China if he could not test into a renowned public school. After Beth moved abroad, her earlier quarrels with Edmond over money were exacerbated by an utter lack of sex. This took her by surprise given their previous time together. In a telephone interview with me, Beth said, "He doesn't have sex with me; he has no needs. We just never have sex . . . I think that is abusive; you know, I can divorce him over just that." It turned out that Edmond had taken Viagra on his trip to China, and now that Beth was in the United States, he decided to stop taking the erectile dysfunction drug.

Two years after Beth moved to the United States, we got together with Ms. Mei at a beachside resort in California. Beth looked older than before, having developed dark undereye circles and a few wrinkles. Nevertheless, she still took meticulous care of her appearance. One evening, as I watched her perform her nightly facial massage, Beth revealed that she had a lover on the side. He was also Chinese, several years her junior, and they had met as coworkers at the supermarket where both were employed. Beth was rather forthcoming with her lover, and told him that she had no plans to divorce Edmond, since she relied on him for her green card so that her son could stay in the United States to attend college. To distract Edmond from her frequent absences from home, Beth even bought him a pet cat.

Beth attributed her failing marriage not only to their lack of sex, but also to differences in their spending styles and gender ideologies. According to Beth, Edmond was obsessed with saving money even though he earned a decent salary. For example, while Beth enjoyed eating out and traveling, Edmond spent most of his free time sitting at home. Moreover, he refused to buy health insurance and self-medicated with over-the-counter drugs. This was unthinkable to Beth, who immediately got a job so that she could pay for her own insurance. "We don't get any assistance from him," Beth said, "except he gave me his eleven-year-old car and let us live in his house rent-free. We still have to pay for our own gas, cellphone bills, insurance, and even food because we don't eat the American stuff he buys." Deeming breadwinning a man's responsibility, she called Edmond "stingy, calculating, and selfish."

As Beth spoke, the dim bedroom light cast a silhouette of her dainty, heart-shaped face on the wall. Before long, she peered into the kitchen to make sure Ms. Mei had not overheard our conversation. Then, she trotted back into the bedroom to show me an intimate selfie of her and her lover and explained, "You know, living with Edmond is like being in dead water. There is no future, no hope. I just get up, eat, work, and sleep, like a robot. I want more passion and meaning in life."

For both Beth and Emily, passion was an important part of marriage. When their Western husbands failed to deliver on this aspect of their relationship, they developed coping mechanisms in the form of lovers or vacations away. Their ability to work outside the home did not automatically translate to a more equitable marriage, either, and often it only opened more avenues by which differing gender ideologies could prove problematic in these transnational relationships. Yet, they chose to stay in these difficult marriages due to their financially burdened status and their reliance on their husbands for a green card.

ALL HUMAN HEARTS ARE MADE OF FLESH

While Meredith, Emily, and Beth all fought with their Western husbands over the sharing of household fiscal responsibilities, another bride, Daisy, did not encounter this problem, even though she also worked outside the home. Daisy's marriage was still far from perfect, however. There was a persistent lack of sexual passion, which bothered Daisy, but she accepted her husband anyway due to her financially burdened status.

I first met Daisy in 2010 when Ms. Mei, her agency manager, invited me and a few clients to her home to play mah-jongg. With rosy cheeks and round, gleaming eyes, Daisy had a doll-like appearance. She was divorced, in her mid-forties, and worked as a department store salesclerk. At that time, Daisy was dating Anthony, a well-off business owner from Florida. When I revisited Tunyang in 2011, however, their relationship had soured. After more than ten months of email exchange and a visit to China, Daisy received an email from Anthony's children stating that he had to give up on their relationship due to an illness. Upon hearing the bad news, Daisy cried day and night. That summer, I met with her every other week to help her translate emails and phone calls to Anthony, most of which he never answered.

Suspecting that Anthony had married someone else, the agency translators advised Daisy to seek out other men. She then started dating Peter, a divorced mechanic from France who soon visited her in person. On one brisk and sunny October morning, Daisy, Peter, Ms. Mei, two other female clients, and I met up at the local train station to embark on a weekend excursion to tour China's Three Gorges, a mountainous reservoir region along the Yangtze River. From afar I spotted Peter, a man in his early fifties. Although he was not particularly tall or handsome, everyone complimented Peter on his "baby face" and youthful looks. After getting to know Peter, they liked him even more, as he was always smiling and never complained. During our three-hour train ride to the Three Gorges, Daisy played cards with her Chinese friends the whole time and left Peter to sit alone. Despite her standoffish attitude, he remained cheery. On the last day of our trip, when another female client sprained her ankle, Daisy volunteered to stay behind with her at the hotel while everyone else went hiking. Instead of acting disappointed, Peter praised Daisy for being a good friend to the injured woman.

After observing Peter's considerate personality and clear attraction to Daisy, everyone told her to forget Anthony, who had not visited China for months. Despite this, Daisy was reluctant. She was not attracted to Peter, as he was not tall, handsome, or muscular like Anthony, whom she called an "Arnold Schwarzenegger look-alike." After spending one night with Peter, Daisy frowned and said of their sex, "I had zero juice down there! All dry!"

After Peter left China, Daisy's translator continued writing to him on her behalf. Nevertheless, Daisy was still emotionally invested in Anthony. One morning, she begged me to help her contact Anthony again. She seemed so distressed that I skipped breakfast and rushed over to her apartment. Upon my arrival, Daisy cooked many dishes for me, but she barely ate anything herself because she had lost her appetite due to her distress over Anthony's lack of response. As she watched me eat her homemade dumplings and spicy beef noodle soup, she muttered: "Everyone says Peter is a nice guy, but I have no *gan jue* [passion] for him. You know, he is a bit *yu* [foolish and clumsy], like a *nong min lao da ge* [someone from the peasant class] . . . he has no flexibility or sophistication in his thinking. He just feels like a big brother to me. But I am looking for a husband, not a brother!"

Yet, she also admitted that she had to move on if Anthony continued ignoring her. Daisy was particularly worried because she had quit her depart ment store job after meeting Anthony, who wired her US$2,000 each month for the duration of the year they dated. After the breakup, she had to take on temporary jobs, such as food sampling at a supermarket, to make ends meet. Shaking her head, Daisy exclaimed, "Quitting my job and relying on men was a bad idea. Now I live in fear every day . . . but I cannot go back to my old workplace, either. Everyone would ask me, why are you coming back? What happened to your rich boyfriend? We thought you were moving to America? It would be such a huge loss of face." Finally, she looked up at me, teary-eyed, and said, "[Monica], do you think Chinese women like me are pathetic?"

In China, Daisy had dim employment prospects. Even if she did go back to the department store, she would still face the risk of unemployment in the long run because China engages in "beauty economy" market practices,[9] whereby only young, attractive women get hired to promote commercial products. In fact, job stability was one of the primary factors that motivated Daisy to seek marriage migration in the first place. Ultimately, Daisy decided that she could not afford the risk of waiting, particularly when her translator told her that "we really cannot guarantee that you will come across another sincere suitor anytime soon," and she accepted Peter's proposal. However, she still cried her heart out on the night before leaving China, as she felt forced—out of financial desperation—to marry someone for whom she felt no romantic attraction.

Two years later, in the summer of 2018, Daisy and I met up once again when we both returned to China for vacation. When she spotted me in front of the restaurant where we met for dinner, she ran excitedly toward me and we hugged. Daisy looked somewhat different from how I remembered, as she no longer wore false eyelashes or had red highlights in her hair. She showed up in a T-shirt, jeans, and a simple ponytail, a very different look from the frilly dresses and heels she used to wear. Interestingly, she had picked up a heavy Taiwanese accent, possibly from socializing with Taiwanese immigrants whom she befriended in France.

Recalling Daisy's initial reluctance to marry Peter, I was extremely surprised to see how much she was now enjoying her marriage. Over dinner, Daisy whispered to me, "Peter really spoils me; he lets me do whatever I want!" Unlike many other Western men Daisy knew, who went out of their way to prevent their Chinese wives from socializing with other people, Peter always welcomed Daisy's friends. This being the case, she excitedly invited me to visit Europe and stay in her Paris home. As we chatted, Daisy pulled out her cellphone to show me photos of their two-story townhouse. In Paris, Peter owned two properties, one of which he rented out to generate extra cash flow. Grinning and sounding contented, Daisy said, "Peter is not a rich man, but he makes enough money for me to live comfortably without having to worry about food or shelter." Here we can see how Daisy's satisfaction with Peter directly aligns with entrepreneurial C-feminist perspectives on marriage. The utilitarian understanding of marriage posits obtaining personal economic security at the center of a woman's agency.[10] In freeing her from having to worry about food or money, especially as a financially burdened woman, Daisy's marriage was innately a successful one.

At home, the couple resorted to a traditional gendered division of labor, where Peter paid all the bills while Daisy cooked and cleaned. To supplement the paltry sum of pocket money Peter gave her, Daisy worked part-time as a waitress at a Chinese restaurant and kept all her earnings as her private income. Making US$1,500 per month, she excitedly exclaimed, "I worked way more hours in China but never made this kind of money!" Not only did this job ensure her plenty of money to spend on clothing and gadgets, but it also enabled her to send remittances to her grown daughter in China, who struggled to hold a steady job. Here we can see that, although Daisy worked outside the home, the couple experienced no clash in gender ideology because both parties subscribed to a gendered economic deal in line with the values of entrepreneurial C-fem, where the husband took on full responsibility for the household regardless of whether the wife held an outside job.

When it came to their sex life, however, Daisy saw no significant improvement. She said it was "tolerable but not ideal." When I asked her if she still thought about Anthony, she confessed, "To be honest, if Anthony wanted me now, I would leave Peter and go back to him in a heartbeat. Anthony is the one I am attracted to, not Peter." Clearly, Daisy valued passionate love. Yet, she still made do with her existing marriage to Peter. In fact, she used the term *ren xin dou shi rou zhang de* (all human hearts are made of flesh) to describe her current marriage. In this context it means that appreciation for one another can be cultivated through kindness. Despite their uninspiring sex life, Daisy appreciated Peter's devotion to her, and she decided to requite him with the same kindness. This concession shows that the financial component of her marriage trumped all other concerns, once again emphasizing a C-fem understanding of the role of marriage in a woman's life.

CONCLUSION

While Western feminists often assume that women become more empowered when couples share breadwinning and domestic duties, my respondents did not agree with this view. Subscribing to entrepreneurial C-feminism, they believed women can be just as empowered when they acquire wealth indirectly by controlling men's wallets in exchange for performing conventional femininity. Hence, their ability to work outside the home did not translate to greater marital satisfaction. In fact, their employment sometimes led to marital conflict if their Western husbands did not allow them to keep all of their own earnings for themselves. Moreover, comparing the women in this chapter (Meredith, Emily, Beth, and Daisy) with the homemakers in the previous chapter (Joanne, Susan, and Lindsay), there does not seem to be a primary divide in marital happiness based on whether or not the women worked for pay. This observation again challenges the Western-centric, middle-class assumption that women who work for pay would experience greater marital satisfaction than women who are full-time homemakers.

It is important to investigate the Chinese women's marital dissatisfaction and the East-West clash in gender ideology that caused it, because this helps us better understand and predict their behavior. Nevertheless, I am not using their marital dissatisfaction here as evidence to discredit the general tenet that participation in the paid labor force can empower women. Instead, I highlight the Chinese women's internalization of entrepreneurial C-feminism, an inherently flawed gender ideology, as the root of the problem. Recall that entrepreneurial C-feminism emerged in China when wealth suddenly became concentrated among a small subset of men, while women's social position worsened. It is a short-term response to gender inequitable conditions of the postreform era. The gender strategies that this strand of feminism endorsed sometimes worked for young women who could capitalize on their sexuality in exchange for men's money and power, but its long-term efficacy remains questionable, given that women lose their sex appeal, from many men's perspective, as they age.

In line with entrepreneurial C-feminism, my respondents wished to find a wealthy husband who paid all the household bills while at the same time remaining devoted and caring to his aging homemaker wife. When they could not find such a man in China, they turned to the West. Unfortunately, the stories from this chapter show that their search for the right Western man also failed, and that their ideal husbands existed only in their imagination. In essence, the unattainable goals that these women had set for themselves, based on the flawed gender ideology they were conditioned to adopt while living in postreform China, left them in a no-win situation.

As we have seen, clashes in gender ideology certainly had a significant negative impact on the women's marital satisfaction. Nevertheless, other factors such as sexual compatibility, gaps in cultural capital, and, as we will see below, geographical location also influenced their satisfaction. Conflict over gaps in cultural capital were more salient among women like Emily, who joined China's emerging middle class in the new capitalist era but later experienced downward mobility and ended up marrying working-class Western men. In contrast, this type of conflict was less common among women who had always been stuck at the bottom of China's socioeconomic ladder and thus never accrued cultural capital themselves.

Geographical location, as mentioned, played a role in marital satisfaction as well. While Meredith ended up in a remote rural area and had to live away from home for work, Daisy was based in Paris. This allowed her to quickly integrate into the local ethnic community and enjoy their support while maintaining physical proximity to her husband, all of which enhanced her marital satisfaction. In summary, the intersectionality of other factors beyond gender ideology affected the women's marital satisfaction.

The stories in this chapter also show that, compared with the financially flexible women described in chapters 2 and 3, financially burdened women were more inclined to compromise on their mate-selection standards, and this accounts for their higher rate of marriage (more than three-quarters as opposed to only one-third). After moving abroad, financially burdened women were also more likely to remain in imperfect marriages out of economic need.

In Daisy's case, she married Peter despite a lack of romantic attraction. Her decision was informed by her own precarious position on the Chinese labor market as an older woman facing age discrimination in the service sector. In Meredith's case, she married Robert despite her knowledge of his financial shortcomings, only because she wanted to help her handicapped son immigrate abroad. In Emily's case, after experiencing business failure in China, she wanted to finance her own retirement and help her unemployed daughter, which led her to stay with Joe. For Beth, it was her son's education timeline that rushed her into marrying Edmond, even though she did not think he was good enough. In all these cases, the women's decisions hinged on pragmatic economic goals. Upon moving abroad, these women continued to tolerate their less-than-perfect marriages out of financial need. Meredith, Emily, and Beth all stayed in the United States despite their clash in gender ideology with their husbands. In Daisy's case, the lack of sexual chemistry was not reason enough to leave Peter. For Emily and Beth, even an utter lack of sex life—which they had not anticipated after the men previously used Viagra to mask issues with their sexual functioning—did not cause them to end their marriages.

Certainly, we cannot assume that all financially burdened women ended up in unhappy marriages and all financially flexible women ended up in happy ones. In reality, I have observed both happy and unhappy marriages among women in both groups. However, it is safe to say that financially burdened women faced an overall higher risk of getting *trapped* in an unhappy marriage for the long haul. This is because financially burdened women were more likely to *compromise* on their mate-selection standards during the courtship process for the sake of money or a green card. By compromising, they subjected themselves to *higher odds* of marital dissatisfaction, particularly if they chose someone whom they knew had significant shortcomings, such as an incompatible gender ideology.

While some women were fortunate in that their marriages ultimately turned out to be reasonably happy even if not ideal, as in the case of Daisy, others were not so lucky. Among those unlucky women who ended up in a conflict-ridden marriage, they were more likely to let things drag on, rather than getting divorced quickly, due to their own financially burdened positions. For this reason, it is important to investigate the leading causes of conflict in these women's marriages and, in particular, the clash of Chinese-style feminism with Western-style gender egalitarianism, rather than relying on blanket statements about marriage migrants to describe these kinds of women and their complicated, nuanced relationships.

6 | SURROGATE DATING

Translators behind the Screens

I ONCE WITNESSED A TRANSLATOR at Ms. Mei's agency resign because she could not come to moral terms with her job. Her name was Lingfang. At the time, Joanne, one of Lingfang's female clients, was already engaged to an American man. Yet, against the advice of Lingfang and Ms. Mei, Joanne insisted on accepting money and presents from Ken, one of her other suitors. This meant that Lingfang continued to write Ken on Joanne's behalf and to accept his money for months before Joanne finally agreed to cut ties with Ken. Joanne then excused her own behavior, falsely claiming that she was suffering from stomach cancer in her final letter to Ken. Soon after, Lingfang received an email from Ken's son, asking what they had done to his father, who had died suddenly from a heart attack. Reading the email, Lingfang felt overwhelmed with shame and guilt. After all, she was the messenger in this misleading relationship. As a result of this incident and some other disagreements she had with Ms. Mei, Lingfang later resigned.

At these dating agencies, translators play a pivotal role in facilitating their clients' courtships. First, they assist the female clients in creating online profiles and contacting male clients. When the men write back, translators forward the emails (in English) to the women, give them a brief summary in Chinese via phone call or text message, and then help the women craft a response.[1] Couples typically correspond for several months before some men take trips to visit China, and during those visits the same translator also facilitates verbal communication. Although the agencies extract revenue from a variety of sources, such as female client membership fees (US$1,000 per year) or charges for online live chat translation, the e-letters written by the translators—with male clients paying up to US$10.00 for a single letter—furnish the bulk of the profit.

Like most of the agency's translators, Lingfang was a recent college graduate. Born and raised in a rural region, she initially relocated to the city for college and later settled there for work. In fact, the agency managers have told me that they typically like to hire translators of rural origin, who do not have permanent residency status in the city. In China, a governmental household registration system called *hukou* distinguishes rural residents from urban residents and allocates social benefits to each group differently.[2] Employees with rural *hukou* face greater discrimination on the urban labor market. Thus, they are more likely to endure the long hours demanded by their job.

Translators typically work six days a week and more than ten hours per day. This is because the male and female clients they serve are eager to hear back from each other. Every morning, translators start arriving in their offices at eight a.m. and type away assiduously at their desks. At lunchtime, some translators who live close by walk home to cook their own meals, while others stay in the office and order noodles or fried rice from street vendors downstairs. Between one and two p.m., the entire office shuts down so that everyone can take a nap, either face down on their desks or on a "bed" they make with two chairs facing each other. Then work resumes until five p.m., when the first batch of translators starts leaving early, hoping to beat the city traffic. After dinner, they continue their work from home, while those without a personal computer often stay at the office past eight p.m. Although this job requires long hours, the translators are also paid handsomely. They receive substantially more than 1,798 yuan (US$266) a month, which was the national average starting monthly salary for recent college graduates in China in 2008.[3]

When I first met twenty-two-year-old Lingfang in the summer of 2008, she had just started her job. Rooming with three other translators, she lived in a shabby, poorly ventilated two-bedroom apartment located in a dark alley behind the bustling skyscraper where Ms. Mei's agency stood. Lingfang walked to work with her housemates every day and spent much of her evenings and weekends at the office. When I saw Lingfang the following summer, she had saved up enough money to buy a personal computer and was frequently working from home. Nevertheless, her frustration with never being able to take a "real vacation," alongside the previously mentioned incident with Joanne, led her to resign. Like Lingfang, most translators stay at their jobs for only a year or two to earn some quick cash. After that, they seek work in other industries with shorter hours, better benefits, and greater potential for long-term growth. This pattern contributes to the dating companies' high rate of turnover.

Here we turn our attention from the agencies' clients, female and male, to the translators and managers, examining how macro-level economic and social changes in China have shaped their livelihoods and considering their individual perspectives on the challenges and rewards of their job. How did these staff members feel about their clients? What were some of the obstacles they faced, and what aspects of their work did they find gratifying? Moreover, did joining this industry present them with new opportunities for upward social mobility and other forms of empowerment for themselves?

The challenges involve the various forms of insecurity that translators faced, including the precarious legality of their industry and the financial pressure to churn out successful relationships. These complex, competing interests incentivized them to police the morality of their clients. We can view their work as emotional labor that is driven not only by economic incentives, but also by their personal investment in their clients' relationships. They struggle to balance profit-making goals with their conscience while living through a chaotic period of social transition in China, when many traditional norms, regulations, and morals have been upturned.

YOUNG TRANSLATORS' PRECARIOUS POSITION

To understand how the translators come to judge their clients' morality, we must first understand the chaotic sociocultural climate in which they live. Some scholars argue that China is in a state of moral decay[4] due to both a loss of traditional values and a failure to build new ones. While traditional religions, such as Confucianism, Daoism, and Buddhism, served as the bedrock of morality and spirituality for centuries, they were uprooted and replaced by Maoist ideology when the Communist Party seized power in 1949. Yet, after 1976, Maoism became discredited following China's Cultural Revolution, a failed sociopolitical movement that cost the nation a decade of economic growth. Since then, Chinese people have been left without a uniform ethical belief system to guide their decision-making in everyday life.[5]

In the 1990s, Deng Xiaoping's pragmatic push for economic reform led moneymaking and materialism to become China's most conspicuous public values.[6] During this period, some people resorted to unscrupulous behavior for material gain. At the institutional level, reports of government corruption and production of substandard food for profit were repeatedly seen in the news.[7] At the individual level, pedestrians even became chary of helping elderly people who fell in the street, after they saw multiple incidents of extortion for compensation by opportunistic "victims."[8]

Clearly, values of moneymaking and materialism leave something to be desired, as many people seek out a greater sense of meaning and fulfillment in their lives.[9] Because there is no longer a single collective ethic to guide people in their everyday decision-making,[10] many struggle with questions such as "How can I be a good person?" or "How can I create a sense of meaning beyond making money?" These questions plague translators as much as any other modern Chinese citizen. China's current social climate puts translators in a difficult position of having to choose between profit-making and upholding their personal moral ideologies. To better understand their struggles, we need to consider their unique roles within their dating agencies.

Each week, the managers hold a staff meeting, during which each translator reports on their clients' dating progress, while everyone helps brainstorm ideas on how to handle difficult situations. Through these meetings, I learned about the translators' personal feelings toward their clients and witnessed how those sentiments impacted their professional conduct. Interestingly, the translators' values and beliefs frequently clashed with those of their female clients. Often, these clashes resulted from significant differences in generational characteristics and life experiences.

More than 90 percent of translators are in their early to mid-twenties, and some have never yet been involved in a serious romantic relationship. In contrast, many clients have already experienced infidelity, divorce, domestic abuse, career failure, or unemployment. Thus, they tend to be more jaded and more pragmatic. The management values the translators' youth and emotional inexperience, as these qualities help them write letters with a "freshness and innocence" that their middle-aged clients lack. However, this same freshness and innocence renders them unprepared for the lying, cheating, and "gold-digging" they sometimes see from their clients, leaving them horrified and outraged, as they bear witness and even contribute to behavior they find morally despicable.

In addition, translators are under intense financial pressure to perform. Just to receive a base pay, they must meet a quota of letters written and reach a certain rate of reply from the men. Even then, their base salary is not a living wage and the bulk of their income hinges on monthly bonuses. To add to the monetary pressure translators face, the managers foster a competitive workplace culture. During the weekly company meetings, the managers announce each translator's earnings, and those who do not meet the goal are criticized publicly. If no improvement is seen over time, low earners are fired.

Beyond this pressure to make a profit, translators must also satisfy their customers, given the precarious position of their agency in the global business chain. Compared with the Western partner companies, the local Chinese agencies have much less money, resources, and power. Back in the early 2000s, when a Western company invited Ms. Fong to join them, she was running a tiny domestic Chinese dating agency. By contrast, the foreign company already had more than 1 million male members and partnered with numerous female-supplier agencies across China, Eastern Europe, and Latin America. In the way of profit-sharing, the Chinese agencies receive only a small fraction of income from the letters, even though they translate all the letters. Moreover, whenever a Western man files a complaint for feeling "scammed" or for unsatisfactory translation service, the foreign company launches an investigation that may result in a hefty fine for the Chinese translators. Yet no such mechanism exists in the reverse. Despite this lopsided situation, the Chinese agencies still accept these terms and conditions, as they do not have the financial or legal means to recruit Western men themselves.

The Chinese agencies face another challenge as well: cross-border matchmaking is illegal in China due to the government's concerns about human trafficking.[11] To work around this, the agencies in my study identify as cultural mediation companies rather than as "matchmakers" pairing couples at the translators' behest, and the government has therefore issued them official work permits. Nevertheless, the state could also claim they are matchmakers in disguise and shut them down at any time. For example, in 2009 I witnessed the government shut down two agencies in Tunyang when several female clients sued them for fraud. In November 2011, the agencies experienced yet another crackdown scare after *Topics in Focus*, a news program on China's Central Television, featured an "Overseas Matrimonial Agencies and Fraud" episode.

This murky legal status puts the staff under pressure to please their female clients and avoid any legal disputes that might bring unwanted government attention. Just as with dissatisfied male clients, they fear unhappy female clients suing their agency. For example, even when some female clients refused to pay the previously agreed-upon 3,000 yuan (US$440) "success fee" that is due when couples marry, the agencies chose not to sue them. When this became an overwhelming problem, the managers altered the payment structure so that all women paid the same fee up front, regardless of their marital outcome. Additionally, even when some translators later started their own dating agencies and took their previous clients with them—a breach of business ethics that hurts their former colleagues—the managers chose not to sue and risk bringing attention to the agencies.

Despite their lack of legal and financial power, the agencies must still create profits, please their clients, and, at the same time, balance their pragmatic goals with their own moralistic concerns. How does this play out? Let's first look at situations where the clients' behavior, interpreted by the translators as immoral, interferes with the agencies' profit-making bottom line, thereby forcing the translators to attempt some level of moral regulation just to maintain normal business operations. Then we'll turn to cases in which the translators' business goals do not align with their personal moral values. These cases will unveil how the staff members act in situations where their business interests conflict with their personal moral ideologies.

CENSURING LIARS, CHEATERS, AND GOLD-DIGGERS

Why do the young translators feel compelled to censure their clients? What moral rules are their clients bending in the first place? To better understand these issues calls for a closer look at China's so-called moral crisis in the intimate sphere. We have seen how China's reform led to the emergence of a nouveau-riche capitalist class dominated by men who consume feminine youth and sexuality, while women face an increasingly precarious capitalist labor market.[12] These shifting structural factors have led women to emphasize men's financial capability as a measure of their desirability. In popular culture, romantic unions between middle-aged *da kuan* (sugar daddies) and young, white-collar office workers are praised and admired.[13] Mottos such as "better to marry well than to study well," or "laugh at the poor girls but not the call girls" are ubiquitous. Some women who seek to date or marry rich even do so at the expense of having extramarital affairs with married men.

The Chinese government certainly considers the nation's dating and marriage culture to be in a moral crisis. In 2011, China's Supreme Court issued a new interpretation of the country's marriage law to state that, after divorce, marital real estate belongs solely to the person who took out the mortgage.[14] Many media outlets interpret this new policy as an "anti-gold-digging measure" to discourage women from making homeownership a precondition of marriage, and to protect the rights of the groom's parents in the event of a divorce, since Chinese parents often provide mortgage assistance to their grown sons.

While affairs between young, unmarried women and wealthy, married men have increased dramatically in the postreform era, married women are also starting to cheat on their husbands.[15] A 2012 study showed that rates of infidelity among Chinese women surpassed those of women in all but three of thirty-six countries surveyed, trailing only Norway, Britain, and Cameroon (while topping the United States, France, Australia, and Italy).[16] Considering that historically only Chinese men were allowed multiple partners, sociologist James Farrer attributes the rising female infidelity rate to the legacy of state socialism, a time when society emphasized women's independence and equality. This, alongside China's sexual opening up in the postreform era, has led many married women to believe they now have a right to pursue extramarital love just like men.

Given China's increasingly consumeristic dating culture and rising rates of infidelity, it is no surprise that some of the female clients in my study pursued dating strategies that subverted traditional norms of fidelity, earnestness, and honesty. Interestingly, the commercial agencies proactively regulated this kind of behavior, given that the female clients' cheating and hustling sometimes interfered with the companies' profit-making bottom line. For example, when Kristin, a Chinese client, rejected her Western suitors after she took them on shopping sprees and asked for expensive presents, such as an Apple computer or high-end jewelry, Ms. Mei called her into the office to scold her: "If you're not planning on marrying these men, then why do you ask them to buy all this stuff? You are literally pressuring men by dragging them out to the most expensive department stores and making it embarrassing for them to say no on the spot. We're worried that these men will *tou su* [file a complaint] to our partner companies, who will think we encourage women to trick men for money!"

Not only are the managers worried about male clients filing complaints to their partner companies, but they are also concerned about the men posting about their overseas dating experiences in various internet forums. In this cyber age, just a few negative reviews targeted toward a particular agency can impact its business prospects. Mr. Li, another manager, describes this situation as "having one bad mouse spoiling an entire pot of soup."

Aside from fending off bad reviews from the Western men, the agencies also feel compelled to foster their clients' relationship longevity. This is because they must continually showcase examples of successful marriages in order to entice new clients to join. As described in chapter 2, the companies rely on their promotional blog articles, which chronicle tales of happily married couples. Thus, it is in their business interest to foster fidelity, earnestness, and honesty—which contribute to long-term relationship success—while subverting behavior that bends these morals.

To this end, the agencies discourage the women from having affairs with married Chinese men, since these affairs decrease their probability of marrying the Western men. For example, at a company meeting, one translator reported that her female client, who was picking up a Western suitor at the airport, ran into the bathroom as soon as she saw her married Chinese lover at the departure terminal. This woman hid in the restroom for an entire hour, even though her Western beau had already spotted her from a distance and continually called her cellphone. On their cab ride back to his hotel, she pretended to have had an upset stomach. Later, she even rerouted their vacation itinerary away from her hometown to a national park several hours away, just to avoid running into her Chinese lover. Concerned that the Western suitor might get suspicious, this woman's translator sought their coworkers' advice on how to persuade this woman to cut ties with her Chinese lover. Interestingly, this situation occurs frequently among clients with married local lovers. In fact, many translators tell me this type of woman is the most difficult to marry off, as their heart is never truly with the Western men.

The story of Beth also illustrates a conflict of interest between the agencies and their cheating female clients. Beth always felt she could have married someone better looking and higher earning than her husband, Edmond, an American firefighter. As we have seen in chapters 1 and 5, Beth rushed into marriage with Edmond out of concern for her son's education. A month prior to her US departure, she invited me, Ms. Mei, and several other female clients to lunch. That day, Beth arrived with a tall, athletic-looking Chinese man, whom she introduced as her personal trainer. From their intimate body language, it was obvious to everyone that they were romantically involved.

That day, as Ms. Mei and I walked home together after lunch, she shook her head and vented her frustration: "Everyone knows Beth is engaged to Edmond, and now she has a *qing kuang* [extramarital lover]. Why is she showing him off? What does she want to express? Her ability to attract a lover on the side? What kind of role model does she think she is setting for our other women?" Clearly, Ms. Mei worried that Beth's behavior would encourage other clients to follow her example, thereby disrupting Ms. Mei's business.

On-site, I certainly witnessed more staff complaints against women's missteps than the men's. When I asked the translators for their impressions of the men, "sincere" and "naïve" were the two words I heard most often. Nevertheless, I also witnessed many situations where the staff policed Western men who tried to take advantage of their female clients. As much as these agencies care about retaining Western men, they are also concerned about pleasing the Chinese women, who not only provide a substantial chunk of revenue, in the form of their hefty annual membership fee, but also wield the power to sue if they feel swindled, particularly if their agencies promised them the potential of marriage but instead matched them with Western suitors who treated their China trips as sex tours.

The way the translators dealt with Eric, a divorced male client in his sixties, exemplifies their policing of the men. In 2011, Eric moved from Texas to China in search of new career opportunities after his American company declared bankruptcy following the 2008 financial crisis. He asked Ms. Mei to set him up with Chinese women in business because, along with seeking a romantic partner, he needed help launching his company. Ms. Mei first introduced him to Tracy, a retail manager fifteen years his junior. Two weeks later, however, Tracy told us she broke it off with Eric because she felt he was only interested in her for sex.

Next, Ms. Mei set Eric up with Julia, a retail shop owner who wanted to move abroad so that her teenage children could attend college overseas. Their relationship progressed quickly. Within two weeks, Julia started spending nights at Eric's place. At one point, marriage was on the table, and so was a joint business venture. Julia told us Eric had promised to pay for her daughters' college tuition in the United States. But she also complained about his stinginess, as he never bought her presents and only took her to low-end restaurants when they dined out. Moreover, Julia was annoyed by the fact that Eric had asked to move in with her, but later backed out when she asked him to share rent.

Whenever they fought, Eric would go to the agency and ask Ms. Mei to give him a new list of businesswomen to choose from. By now, the translators suspected that Eric was really seeking free sex and free business connections from their female clients. For this reason, they warned Julia not to marry him or invest money in his company, and they canceled his membership, while moving quickly to help Julia find someone who could help her children study overseas. Their hunch was right. Over the years, Eric never married. After leaving Ms. Mei's agency, he continued dating various local Chinese women and as of 2021 he remained single.

BALANCING PROFIT WITH CONSCIENCE

Thus far, we have discussed various ways in which the translators serve as moral regulators during the courtship process because doing so works in favor of their business interests. But what about situations in which enacting moral regulation works against their profit goals? In such case, employees struggle to balance their materialistic desires with their conscience.

A translator who no longer works at the agency once said to me, "I feel that if you want to survive and make money, you cannot always be a good person. You have to hurt others in the process. Translators with the kindest hearts do not always make the most money." One strategy I witnessed the translators and managers pursue, which had the potential to hurt others in the process, was writing to men on behalf of women who were not interested in marrying those men. If those men eventually traveled to China, the translators would offer to introduce them to other female clients after their original partner met with them and rejected them.

Although most men agree to consider alternative candidates and many even end up marrying them, for the minority who refuse to meet new women, they leave China with a broken heart and thousands of dollars wasted through months of email exchanges and international flight tickets. In fact, I often heard stories of men breaking down when they got rejected. Some cried in the manager's office. Others even threatened to commit suicide. The following excerpt, taken from my fieldnotes, shows a man becoming depressed after the woman he liked rejected him:

> One afternoon as I was walking into the agency, I saw someone sitting in Ms. Mei's office. Through the glass window, I saw a very thin, balding man with deep lines on his face. He looked stern and depressed. The door was not completely shut, and I kept hearing him repeat, "Well, she saw my photograph, so I don't understand why she didn't like me in the end," over and over. I halted my footsteps. The other translators sitting outside told me that he was crying because he just got rejected. Another translator reassured me that "Ms. Mei is very good at comforting the men and helping them get over rejection. First, she lets them cry. Then, she will introduce

them to other ladies at the agency." In this case, Ms. Mei suggested a different woman and he agreed to meet her after seeing her photo.

The translators certainly acquired permission from their female clients before engaging in this practice of allowing men to visit despite the women not having serious intentions of marrying them. Although translators also empathized with men who experienced pain from this rejection, they justified their own legitimacy by pointing out that many couples who fall in love over email still break up after meeting face to face, while some couples who never exchanged emails end up hitting it off in person. Hence, although the translators recognized that this practice could be financially and emotionally taxing on the men, they deemed it morally acceptable so long as they made an effort to help the men find a new partner once they arrived in China.

While some translators believed they could not be "good people" and still make money at the same time, others disagreed. For example, another translator who initially ignored her personal morals for financial gain later realized that her approach was problematic. Although her writing elicited very high response rates online, she later came to realize that leading the men on or matching clients for reasons other than love made her job stressful in the long run, as she eventually felt haunted by unhappy couples whom she paired together for profit at the cost of compromising their compatibility. In an interview, she stated:

> If you have love in your heart, you will try to think from her perspective and pick a fitting person for her. Otherwise, you would say, "Marry him! Look! He has money!" Many women may be tempted by your words and marry someone they don't love. But at the end of the day, if they're unhappy with their marriage, they will come back and blame you. You will feel guilt and pressure and put the company in a bad position too. It is a vicious cycle. Over time you will feel like you owe so much to so many people that your guilt will force you to quit.

The feelings translators experience on their job—whether anger, repulsion, or sympathy—have a real impact on the way they treat clients. One salient way their personal moral ideology interferes with their profit-making goal shows up during the email translation process. Many translators stigmatize women who only seek foreigners for money or a green card. One translator said, "We don't agree with this kind of behavior, and we believe it is a loss of face for Chinese people." More important, this attitude hurts the quality of their letters, as shown by the passage below, drawn from one translator's personal blog:

> After a lot of hard work, I finally got a Western man to take interest in Ms. Fu. I told Ms. Fu excitedly, but she only said to me, "Just ask him if he has money, if he owns a house, and whether he could help me take my kid abroad." All in all, she was not interested in anything but that. I really did not like her attitude, so I could not write nice letters for her.

Thus, despite stereotypes of commercial dating companies as entities that care for nothing but profit, at the agencies where I conducted research, morality, conscience, and justice mattered greatly to the staff.

Not only did the staff criticize Chinese women seeking relationships for the wrong reasons, but they also condemned Western men. For example, Sisi, a bright-eyed, outspoken young woman who was the head translator at Ms. Mei's agency, told us she encountered a male client who claimed he lost his debit card in China and thus wanted to move into a female client's home. When Sisi referred him to the US embassy for assistance, he refused. Sisi then lashed out in anger at a staff meeting: "We are not so stupid as to let you trick our women. What do you want? Free room, board, and sex in China? How shameless could a man get?" Sisi believed that the debit card loss was just an excuse he made up in order to save on expenses while traveling in China.

The translators were also repulsed by men who wrote overly sexualized letters. In fact, they referred to those men as *se lang* (perverts). One translator even said, "After working this job, I have met so many disgusting foreigners. Sometimes we see emails with nude selfies attached. At first, when we were not yet used to it, we would scream!" When writing to *se lang*, SiSi felt no qualms about crafting wild sexual fantasies with little input from the women. Those men, who she believed treated the transnational dating process as an online fantasy, deserved to be treated like cash cows.

Sisi labels her clients as either "good people" or "bad people." Aside from "cheaters," "gold-diggers," and "perverts," other "bad people" include those whom she considers greedy for aiming too high and setting their standards well above their own value on the marriage market. Genuinely concerned for her "good" clients' emotional and financial well-being, Sisi often takes extra time to assist them, as she believes "good people deserve a good life." In contrast, I often heard her wishing the "bad" clients a failed marriage. Sometimes Sisi gets so frustrated that she lashes out at "bad" clients to their face. For example, she once said to a "greedy" woman: "To be honest, you are not beautiful like a celebrity, so why in the world do you expect handsome, rich men to take interest in you?"

At these agencies, negative sentiments against female clients can run so deep that the managers must continuously remind translators to view the women in a more positive light. One phrase I often heard Ms. Mei and Ms. Fong repeat during staff meetings was, "No matter how you feel about these women, you must focus on their best qualities and overlook their imperfections in order to deliver the best service." Not only do they encourage translators to view the women more positively, but they also criticize them for making moral judgments about their clients. Ms. Fong's exchange with Liyi, a translator-turned-interim-manager who later left her job, offers an example.

Liyi told me she could not stand her "lazy, selfish, and greedy" clients. She referenced one woman in particular—Sally, a laid-off factory worker who spent much of her time playing mah-jongg but who enlisted herself as employed and even uploaded a ten-year-old profile photo. This outdated photo attracted an American man who later became extremely devoted to her. In contrast, she rarely read his long emails and told her translators to "write whatever you want" when they reached out to her. It seemed to Liyi as though Sally wanted nothing but the monthly stipend the American sent her to foot her mah-jongg expenses. Eventually, Liyi grew so frustrated that she tried to match him with someone else, but, to her surprise, he declined. Later on, when Liyi cut back on Sally's letters out of pity for this man, he stopped using their service altogether. At this time, Ms. Fong criticized Liyi for intervening: "As a service provider, you should not make moral judgments on your clients and meddle with their relationships like that. Remember, these people are not your friends. Don't judge, don't get personally involved, just do your job."

Although the managers are more skilled than the translators at separating their business interests from personal judgments, they are not always in perfect control, either. I have certainly heard multiple clients complain about the moral judgments that agency managers made against them. To give an example, Vivien, whose story I told in chapter 3, accepted thousands of dollars from her American fiancé, John. Yet she refused intimate physical contact with John while simultaneously engaging in a secret sexual affair with a married Chinese man. As soon as Vivien's translator brought up her case at a company meeting, another translator who knew of her dating history jumped in: "Oh, her heart is deep and dark. She was abused by Chinese playboys earlier in her life, so now she wants to abuse foreign men." Instead of rebuking this translator, Ms. Mei agreed and added: "Indeed, Vivien is a terrible person."

Several days prior to this company meeting, I even witnessed Ms. Mei criticize Vivien to her face over this matter, when we ran into Vivien while walking down the street together. When Vivien told us she was disgusted by John's body and that she much preferred her thinner Chinese lover in bed, Ms. Mei said:

> Vivien, in my view, we should all be *fu dao ren jia* [moral women]. When a woman loves a man, she should love everything about him. You cannot just treat one man as your ATM machine and then go to bed with another. John has traveled to China to visit you multiple times, spent lots of money on you. *Jiang xin bi xin* [Putting yourself in his shoes], you would not want to be treated the same way you treat him, would you?

If Ms. Mei simply wanted to win more business, she could have framed the concern around her own fear of John filing a complaint with the Western partner company. Yet, Ms. Mei chose to condemn Vivien over her moral conduct, even though it put her at risk of offending Vivien.

During the company meeting, Ms. Mei recounted her conversation with Vivien to the group of translators. At this time, another translator reported that one of her clients, a pyramid scheme telemarketer, was selling health care products to the Western men. Shaking her head, Ms. Mei said, "These men are so *zhao nie* [pitiful], getting tortured by women who are out to empty their wallets."

At the same time, I also saw Ms. Mei lend her own money to women whom she pitied and deemed worthy of assisting. These were usually women who she thought were kind-hearted and sincere but who had ended up in a financial struggle. Some were divorcées who had lost their homes to their Chinese ex-husbands and were thus forced to move in with their parents. Moved by their plight and their determination to strive for a better life abroad, Ms. Mei took on some personal financial risk to help them.

These discussions lead us to the question of why the staff go so far as to give up profit to uphold their personal moral ideology. Why not turn a blind eye to their clients' unscrupulous behavior or personal plight and focus on moneymaking? Does their intervention simply reflect the fact that "fundamental notions of right and wrong are too deep in Chinese culture to allow people to feel comfortable with a formula that says only money counts no matter how it's obtained"?[17] Or is there something that differentiates the global dating industry from other service sector jobs? In this context, the concept of "surrogate dating"[18] is relevant. In serving as the online voice of their clients, the translators often find it difficult to detach their personal identity from their professional identity, which leads them to subconsciously project their own moral ideology onto their work.

SURROGATE DATING AND EMOTIONAL LABOR

Unlike conventional "picture brides" who select their mates based on photographs and the occasional exchange of postal letters, the couples in my study engage in extensive translator-assisted online communication for months. I call this "surrogate dating" because the translators essentially act as their clients' online self. This process requires intensive "emotional labor." This term, introduced by Arlie Hochschild, refers to the process by which workers manage feelings and expressions to fulfill the emotional requirements of their job.[19] In some service sector jobs, workers are required to display particular emotions in order to trigger desired emotional states in their customers. For example, waitresses at restaurants smile and greet their customers with enthusiasm to create a positive dining experience; child care workers suppress emotions of frustration or sadness so as not to upset or scare children.

During the surrogate dating process, clients pay for translators to act as cyber versions of themselves to increase their competitiveness on the global dating market. In this role, translators can suffer from the emotional labor required to successfully create and maintain these online images of their clients. We have seen this already in how the translators struggle to represent clients who act in morally questionable manners. The question we must then ask is, why do translators find this process so difficult? I suggest it is because translators must utilize their cultural capital,[20] which includes not only their mastery of English but also their knowledge of China's contemporary sex culture and youth culture, to help their female clients develop attractive online personas. In providing such cultural capital, translators are inserting themselves intimately into the dating process, and, as a result, they experience a heightened sense of emotional involvement in their work.

For an example of how providing cultural capital leads translators to experience an increased sense of emotional investment, let us consider the following circumstance. Most female clients of today grew up during China's prereform and early reform eras, when the dating and courtship culture was far more restrictive than today. Back then, a person's "work unit," or place of employment, imposed age restrictions on dating, and people started courting only when they were ready for marriage.[21] Society placed a high value on female virginity,[22] while the state monitored and regulated premarital sexual behavior through both work units and schools.[23] In contrast, when the translators were growing up throughout the 1990s, work unit and parental involvement in dating greatly decreased.[24] People started dating at a much earlier age, and romantic relationships became more emotionally engaging and sexually involved.[25]

Given the social and institutional differences between the generations, it is not surprising to see differences in their rhetoric. Many clients at the agencies I studied appeared to be uncomfortable with, or to lack knowledge of verbal expressions of love, romance, sex, and intimacy. Some clients said, "I do not know how to say this mushy stuff; I am not good with men." The translators, being younger, were more accustomed to such expressions. Translators therefore used their own cultural capital to help their female clients convey sexual confidence in their letters. For instance, one letter that was paraphrased by a translator read, "I often dream that we kiss each other and I touch your body softly," and went on to speak of masturbation and foreplay, thus making the client appear sexually open and skilled to her Western suitor. The seductive tone achieved in this line was due to the translator far more than to the original author of the letter.

The translators also attributed their successful letter-writing to their familiarity with China's youth culture. As members of the *ba ling hou* (post-1980s generation), which the popular media depict as "China's first generation of couch potatoes, addicts of online games, patrons of imported fast-food chains, and loyal audiences of Hollywood movies,"[26] many of the translators felt that their means of self-expression were more in tune with the thoughts of the male clients. For instance, one letter read, "So I want to write this letter to you, and to show my miss to you. Big kissssssssssss for you. I have seen the American movie, named, P.S. I LOVE YOU. I have been touched totally." These words showcase a comfort with sexuality as well as a familiarity with Western movies, thus making the client seem fun, relatable, and sexually appealing to a Western man.

The translators noticed that the female clients who decided to write emails without their help often ended up losing the men. One translator said of her clients: "Many of them just talk about what you do today, what I do today, etc. That is so boring! Eventually the couple will lose passion. On the other hand, the letters we help them write are sizzling hot with passion, energetic, and ultra-hip."

This extensive use of their personal cultural capital results in the translators sometimes becoming emotionally engrossed in their clients' lives. For example, one translator spoke of her experience as follows: "I feel like I am the woman I write for, and I think of her man as my own boyfriend." Another translator reflected that some male clients wrote very touching letters and that she could not help but weep when she read them. For others, seeing clients get married feels "as if I just created a new baby!"

In these ways, translators often experience the same emotional ups and downs as their clients. For example, one translator said, "I like reading the men's letters to the ladies and watching their reaction. When things go well, her face would light up, and it makes me happy, too." Similarly, when clients experience an emotional downturn, it may also dampen the translator's mood. For example, another translator stated, "Sometimes when the men leave China and I see him crying as he gets out of the taxi and walks toward the airport, it makes me feel so sad."

As we can see, the surrogate dating process can be mentally taxing for translators, as their productivity depends upon not only their mastery of English, but also their personal knowledge of China's contemporary sex culture and youth culture, and their ability to use this information to construct an identity to which Western consumers will relate. In some ways, their emails reflect themselves more than their clients, which leads to them experiencing distress over their inability to separate their personal identity from their professional work. For example, one translator said:

> There had been a time when I felt very confused and could not accept it ethically. I was communicating with several men and sometimes I was writing to one but thinking about the problems another man was having. So suddenly I thought to myself that if I were a woman who simultaneously got into relationships with multiple men, I would feel so *eh xin* [disgusted].

One major challenge these translators face, then, is detaching their personal identity from their professional identity. Hochschild points out that some workers who are unable to separate their self-identity from their displayed identity will strive to "depersonalize the situation" or "withdraw" altogether. That is, they become remote and detached from the people they service. Kalindi Vora cites a similar phenomenon among the Indian call center agents in her study, who work with an American clientele. Vora observes that, as a result of prioritizing the emotional capacity of their false, professional identities on the phone, the call center workers experience an acute sense of loneliness and an eventual repression of their genuine feelings and sentiments.[27]

Similarly, the translators in my study developed coping strategies to depersonalize the situation or simply withdrew as they spent more time on the job. Some gradually learned how to maintain their identification with their work role without becoming fused with it. For example, one translator recalled, "When I first came on the job, I often experienced very strong feelings, whether it be passion, love, hate, or disgust. But now, after all this time, I don't feel anything anymore, no matter what happens. I think I have become numb." Among those who still maintained a certain degree of emotional attachment, the strength of their emotions waned over time.

For example, when asked whether she felt in love with her male clients, one translator said, "In the beginning I was more into it, but later on I realized that I cannot take it so seriously because it is just a job."

Although the translators may cultivate emotional distancing over time, few stay long enough to become fully skilled at depersonalization. Given the high rate of turnover at these agencies, most translators are newcomers who struggle. Some translators who feel that their female clients treat the men poorly or unfairly even become too embarrassed, guilty, or sad to face the men. As a result, they may transfer their female clients to someone else or quit their job altogether, just like Lingfang.

The challenges translators face are exacerbated by their lack of professional training. Since the global internet dating industry is new in China, none of the managers has certification in business management or relationship counseling. Prior to entering the dating industry, Ms. Fong worked at a state-owned factory. She recalled writing the agency's employee handbook based on nothing but her "gut feelings." In her own words, she was "crossing the river by feeling the stones." The two managers she hired at her satellite offices—Mr. Li and Ms. Mei—were also former state workers whom she had known for years as personal contacts. Although Ms. Fong knew that Mr. Li was not particularly skilled in business, she chose him anyway because she trusted him not to scam the female clients.

While the managers had at least accumulated some industry experience over the years, the fresh-out-of-college translators had none. Moreover, many of them hailed from rural areas without familial connections in the big cities where they worked. The managers often saw them as children and forgave them for making "childish mistakes," such as forgetting to ask for the men's contact information when they accompanied the women to the airport, and even encouraged them to imagine their middle-aged clients as a lonely aunt or mother. Of course, many businesses in China today, like the agencies I studied, are still in nascent development. Their management style, which emphasizes personal relationships and connections, makes it even more difficult for translators to detach their personal identity from their professional identity.

A PATH TOWARD UPWARD MOBILITY

Given the challenges that staff encounter, what rewards do they reap from working in the global internet dating industry? What new opportunities for upward social mobility do they encounter, in both the short run and the long run? As I have described, many translators are poor, rural migrants who have neither the pedigree nor the right social networks to secure urban jobs at large companies or government-owned enterprises. They do have a college degree, but having a degree in English actually makes employment even more difficult for them, given China's oversupply of English majors.[28] Thus, many translators consider themselves lucky to have found a relatively well-paying job. After working for a year or two, some decide to stay at the agencies and seek internal promotion, while others venture out to start their own businesses. Under such circumstances, the knowledge they acquire through their job as translators—including computer skills, customer service skills, and marketing skills—helps them launch their own businesses.

At the agencies, top performers were rewarded with high earnings, which enabled them to achieve upward mobility. For example, Wenli, who came from a mountainous rural area, worked her way up to become a manager and shareholder at Ms. Fong's company. After ten years of hard work, she could afford to buy a home in one of China's most expensive coastal metropolises. Similarly, Sisi, the head translator at Ms. Mei's agency, saved up enough money to purchase a home for her parents in her rural hometown in just a few years. After achieving what many would consider a mighty feat for a girl under thirty, Sisi decided to venture into entrepreneurship by launching her own startup.

On one hot summer day in July 2017, I reconnected with Sisi after my five-year absence from Tunyang. Upon seeing her, I realized that she no longer looked like the young schoolgirl I remembered, with thick-rimmed glasses and a ponytail. Sisi waved goodbye to glasses after getting LASIK surgery. She appeared much more mature and refined now, with her wavy, permed hair, maroon lipstick, and black Miu Miu purse, which she had recently purchased while traveling in Italy. Sisi now ran several businesses, one of which was a startup that offered online English classes, while another involved selling health and beauty products on social media. Although her parents and relatives all worried about her job stability, Sisi shared none of their concerns. Like many members of the younger generation that grew up in China's internet startup culture, Sisi greatly enjoyed her autonomy and flexibility to work anytime, anyplace. Moreover, she was thankful to have worked at Ms. Mei's agency, where she first learned how to run an online business.

Unlike Sisi, who ventured into another field, many other translators, such as Lingfang, branched out by opening their own transnational dating agencies. In 2012, I met up again with Lingfang, whom I introduced at the beginning of this chapter. In her mid-twenties, Lingfang had bright eyes and a warm laugh. Over dinner, when I saw her ordering nothing but vegetables, I teased her for always wanting to lose weight despite being so slender. As we ate, Lingfang told me that she now worked for a translation company that processed visa applications. Despite her lower earnings, she felt happier due to her lighter hours. Meanwhile, her long-term goal was to save up and launch her own business. Five years later, when we met up again in 2017, Lingfang had accomplished this feat. She and another former translator from Ms. Mei's agency now run their own global dating company. Like Lingfang, many other translators have gone down this path of opening their own dating companies, after they acquired the relevant skills and resources from working at Ms. Mei's, Ms. Fong's, and Mr. Li's agencies.

Aside from entrepreneurship, the translators pursued other career paths as well. For example, Ming Ming saved up enough money to go to graduate school, and she now works as a college English teacher back in her hometown. Several other translators married Western men through their own dating sites and have since become mothers. In the eyes of Ms. Fong and Ms. Mei, immigrating to the West was a big step up in the way of social mobility for these rural girls with no money or connections in China.

The managers, too, just like the translators, gained many new opportunities for upward mobility through their work. Before entering this industry, none of the three managers was particularly well-off: without a college degree, they had all worked low-paying, SOE jobs at one point. Joining the global dating industry dramatically improved their standard of living. For example, when Mr. Li first joined the industry in 2008, he was a poor, jobless man who had been laid off from an SOE. Yet, by 2013, Mr. Li earned so much money that he could afford to give his girlfriend RMB 300,000 (US$42,352).

Likewise, Ms. Mei was grateful to have a job that enabled her to feel more confident, independent, and empowered than ever before. Born and raised in a small town, Ms. Mei always considered herself a "traditional woman" who put her husband's needs before her own. She sacrificed the opportunity to attend college in support of her husband's career, and yet he cheated on her with his secretary after he became successful. Following her divorce, Ms. Mei dated her boss, a well-off businessman who never went through with his promise to leave his wife, thereby wasting many years of Ms. Mei's youth. Single, divorced, and working various secretarial jobs after getting laid off from an SOE, Ms. Mei experienced a long period of depression before Ms. Fong invited her to join her business.

As Ms. Mei's agency grew, she began to enjoy her newfound economic success. Not only did her high income afford her amenities, such as an SUV, exotic travel abroad, and gifts for her family, but it also changed her outlook on gender. For the first time, Ms. Mei started dating men who earned less money than she did, while she experimented with taking on the breadwinner role in relationships. For example, she dated Mr. Jiang, a poor salesman who moved in with her and accepted her financial support. In exchange, he took on a caretaker role to support her busy career. Whenever I visited Ms. Mei at her home, I enjoyed Mr. Jiang's fine cooking and watched him run errands for her. After breaking up with Mr. Jiang, Ms. Mei also dated Josh, a poor but handsome American sales representative several years her junior.

While Ms. Mei eventually sold her company to marry a man from Switzerland, Ms. Fong stayed in China. Compared with the other two managers, Ms. Fong was more dedicated to her job. Before opening her agency, Ms. Fong already had some experience running other businesses, but this one was by far the most financially successful. Nevertheless, Ms. Fong saw her work as more than a means of making money. Having been divorced at one point herself, she empathized with the single ladies at her agency, and took pride in her ability to help them rebuild their lives.

Interestingly, Ms. Fong enjoys working with the financially burdened women more than the financially flexible women, even though they sometimes struggle to pay their membership fees. This is because financially burdened women tend to be more active during the email exchange process, more eager to consult the staff, and more sincere in their efforts to study Western language and culture. All of this leads to a greater chance of marital success, which is ultimately what gives Ms. Fong a sense of accomplishment. Ms. Fong once said to me, "I am not just in it for the money. I really feel that I am doing good for people. Even if the government decides to shut my company down one day, I would look back with no regrets because I once helped more than two thousand women find love and happiness."

Each morning at six a.m. sharp, Ms. Fong starts responding to emails and text messages. On evenings and weekends, her home is constantly filled with clients—including those traveling from out of town—coming to consult her for dating advice. Her hard work has been recognized by her clients, many of whom believe that she genuinely cares for their well-being. At a 2019 client gathering I attended, a plump, dark-skinned woman in a long, red dress went up to the front of the room to acknowledge her appreciation for Ms. Fong:

> One time when Ms. Fong felt I was making a mistake by being too picky, she yelled at me: "Who do you think you are? You old women in your forties and fifties! When you see an opportunity to marry, grab it!" As Ms. Fong spoke, I saw tears in her eyes. I was shocked. Here is a lady who worries so much about my future that she tears up. Who else would ever give a damn about me, an old, single, divorced woman in China?

Moreover, the client went on to say, "On the day before her major surgery, Ms. Fong made phone calls to each one of us to give us personalized guidance, because she wanted to make sure we were okay in case she never woke up again." As this client spoke, tears rolled down her cheeks. Everyone clapped.

Later that afternoon, Ms. Fong chimed in to tell us about the one client whom she will never speak with again. This woman had suffered a third-degree burn following a quarrel with her Chinese ex-husband that led to a hot water bottle–spilling accident. The scarring was so severe that she felt she could never wear shorts or dresses again. Feeling great sympathy for this woman, Ms. Fong allowed her to stay at her own home for several weeks when the client traveled from out of town to seek dating advice. With Ms. Fong's help, this client finally met a Western man she liked.

While in the recovery room following her own surgery, Ms. Fong received a phone call from the lady, asking for help again. When Ms. Fong told her to consult a different staff member because she herself had just woken up from anesthesia, the woman insisted, "No, I need to talk right now because I have a really important question about my relationship." "At that moment I felt so sad," Ms. Fong said, "but took her question anyway." Throughout her recovery over the next six months, a period when many clients showed up at her home with flowers and get-well cards, this client never paid a visit, even though they were both in the same city. From then on, Ms. Fong blocked this woman online, as she felt underappreciated after all her heartfelt assistance. Through this example, we can see that Ms. Fong's relationships with her clients are built on more than just a business partnership. For Ms. Fong, this career became a source of friendship, passion, and inspiration in her life.

It is clear that for managers like Ms. Fong and for many of the translators, they viewed their work as more than a moneymaking endeavor. While the translators often came from rural backgrounds and used their time in the industry as a steppingstone to further entrepreneurship opportunities or to develop other career-building skills, many couldn't help but feel personally invested in their clients outside of the fiscal rewards of their job. These women curated romances they earnestly hoped would end in marriage, and they empathized with both the disillusioned women who didn't find what they were looking for and the heartbroken men who were led on and never made it to the altar. This level of investment even extended to clients the translators may not have been rooting for; the emotional labor of surrogate dating meant that translators often felt a personal moral responsibility not to allow their clients to use Western men without an earnest interest in getting married, just as agency managers felt a moral obligation to protect their clients from men looking for something closer to sex tourism.

From the foregoing, we can see that translators do more than write letters—they use their cultural capital to help clients succeed on the global marriage market, facilitate in-person meetings, and police their clients' morality, at times to help the business succeed and other times to maintain a clear conscience themselves. The stories of Lingfang, Sisi, and Liyi show that even in a national state of moral decay, even when working with women who have become jaded by unfaithful partners and financial ruin, and even when dealing with men and women who engage in international dating for the wrong reasons, there is an underlying morality that guides the translators and allows them to celebrate their role in curating successful unions.

EPILOGUE

AFTER READING THE STORIES IN this book, readers may be asking themselves, is this an accurate representation of Chinese women and Western men? If so, why haven't I ever met, in person, anyone like the people you describe in the book? Interestingly, these are the same questions I receive from my own friends and family, both in China and in the United States. In fact, a translator in China exclaimed, when I asked her what TV shows she enjoyed watching, "TV? What TV? If you work here like me, you will not watch TV. The stuff happening at our agency is more fascinating than any TV show!" As such, it's important to realize that the individuals in this book do not, by any means, represent the "average" woman in China or man in the West. In fact, they may not even represent the typical Chinese marriage migrant, given that it is mostly women without English-language skills who opt for translator-assisted dating, while women fluent in English may bypass third-party agencies to join Match.com or eHarmony directly. Similarly, most men residing in Western countries do not seek foreign wives, let alone seek them through translator-assisted global dating agencies.

Although my respondents in this study represent a unique subset of the population in their home countries, one commonality is that their liveli-hoods have been dramatically altered by structural changes in their local economy. Subsequently, their life goals, values, and gender ideologies have all shifted. Through close analysis of these men's and women's private lives, we can better understand the process by which broader sociostructural transformations reshape intimate relationships at the micro-level. A recap of some of the structural transformations that motivated these men and women to seek a foreign spouse will be helpful here.

CHANGING ECONOMIES CHALLENGE GENDER IDEOLOGIES

In China, the rapid transition from a centrally planned economy to a mixed economy imbued with global market forces created new opportunities as well as constraints for its citizens. After China's 1979 reform, the financially flexible women in this study experienced upward economic mobility, either through their relationships with their nouveau-riche husbands and lovers or through their own career success. In contrast, the financially burdened women experienced downward mobility: they either lost their own state jobs, failed in their business pursuits, or had Chinese husbands who endured these setbacks. While the women later divorced these men, the lingering economic effects of their previous marriages defined their financial status later on, when they entered the dating field as single women.

Not only did these structural changes lead to rising class inequality in China, but they also transformed gender norms at large, affecting women across all economic groups. As wealth and power became concentrated within the hands of a small group of male business elites, there was a revival of traditional patriarchal culture that emphasizes feminine youth and domesticity, alongside the association of masculinity with earning power. Thus, for the financially flexible women, their primary motive in seeking marriage migration was to escape gendered ageism in China, where older women were now deemed unworthy of wealthy men's attention. For the financially burdened women, who faced discrimination on both the Chinese marriage and labor markets, one additional motive for them was to achieve upward socioeconomic mobility.

Just like the Chinese women, the Western men enrolled in global dating agencies faced economic and cultural transformations in their home countries. In light of globalization, agriculture, manufacturing, and small business sectors have dramatically declined in the West. At the same time, gender norms have shifted toward greater "egalitarianism" in the sense that both men and women are now largely expected to pursue independent careers and to share domestic work at home. For some men who are financially well-off, their desire to seek a Chinese bride is rooted in their nostalgia for the gendered division of labor prevalent during the 1950s, which they believe has all but disappeared following the feminist movement of the 1970s. For other men, who have experienced downward economic mobility in recent years, their motive in seeking a Chinese bride is also informed by their inability to find a desirable spouse back home, given their own declining socioeconomic status.

My observation of these couples' courtships and marriages provides some key contributions that will help clear up several misconceptions people have about Chinese women and Western men. First, while the women in this study state that they want more "gender equality," their perception of equality falls outside the scope of what Western feminist scholars typically think of as "egalitarian." Western feminists, particularly second-wave feminists, equate egalitarianism with women's participation in the paid labor force.[1] By contrast, many of my research subjects either do not wish to work or do not want to share their earnings with their husbands. In fact, some women view sharing their income as an insult to their femininity. For them, gender equality means a separation of spheres, while placing equal value in each partner's respective responsibilities.

Subscribing to "entrepreneurial C-feminism," these women have an ideology consistent with the popular Chinese adage, "A man shows his love for a woman by handing her his wallet." The idea here is that a man who loves his wife would let her manage his salary, thereby giving the wife a sense of security and control at home despite her own low earnings relative to her husband's. The women in my study want to retain equal power and control over household finances without having to make fiscal contributions with their personal income. They seek a gendered economic deal in which men serve as the sole household economic providers but women need not be youthful or submissive. Perhaps this ideal exists only in the Chinese popular imagination, fueled by the media's romanticization of wealthy men who also happen to be generous, loving, and utterly devoted to their homemaker wives for life.

In contrast, while the Western men say they want a "traditional" marriage, some were opposed to giving "provider love,"[2] while others could not afford to do so. For many men, the notion of a traditional marriage hinged more on women's submissiveness, domesticity, and devotion to family, rather than on men's responsibility to provide for their wives. Subconsciously, these men may have been influenced by a societal shift in gender norms and dating etiquette in the West following the feminist movement of the 1970s. In many Western countries today, even in so-called "traditional" courtships, couples may split their expenses 30/70 or 20/80.[3] By contrast, in China, there is social expectation for men to show provider love by picking up all dating expenses and giving women cash, cars, and homes.[4] Given this mismatch in the men's and women's expectations, it is not surprising to see conflicts emerge in these unions. While many financially flexible women simply terminated such conflict-ridden relationships during the courtship phase, the financially burdened women often chose to carry on with their marriages despite these underlying disagreements.

Another issue involves the fluidity of race and its close association with class. As we have seen throughout this book, the decentering of wealth across continents and the polarization of wealth within nations has created haves and have-nots in both China and the West. Under such conditions, race becomes less significant during the mate-selection process, while class gains prominence. In China, whiteness still has some currency, as shown by the women's desire to seek white Western husbands and their imagination of whiteness as a symbol of either a global economic elite or an upper-middle-class "family man." This is possibly fueled by the portrayal of white men as wealthy, hegemonic males in Hollywood movies and in the Chinese popular media.

Yet these men's white privilege quickly dissipates when women meet them face to face and discover their lack of wealth, status, and power relative to elite Chinese men who came into prominence in the postreform era. This view was reaffirmed when I visited Meredith on-site at the massage parlor where she worked, located in the Deep South. Her boss, a woman from northern China, said to me, "Twenty years ago when I first came to the United States, I used to look up to white men, but now I look down on them because I have met so many white trash." Again, as Western countries lose their relative economic dominance on the global stage, power and status are defined less across racial lines and more across class lines. Chinese women, who come from a country that was once semi-colonized, "Third World," and filled with "people of color" oppressed by whites, are now challenging the validity of white supremacy as China's rise to economic prominence shakes up the old geopolitical hierarchy.

Finally, there is the misconception that global dating agencies are nothing but ruthless exploiters or even human traffickers in disguise. The assumption is that the agency staff are driven solely by profit motives and care nothing for their clients' personal interests. Yet, we have seen throughout this book that many staff have a strong personal desire to uphold morality. Moreover, while people often question businesses for engaging in unethical practices while excusing consumers from similar concerns, this book explores the reverse. As we have seen, the agency staff often serve as their clients' moral gatekeepers during the dating process. This is because China is currently in a state of anomie, where traditional morals, values, and ideologies have been upturned without a replacement value system. Fueled by a culture of rampant materialism, many clients pursue dating strategies such as cheating, lying, or gold-digging, which short-circuit traditional norms of honesty, fidelity, and earnestness, all of which are bedrocks of long-term marital success. In countries undergoing transition, where there is macro-level moral chaos and dysfunction, meso-level institutions such as dating agencies are forced, for their own survival, to step in and police their clients in order to successfully run their businesses.

DEMOGRAPHIC SHIFTS, TECHNOLOGICAL
ADVANCEMENTS, AND DISILLUSIONED DATERS

Since my goal is to show how macro-level sociostructural shifts reshape intimate relationships, I conclude with some insights about how new changes in economy, technology, and public health may shape the future trajectory of the global dating industry. These new insights are based on my follow-up research in Lingshan and Tunyang, conducted during the summers of 2017–19, when I was invited to give public lectures at the agencies to teach clients about Western culture and lifestyle. On one sunny morning in June 2018, I gave a presentation at Mr. Li's old Tunyang office, attended by thirty female clients. At this time, Mr. Li had left the business, Ms. Mei had immigrated to Switzerland to join her Western husband, and Ms. Fong was getting ready to retire. In fact, she had already transferred a good portion of her stocks to the next generation of young managers.

Following my presentation, Suni and Ming, a young translator couple who had been promoted to managers at Mr. Li's old office, treated me to lunch at a newly opened Asian fusion restaurant. They ordered me a Chinese-style, dessert-like pizza with fruit and sweet cheese. Through our conversations over lunch, I learned that the majority of their female clients are still divorced women with children from previous marriages. Just like their predecessors, these women seek marriage migration partly due to ageism on the Chinese dating market and partly because China's soaring housing prices have further complicated second-chance marriages with local men. Today, Chinese parents are expected to purchase homes for their grown sons,[5] and many people are adamant about passing on their property to their biological children instead of their stepchildren. These uncomfortable financial negotiations have become leading causes of marital conflict or even marital dissolution in China today, thereby causing some women to avoid local men when it comes to second-chance marriages. Beyond these shared motives among the women who joined before 2012 versus those whom I met after 2017, I also noticed some significant differences in aspirations between the two groups.

Rise of the Post-1980s Generation

Since 2012, there has been a demographic shift in the dating agencies' female clientele. Long gone were women born in the 1950s and 1960s, who sought a Western husband to finance their retirement after getting laid off from SOEs. The newer clients were mostly women born after 1980. Financially better off than their predecessors, these women were much choosier and no longer willing to marry just anyone in order to leave China. Moreover, I also noticed a change in these women's perception of money. For example, financial concerns among the female clients I met back in 2008–12 centered on whether Western men owned nice homes and their willingness to add their wives' names to the deeds. By contrast, the women I met in 2017–19 wanted to know how they could transfer funds from China to the West, or how they could protect their Chinese property with a prenuptial agreement. Here we can see these women's changing financial position in the global economic hierarchy. No longer passive recipients of Western funds, many Chinese women today have also become investors who inject their assets into Western economies.

This trend is especially noticeable in Lingshan, where the women are, on average, financially better off than those in Tunyang. Ms. Fong told me that some of her newest Lingshan clients were far richer than the Western men enrolled. Among them, some were relatively young—in their thirties—divorced, and seeking handsome Western men who could be caring step-fathers to their Chinese children. At times, Ms. Fong even helped clients who hesitated about marrying modest-earning Western men to reevaluate their gender ideology. For example, in one case where the woman was sat-isfied with everything about her suitor except his shabby home, Ms. Fong successfully convinced her to sell one of her luxury condos in Lingshan and reinvest in a house in the United States. In the summer of 2017, Ms. Fong invited me to attend a talk she gave at a financial advising company, located in a fancy skyscraper in Lingshan's central financial district. There, Ms. Fong promoted her business to their wealthy female clients who went in for financial advice.

Clearly, this new generation of rich female clients differed from some of the financially flexible women featured in this book. For example, in chap-ter 2, I discussed how wealthy clients were not mentally prepared to marry a lesser-earning man and take on the provider role, even though they could afford to do so. Having internalized China's mainstream gender ideology, which promotes the separation of spheres, these women rejected gender role reversals despite their newfound economic power. Yet, examples from the new generation of college-educated women born after 1980 reveal that they have a different outlook on gender—one that diverges from the main-stream male breadwinner/female homemaker model. If gender ideologies in China continue to diversify, perhaps there will be more successful unions of wealthy Chinese women with modest-earning Western "family men" in the years to come.

WeChat App and Translation Software

Interestingly, China's technological expansion has both fostered and hindered the agencies' growth and development. While internet technology initially enabled the global dating industry to grow, more recent advancements in translation software have caused the agencies to lose profit. For example, China's mobile app WeChat, which emerged in 2012 and quickly became the nation's most popular chat software, can provide real-time translation of all voice and text messages in different languages. This allows couples to bypass third-party translators once they obtain each other's contact information, thereby thinning the agencies' profit margin. As society moves toward a more automated dating landscape, technology itself assumes the role of surrogate and makes the human liaison obsolete.[6] This move toward a more automated future limits the translators' ability to capitalize on the intimate, relational work they once performed.

Accordingly, the agencies have shifted their business focus from translation to date coaching. Since many women are now communicating with the men directly through WeChat, the goal is to teach these women how to present themselves onscreen and carry on an online conversation. Sometimes the women send screenshots of their conversations with the men to translators to seek advice. Beyond this type of advising, Ms. Fong also teaches her clients Western norms, values, and etiquette by inviting psychologists, historians, and sociologists to give lectures. Correspondingly, the agency has raised its membership fees from US$1,000 in 2012 to US$4,000 in 2019.

Despite this new business strategy and fee structure, the agencies are still struggling. More and more local dating companies have emerged in recent years, increasing the women's competition for a limited pool of Western men. Moreover, efforts to compensate for the profit lost to technological advancements can only go so far. In Ms. Fong's words, there will be fewer and fewer women who don't know how to use computers and mobile apps as internet access becomes increasingly prevalent in China. While some women may subscribe to their pricy dating coaching services, many others will opt out and communicate with the men on their own instead.

When I revisited Ms. Fong's Lingshan agency in 2017, I saw how much the business had declined. At the office, there were old computer monitors stacked up in every corner, and thick dust lay on many tables. Ms. Fong confirmed my suspicions when she commented on her recent financial loss.

In fact, she had warned Suni and Ming at the Tunyang office: "If things fail, just close the agency. Don't expect me to save the business because I'm getting ready to retire." Turning toward me, she smiled and whispered, "Don't you think I'm getting old?" "What do you mean?" I asked awkwardly when I saw a tinge of sadness in her eyes. Now in her fifties, Ms. Fong explained, "My body is getting old and achy, my ideas are outdated." For example, she said, she was not keen on collaborating with the financial advising company, and only did so because of Wenli, her Lingshan office manager. Ms. Fong added, "Maybe Wenli wants to tap into a new market; maybe she will invent a new business model . . . I help out when I can, but ultimately I will leave it up to the next generation."

By 2019, the Lingshan office had relocated to a less central location with cheaper rent. Although the new office was in a skyscraper with breathtaking ocean views, it occupied just one tiny room. When the female clients came in, they met with their translators in conference rooms that had to be reserved in advance because they were shared with other companies on the same floor. On one rainy day in July 2019, over a lunch of beef-and-tomato noodle soup, Wenli told me she now focused on the wealthy clientele sector because these women were willing to pay top price for personalized services.

The COVID-19 Global Pandemic

In 2019, the dating agencies were confronted with their biggest challenge to date. The COVID-19 disease, caused by severe acute respiratory syndrome coronavirus 2 (SARS-CoV-2), was identified in December 2019 in Wuhan, China. In the ensuing months, this virus quickly swept across the globe, infecting 504.7 million people and causing 6.2 million deaths as of April 17, 2022.[7] While China and various other East Asian countries managed to bring this virus under control in several months, many Western countries failed to achieve the same success. The United States, for example, currently holds the world's highest number of confirmed cases and deaths.[8] As a result, global travel has waned and visa approval rates have plummeted. At the dating agencies, many clients have been forced to alter their travel plans or even put their marriage search on hold.

Interestingly, as the pandemic progressed, the agencies saw record-breaking male client activity online. Moreover, COVID-19 has not altered the Western men's desire to date Chinese women transnationally, despite the rising cases of racism against Asians in the United States. In fact, more and more men were requesting translator-assisted chat, videoconferencing, and email exchange. The translators believe this rise is linked to Western men spending more time online due to social distancing restrictions and increased opportunity to work from home. Even before the pandemic, the majority of Western male clients never traveled to China and instead used the site to fulfill their fantasies online. By contrast, most of the women hope to marry and move abroad one day. Thus, the agencies have faced new challenges recruiting women since the pandemic began. Facing an uncertain future, many women became hesitant to join or to renew their memberships.

Since 2016, Ms. Fong has invited me to give online lectures to her clients as part of the new business model that focuses on giving the women the tools to successfully represent themselves online. During the Q&A session in one of my lectures in October 2020, I asked clients why they continued their husband search despite the uncertain future. The answers I received included these: "desire for freedom and democracy," "food safety," "high-quality air and water," "to practice Christianity," "to provide a better education for children," "simpler interpersonal relationships and organizational politics," "slower-paced life," and "more responsible, family-oriented men." Nevertheless, they also expressed concern about the practicality of marriage migration in light of the new travel and visa restrictions, high rates of COVID-19 infection abroad, and tattered economies in the West.

Some of these concerns will certainly recede in the near future if the virus is contained. Yet, I cannot help but wonder how Chinese women will reenvision marriage migration after the pandemic ends. Will Western countries, and the United States in particular, remain desirable migration destinations? Throughout 2020, Chinese citizens saw their own government work closely with medical scientists to bring COVID-19 under control. By contrast, they witnessed the politicization of mask-wearing, pursuit of freedom at the cost of compromising public health, and staggering rates of COVID-19 infection and death in the West. Given that many Chinese women once imagined the average Western citizen to be better educated and more scientifically minded than the average Chinese citizen, and Western governments to be more capable of crisis management than the Chinese government, how will they come to terms with a newly revealed reality in the post-COVID-19 world?

FUTURE OF EMAIL-ORDER BRIDES

Throughout this book, we have seen the significant role economic standing played in the lives of Chinese marriage migrants. Whether economic hardship made them more pragmatic about their desire for a life partner, or whether personal financial success allowed them to pursue grandiose dreams of marrying a member of the global economic elite, the mark that China's changing economy left on these women undeniably ricocheted into their marriage decisions. Both women and men carried the collective weight of their personal financial situations alongside the financial reputations of their countries. These reputations, understandings, and yearnings, combined with their differing ideas of gender roles, translated into marriages that often fell short of their expectations.

While this book has shown how cultural and structural factors merged to create happy or unhappy unions thus far, what happens next? How will future global economic policies shape marriage migration? I speculate that the financially flexible women's desire to move abroad will decline drastically as China continues to rise while Western countries, haunted by political division and economic recession, lose their soft power. However, the financially burdened women, many of whom are small business owners and service sector workers—two groups that were hit hardest by COVID-19 in China—are likely to continue seeking marriage migration. Moreover, I predict that China will become a more attractive destination for Western men, particularly retired men, to relocate in the future and possibly seek second-chance marriages with local women, if China is able to maintain economic and political stability alongside high standards for public health and safety. By contrast, the main challenge to the dating agencies' business is the dramatic decline in female client enrollment. This is due not only to the Chinese women's fear of catching COVID, but more important, because COVID travel restrictions hamper the migration process. As COVID-19 eventually gets under control, I hope to visit China once again and update readers on the future trajectory of this rapidly evolving industry.

Notes

Introduction

1. The term "picture bride" stems from arranged marriages in which families sent pictures of brides in their home country to foreign men looking for partners. Nowadays, the term references the multimillion-dollar industry that uses images to market women from developing countries as potential brides to men from industrialized nations, largely presenting these women as "Pearls of the Orient" or "Gorgeous Pacific Women" (Chun 1996).

2. Tajima (1989); Villapando (1989); Constable (2003).

3. Launched by Chairman of the Communist Party of China Mao Zedong in 1966, the term "Cultural Revolution" refers to a series of sociopolitical changes that sought to amplify communism and eradicate capitalist influences in the region. From eliminating material incentives such as production bonuses to forbidding material displays of status difference, the movement sought to achieve widespread social equality by leveling down the elites to the masses (Whyte 2012).

4. Yang (2007).

5. Meszaros (2018).

6. Slater (2013).

7. Between 1991 and 2015, there was an eightfold increase in China's real GDP per capita, from US$800 to US$6,500 (Chen et al. 2018; Ji et al. 2017).

8. Countries of the World (2011).

9. Schaeffer (2013); Starr and Adams (2016).

10. China's history of anti-Black prejudice extends from premodern encounters, in which Black bodies were otherized and imagined as having mystical powers, to more concrete discrimination in the late imperial era (mainly the Ming [1368–1644] and Qing [1644–1912] dynasties), during which many Black and mixed-race children were abandoned and their parents were marginalized in society, going so far as to be banned from formal institutions such as marriage (Castillo 2020; Huang 2020). The discrimination solidified during the international slave trade and expansion of European colonialism, in which assumptions of Black people as savage, hypersexual, and violent became more widely accepted in the East Asian social consciousness (Huang 2020). In China today, *waiguoren*, or "foreigner," is used to understand white Europeans, Americans, and Australians rather than directly classifying them as white. However, Black people from wealthy Western nations are generally not referred to as *waiguoren* and instead remain classified by race, as *heiren* (Black person) (Farrer 2010). This linguistic differentiation emblematizes a broader distinction in which Black foreigners are excluded from the narrative of transnational masculinity in China.

11. Farrer (2010).

12. Thornton and Lin (1994); Xu et al. (2000).

13. Davin (1975); Shu (2004).

14. Wolf (1985); Zuo and Jiang (2009).

15. Mu and Xie (2014).

16. Cook and Dong (2011); Song and Hird (2014).

17. Berik et al. (2007).

18. Ji et al. (2017).

19. Otis (2012); Xu and Feiner (2007).

20. Yang (2007). During this period, more than 30 million workers across the nation lost their jobs (Giles et al. 2006). Women were laid off at much higher rates than men and had more difficulty finding reemployment (Berik 2007; Parish and Brusse 2000). Following their layoffs, many had to take low-paying jobs in the contingent sector, working as nannies or street vendors without health care or social security benefits (Appleton et al. 2002; Giles et al. 2006).

21. Lin (2003).

22. Osburg (2013).

23. Mu and Xie (2014); Xie (2013).

24. Yang (1999); Zhang (2010).

25. Osburg (2013); Xiao (2011).

26. Berik et al. (2007).

27. Zhang C. et al. (2014).

28. Mu and Xie (2014).

29. Terry (2019).

30. "C-fem" is short for "Chinese feminism." Wu and Dong (2019).

31. Fincher (2014). Noncooperative C-fem emerged in response to the so-called "leftover woman" media campaign, which was launched by the state to shame urban professional women in their late twenties and beyond into marrying China's surplus men, who are seen as a potential threat to social stability.

32. Wu and Dong (2019).

33. Wu and Dong (2019).

34. Wu and Dong (2019).

35. Harvey (2012).

36. Forbes (2020).

37. Harvey (2012).

38. Eitzen et al. (2017).

39. US Department of Labor (2021).

40. Schaeffer-Grabiel (2006b); Starr and Adams (2016).

41. Wade and Ferree (2019).

42. Ellingsæter (1998); Zulehner and Volz (1998).

43. Wade and Ferree (2019).

44. Schwartz (2013); Streib (2020); Steward (2018).

45. Ellingsæter (1998); Wade and Ferree (2019); Zulehner and Volz (1998).

46. Schaefer (2013).

47. Atanasoski and Vora (2019).

48. Link et al. (2013).

49. Xu (2017); Link et al. (2013).

50. Link et al. (2013).

51. Hoang (2015).

52. CEBR World Economic League Table 2021.

53. Constable (2003); Schaeffer (2013).

54. Novikova (2000).

55. Meszaros (2018).

56. Interview with Julia Meszaros, assistant professor of sociology at Texas A&M University—Commerce, November 27, 2021.

57. Durkheim (1897).

58. Wang and Chang (2002).

59. Berg (2004).

60. Heyl (2001).

61. Berik et al. (2007).

Chapter 1

1. Xie and Zhou (2014).

2. Harvey (2012).

3. Harvey (2012).

4. Wei et al. (2017).

5. See Wong (2016).

6. There are great variations in Asians' immigration histories and reasons for immigration, and striking disparities in their current well-being (Portes and Rumbaut 1996;). Some Asian groups immigrated voluntarily, while others were forced to do so by dire conditions in their native countries. Some came for education and employment; others, for family reunification; and still others, to avoid genocide, wars, and political persecution (Chan 1991). See also Chen et al. (2009, 858).

7. Among the 1,740 women enrolled across the three agencies, 996 (57%) were divorced and 1,144 (66%) were over the age of forty.

8. Livingston (2014).

9. Fincher (2014).

10. Treiman (2013); Wu and Song (2010); Mu and Xie (2014).

11. Mu and Xie (2014).

12. The average annual wage of workers in Shenzhen (city) was US$7,197 in 2009 and US$8,495 in 2011; the average annual wage of workers in Wuhan (city) was US$4,660 in 2009 and US$7,031 in 2011 (China Data Online).

13. Zurndorfer (2018).

14. Osburg (2013).

15. Song and Hird (2014).

16. Zhang (2010).

17. Zhang et al. (2014).

18. Osburg (2013).

19. Xiao (2011).

20. Constable (2003).

21. Osburg (2013).

22. Xiao (2011).

23. Zurndorfer (2016).

24. Hakim (2011).

25. Connell (1987).

26. Otis (2012); Xu and Feiner (2007).

27. Meszaros (2018).

28. Merton (1941); Edwards (1969).

29. Berik et al. (2007).

30. Hochschild (1990).

31. Berik et al. (2007); Ji et al. (2017).

32. Constable (2003).

33. Sandy To (2013, 1–2) writes that "increasing numbers of single, unmarried Chinese women in affluent Chinese cities such as Shanghai has given rise to the phenomenon of *sheng nu* or 'leftover women.'"

34. Stark and Taylor (1989).

35. Portes and Rumbaut (2006, 365).

36. Yang (2007).

37. Parish and Busse (2000).

38. Appleton et al. (2002); Chi and Li (2008).

39. Otis (2012).

40. Otis (2012).

41. Bourdieu (1978).

42. "Today in China, just as had been the case for in the past 1,400 years, the idea of '万般皆下品, 唯有读书高' [All pursuits are of low value; only studying the books is high] is still the dominant view of education . . . Per the China Education and Human Resource Report, in 2003 family expenditure on education amounted to 12.6 percent of the family budget and surpassed both housing and clothing to become, after food, the second highest expenditure in Chinese cities" (Yu and Suen 2005, 18; citations omitted).

43. Li et al. (2014).

44. Li et al. (2014).

45. Ponzini (2020).

46. Osburg (2013, 9) writes that "the smashing of the 'iron rice bowl' (*tiefanwan*)—the end of the state systems guaranteeing social services, lifelong employment, and housing—has generated greater uncertainty for most Chinese, but it also has created opportunities for individuals to dramatically alter their material wealth and social status."

47. "The explosive growth of China's emerging middle class has brought sweeping economic change and social transformation—and it's not over yet. By 2022, our research suggests, more than 75 percent of China's urban consumers will earn 60,000 to 229,000 renminbi ($9,000 to $34,000) a year" (Barton et al. 2013, 2). See Barton et al. (2013).

48. Xiao (2011).

49. Osburg (2013, 11).

50. Bourdieu (1978).

51. Hakim (2010).

52. CEBR (2020).

Chapter 2

1. Hershatter (2019).

2. Wade (2019).

3. Osburg (2013, 10) writes that "intellectuals and reformers decry the betrayal of socialist goals of gender equality by young women who cultivate their feminine charms in the hope they can marry well or 'live off moneybags' [*bang dakuan*]." In urban centers such as Shanghai, homemakers make up nearly 10 percent of married women, many of whom are young, fashionable, well educated, and previously held high-paying, high-status, white-collar jobs.

4. Xiao (2011).

5. Osburg (2013).

6. Song and Hird (2014).

7. US Census Bureau (2013).

8. The "gendered social imaginary," a term for how potential migrants imagine the nature of gender relations in their future migration destinations, plays a significant role in these women's desire to date transnationally and migrate to marry (Mahler and Pessar 2003).

9. Hunter (2010).

10. Women can save money in not having to buy gifts because women can use their personal charm as a substitute for gifts. Furthermore, many men feel obliged to take care of women, since they are considered more dependent in life (Yang 1994; Choi and Peng 2016).

11. For example, among the 2012 *Forbes* ranking of the world's richest self-made women billionaires, the largest number came from China (7 in the top 14), with real estate developer Wu Yajun topping the list. See The Richest (2012).

12. Farrer (2010a).

13. "Throughout Chinese history, the country's patrilineal family system has led to the practice of paying for brides, a social phenomenon closely related to the issue of surplus males in China" (Jiang and Sanchez-Barricarte 2012). See also Watson et al. (1991).

14. Farrer (2002); Jiang and Sanchez-Barricarte (2012).

15. This is a major social problem for lesser-earning men in China. In fact, it is not uncommon for parents to tap into their retirement savings or even borrow money to help their grown sons get married. See Farrer (2002); Jiang and Sanchez-Barricarte (2012).

16. Prior to the twentieth century, most Chinese women lacked economic

roles outside the home (Mann 2000). It was not until the post-1949 socialist era that urban women were encouraged and sometimes forced by the state to work in the formal economy (Shu 2004). Yet, the state later changed its stance on this issue after 1979. As part of China's transition from a collectivist to a market economy during the 1980s and 1990s, many state-owned enterprises either closed or downsized, and women were laid off at disproportionately higher rates than men. To promote social stability, the government encouraged women to return home (Dong and Pandey 2012).

17. Jeffreys (2008).

18. In the West, there has been a sharp decline in men's provider role during the past forty years. This resulted from Western women's increased labor participation as well as men's rising rates of unemployment and underemployment (Ellingsaeter 1998; Zulehner and Volz 1998). While working-class families could once afford to have only a working husband/father during the 1950s, this is no longer economically feasible in many Western countries. In contrast, "new man" masculinity, emphasizing the sharing of breadwinning and child care between the sexes, has emerged. Among dual-career professional couples, sharing breadwinning is even associated with gender progressiveness and modernity (Coltrane and Adams 2008).

19. Kimmel (2003).

20. Wade (2019).

21. Farrer (2002).

Chapter 3

1. Connell and Messerschmidt (2005).

2. In the Chinese popular imagination, the wealthy man is also the male sexual ideal. "Unlike the US, where working-class and black men are sometimes constructed as hypersexual, with strong abilities to seduce and consume women . . . in China, hypermasculine sexuality is constructed as a privilege of the rich, just like other forms of consumption" (Song and Hird 2014, 74). As the fashion trendsetters and patrons of China's most exclusive dining and shopping venues, nouveau-riche businessmen embody an elite masculinity that became "the normative masculinity around which all urban men's practices are oriented and measured" (Osburg 2013, 10).

3. In a widely circulated article titled "Chinese Men Do Not Deserve Chinese Women," the author describes a "'lack of manliness' among urban Chinese men in the way they walk, stand, and sit, as compared with Western men represented by 'American GIs'" (Song and Hird 2014, 11).

4. Constable (2003); Espiritu (1997).

5. Harvey (2012); Hoang (2014b).

6. Farrer (2010a, 82).

7. Farrer (2010a).

8. Connell (2005).

9. "Erotic capital" refers to a nebulous but crucial combination of sex appeal, beauty, and physical and social attractiveness that makes some men and women agreeable companions and colleagues. Erotic capital is as important as human and social capital for understanding social and economic processes, and in affluent modern societies it is increasingly important. See Hakim (2011).

10. Compared to Vivien's Chinese ex-husband and lovers, Kuan does not embody the epitome of elite Chinese masculinity either. Among China's new rich, there is further distinction between the *di suzhi* (low quality), *baofahu* (suddenly rich person) of rural, less-educated background who engages in excessive banqueting and wears flashy designer clothing, and the *gao suzhi* (high quality) metropolitan businessmen who is more low-key and displays more sophisticated *pinwei* (taste) (Osburg 2013; Song and Hird 2014). Two of Vivien's previous lovers fall into the *gao suzhi* category. One was a well-traveled son of Tunyang's mayor, while the other was a media mogul who spoke fluent English and excelled in calligraphy. By comparison, Kuan falls somewhere in between. While he embodies some characteristics of a *baofahu*, he also pursues various forms of self-improvement, such as learning English, playing sports, and pursuing leisure travel, which is more characteristic of men with *pinwei*.

11. A random sample of 1,000 male client profiles shows a self-reported salary of US$15,000–$34,000 among 29 percent of the men and US$35,000–$49,000 among 21 percent of the men, while less than 7 percent earned above US$150,000.

12. Sumra (2019).

13. Connell and Messerschmidt (2005).

14. "Characteristics such as being impeccably and smartly dressed, dashing appearance, mental and physical quickness, aggressiveness, and vigor reference the default upper-classness, maleness, whiteness, and heteronormativity of ideal investment bankers" (Ho 2009, 39–41).

15. Osburg (2013); Song and Hird (2014); Uretsky (2008).

16. Simple comparisons of mean wages typically find Black–white wage differences in excess of 30 percent. See Fryer and Spenkuch (2013).

17. More than half of Asian American adults have a bachelor's degree or higher, compared to 37 percent of whites, 27 percent of African Americans, and 18 percent of Latinos. But they do as poorly as other minority groups in gaining management and executive-suite jobs in major corporations. See Chin (2016, 70–71).

18. This is an instance of typecasting, as described in Yuen (2017).

19. See Ambler (2017).

20. CEBR 2020.

Chapter 4

1. Wade and Ferree (2019).

2. Espiritu (1997).

3. Connell (1987).

4. Hunter (2010).

5. Song and Hird (2014).

6. Fox and Luxton (2001); Stack (1974).

7. Constable (2003).

8. Connell (1987).

9. Coltrane and Adams (2008); Wade and Ferree (2019).

10. Wu and Dong (2019).

11. To (2013, 14).

12. Wu and Dong (2019, 16–17).

13. Wu and Dong (2019, 16–17).

14. Hershatter (2007).

15. Osburg (2013).

16. Osburg (2013); Song and Hird (2014).

17. Parish and Brusse (2000).

18. Cook and Dong (2011); Song (2011).

19. Wu and Dong (2019).

20. Wu and Dong (2019).

21. Wu and Dong (2019, 11).

22. Susan initially asked me to keep her prenuptial agreement a secret, but later changed her mind and shared her story with the dating agency managers and clients.

23. Ansari and Klingenberg (2015); Cherlin (2010).

24. Tajima (1989, 309).

Chapter 5

1. Coltrane and Adams (2008).

2. Wu and Dong (2019, 10).

3. Wu and Dong (2019).

4. Coltrane and Adams (2008).

5. To (2013).

6. Wu and Dong (2019, 11).

7. Bourdieu (1984).

8. Wu and Dong (2019).

9. Otis (2012).

10. Wu and Dong (2019, 16–17).

Chapter 6

1. Even though the translators encourage women to provide Chinese-language content for the letters, some women fail to do so, and under these circumstances, translators may end up crafting reply letters with little client input.

2. Kong (2017).

3. From the "2007 Employment Situation for College Graduates Survey" conducted by the Education and Economic Research Institute of Peking University and the Institute for Higher Education (Changjun 2014).

4. Link et al. (2013); Xu (2017).

5. Link et al. (2013). As early as the 1980s, Chinese media outlets issued warnings about a looming moral crisis from the loss of moral values, beliefs, and confidence in Communist ideology (Yan et al. 2011).

6. Link et al. (2013).

7. One example of this kind of highly publicized, lethal incident was the 2008 milk scandal. When sixteen babies developed kidney stones, it was discovered that milk powder formula was being adulterated with melamine, a harmful chemical. In this instance, the combination of corruption and poor regulation led to an estimated three hundred thousand babies becoming ill and six reported fatalities (Huang 2014).

8. Yan (2009).

9. Link et al. (2013); Yan et al. (2011).

10. Yan et al. (2011).

11. Wang and Chang (2002).

12. Parish and Brusse (2000).

13. Osburg (2013).

14. Beach (2011).

15. Farrer (2014).

16. Frecklington (2014).

17. Link et al. (2013).

18. Liu (2015).

19. Hochschild (1983).

20. Bourdieu (1984).

21. Farrer (2002, 157).

22. Zhou (1989, 279).

23. Farrer (2002).

24. Farrer (2002); Tang and Parish (2000).

25. Farrer (2002).

26. Li (2008).

27. Vora (2010).

28. According to China's Ministry of Education, the number of graduating college students increased from 1.45 million in 2002 to more than 6 million in 2009. Yet the rate of employment for graduates in 2008 was less than 70 percent, thus leaving as many as 2 million graduates without work (Zhou and Lin 2009). Moreover, the "2010 Chinese College Graduate Employment Report" published by the McCarthy Institute lists English as one of the majors with "high risk of unemployment and low wage" due to China's low market demand for English majors relative to supply. See China News 2010.

Epilogue

1. Coltrane and Adams (2008); Wade and Ferree (2019).

2. Hunter (2010).

3. Schwartz (2013).

4. Farrer ((2002); Song and Hird (2014).

5. Shi (2017).

6. Atanasoski and Vora (2020).

7. Worldometer (2022).

8. As of April 2022, the United States had 82 million confirmed cases and 1,015,451 deaths (Worldometer 2022).

References

Acker, Joan. 2004. "Gender, Capitalism and Globalization." *Critical Sociology* 30(1):17–41.

Agunias, Dovelyn. 2009. "Guiding the Invisible Hand: Making Migration Intermediaries Work for Development." Human Development Report Office, United Nations Development Programme, Human Development Research Papers (2009 to present).

Almeling, Rene. 2007. "Selling Genes, Selling Gender: Egg Agencies, Sperm Banks, and the Medical Market in Genetic Material." *American Sociological Review* 72(3):319–40.

Ambler, Pamela. 2017. "Asia Is Now Home to the Most Billionaires, with China Leading the Pack, Report Says." *Forbes,* 30 October. https://www.forbes.com/sites/pamelaambler/2017/10/30/where-young-chinese-billionaires-are-making-their-wealth-and-spending-it/#6c2074df7fb6.

Angeles, Leonora, and Sirijit Sunanta. 2007. "'Exotic Love at Your Fingertips': Intermarriage Websites, Gendered Representation, and the Transnational Migration of Filipino and Thai Women." *Kasarinlan: Philippine Journal of Third World Studies* 22(1):3–31.

Ansari, Aziz, and Eric Klinenberg. 2015. *Modern Romance.* New York: Penguin Press.

Appleton, Simon, John Knight, Lina Song, and Qingjie Xia. 2002. "Labor Retrenchment in China: Determinants and Consequences." *China Economic Review* 13(2–3):252–75.

Atanasoski, Neda, and Kalindi Vora. *Surrogate Humanity: Race, Robots, and the Politics of Technological Futures.* Durham, NC: Duke University Press, 2019.

Barenholdt, Jorgen Ole, and Brynhild Granas. 2008. *Mobility and Peace: Enacting Northern European Peripheries.* Farnham, UK: Ashgate Publishing.

Barlow, Tani E. 2001. "Globalization, China, and International Feminism." *Signs* 26(4):1286–91.

Barton, Dominic, Yougang Chen, and Amy Jin. 2013. "Mapping China's Middle Class." *McKinsey Quarterly* (3):54–60.

Beach, Sophie. 2011. "China's New Marriage Law May Exacerbate Gender Wealth Gap." *China Digital Times.* https://chinadigitaltimes.net.

Belleau, Marie-Claire. 2003. "Mail-Order Brides in a Global World." *Albany Law Review* 67(2):595–607.

Berg, Bruce L. 2004. *Qualitative Research Methods for the Social Sciences.* 5th ed. Boston: Pearson.

Berik, Günseli, Xiao-yuan Dong, and Gale Summerfield. 2007. "China's Transition and Feminist Economics." *Feminist Economics* 13(3–4):1–33.

Bernstein, Elizabeth. 2001. "The Meaning of the Purchase: Desire, Demand and the Commerce of Sex." *Ethnography* 2(3):389–420.

Bourdieu, Pierre. 1978. "Sport and Social Class." *Social Science Information* 17(6):819–40.

Bourdieu, Pierre. 1984. *Distinction: A Social Critique of the Judgement of Taste.* Cambridge, MA: Harvard University Press.

Brennan, Denise. 2001. "Tourism in Transnational Places: Dominican Sex Workers and German Sex Tourists Imagine One Another." *Identities* 7(4):621–63.

Bridges, Tristan, and C. J. Pascoe. 2014. "Hybrid Masculinities: New Directions in the Sociology of Men and Masculinities: Hybrid Masculinities." *Sociology Compass* 8(3):246–58.

Budnick, Jamie. 2016. "'Straight Girls Kissing'? Understanding Same-Gender Sexuality beyond the Elite College Campus." *Gender & Society* 30(5):745–68.

Bürkner, Hans-Joachim. 2012. "Intersectionality: How Gender Studies Might Inspire the Analysis of Social Inequality among Migrants: Intersectionality and the Analysis of Social Inequality among Migrants." *Population, Space and Place* 18(2):181–95.

Buss, David M., Todd K. Shackelford, Lee A. Kirkpatrick and Randy J. Larsen. 2001. "A Half Century of Mate Preferences: The Cultural Evolution of Values." *Journal of Marriage and the Family* 63(2):491–503.

Cai, Rong. 2003. "Problematizing the Foreign Other: Mother, Father, and the Bastard in Mo Yan's 'Large Breasts and Full Hips.'" *Modern China* 29(1):108–37.

Castillo, Roberto. 2020. "'Race' and 'Racism' in Contemporary Africa-China Relations Research: Approaches, Controversies and Reflections." *Inter-Asia Cultural Studies* 21(3):310–36. doi: 10.1080/14649373.2020.1796343.

CEBR. 2016. *World Economic League Table 2017: A World Economic League Table with Forecasts for 180 Countries to 2030.* London: Centre for Economics and Business Research.

CEBR. 2020. *World Economic League Table 2021: A World Economic League Table with Forecasts for 193 Countries to 2035.* London: Centre for Economics and Business Research.

Chang, Lei, Yan Wang, Todd K. Shackelford, and David M. Buss. 2011. "Chinese Mate Preferences: Cultural Evolution and Continuity across a Quarter of a Century."*Personality and Individual Differences* 50(5):678–83.

Changjun, Yue. 2014. "A Comparative Study of Graduate Employment Surveys: 2003–2011." *Chinese Education & Society* 47(6):12–35.

Charmaz, Kathy. 2006. *Constructing Grounded Theory.* Thousand Oaks, CA: Sage Publications.

Chen, Juan, Gilbert C. Gee, Michael S. Spencer, Sheldon H. Danzinger, and David Takeuchi. 2009. "Perceived Social Standing among Asian Immigrants in the US: Do Reasons for Immigration Matter?" *Social Science Research* 38(4):858–69.

Chen, Mengni, Chi Leung Kwok, Haiyue Shan, and Paul S. F. Yip. 2018. "Decomposing and Predicting China's GDP Growth: Past, Present, and Future." *Population and Development Review* 44(1):143–57.

Chen, Ruoxi, Jason P. Austin, John K. Miller, and Fred P. Piercy. 2015. "Chinese and American Individuals' Mate Selection Criteria: Updates, Modifications, and Extensions." *Journal of Cross-Cultural Psychology* 46(1):101–18.

Cherlin, Andrew J. 2010. *The Marriage-Go-Round: The State of Marriage and the Family in America Today.* New York: Vintage Books.

Chi, Wei, and Bo Li. 2008. "Glass Ceiling or Sticky Floor? Examining the Gender Earnings Differential across the Earning Distribution in Urban China, 1987–2004." *Journal of Comparative Economics* 36(2):243–63.

Chin, Margaret M. 2016. "Asian Americans, Bamboo Ceilings, and Affirmative Action." *Contexts* 15(1):70–73.

China Data Online. https://www.china-data-online.com.

China News. 2010. "College Student Employment Report: English and Computer

Science Majors Struggle with Employment" (in Chinese). Chinanews.com, 4 June. http://www.chinanews.com/edu/news/2010/06-03/2320032.shtml.

Choi, Suzanne Y. P., and Yinni Peng. 2016. *Masculine Compromise: Migration, Family, and Gender in China.* Oakland: University of California Press.

Choo, Hae Yeon. 2016. "Selling Fantasies of Rescue: Intimate Labor, Filipina Migrant Hostesses, and US GIs in a Shifting Global Order." *Positions* 24(1):179–203.

Chun, S. Y. Christine. 1996. "The Mail-Order Bride Industry: The Perpetuation of Transnational Economic Inequalities and Stereotypes." *University of Pennsylvania Journal of International Economic Law* 17(4):1155–1208.

Cliff, Tom. 2015. "Post-Socialist Aspirations in a Neo-*Danwei*." *China Journal* 73:132–57.

Coltrane, Scott, and Michele Adams. 2008. *Gender and Families.* Lanham, MD: Rowman & Littlefield.

Connell, Raewyn W. 1987. *Gender and Power: Society, the Person, and Sexual Politics.* Stanford: Stanford University Press.

Connell, Raewyn W. 1998. "Masculinities and Globalization." *Men and Masculinities* 1(1):3–23.

Connell, Raewyn W. 2014. "Rethinking Gender from the South." *Feminist Studies* 40(3):518–39.

Connell, Raewyn W., and James W. Messerschmidt. 2005. "Hegemonic Masculinity: Rethinking the Concept." *Gender & Society* 19(6):829–59.

Constable, Nicole. 2003. *Romance on a Global Stage: Pen Pals, Virtual Ethnography, and Mail Order Marriages.* Berkeley: University of California Press.

Constable, Nicole. 2009. "The Commodification of Intimacy: Marriage, Sex, and Reproductive Labor." *Annual Review of Anthropology* 3:49–64.

Constable, Nicole. 2016. "Reproductive Labor at the Intersection of Three Intimate Industries: Domestic Work, Sex Tourism, and Adoption." *Positions* 24(1):45–69.

Cook, Sarah, and Dong, Xiao-yuan. 2011. "Harsh Choices: Chinese Women's Paid Work and Unpaid Care Responsibilities under Economic Reform." *Development and Change* 42(4):947–65.

Countries of the World. N.d. "China Economy 2011." https://theodora.com/wfb2011/china/china_economy.html.

Davin, Delia. 1975. "Women in the Countryside of China." *Current History* 69(408):93–96.

Davin, Delia. 2005. "Marriage Migration in China: The Enlargement of Marriage Markets in the Era of Market Reforms." *Indian Journal of Gender Studies* 12(2–3):173–88.

Davin, Delia. 2007. "Marriage Migration in China and East Asia." *Journal of Contemporary China* 16(50):83–95.

Davis, Shannon N., and Theodore N. Greenstein. 2009. "Gender Ideology: Components, Predictors, and Consequences." *Annual Review of Sociology* 35(1):87–105.

Decatur, Mary-Anne. 2012. "Consuming Cuteness in Japan: Hello Kitty, Individualism and Identity." Honors thesis, Western Michigan University.

Donato, Katharine M., Donna Gabaccia, Jennifer Holdaway, Martin Manalansan, and Patricia R. Pessar. 2006. "A Glass Half Full? Gender in Migration Studies." *International Migration Review* 40(1):3–26.

Dong, Xiao-yuan, and Manish Pandey. 2012. "Gender and Labor Retrenchment in Chinese State Owned Enterprises: Investigation Using Firm-Level Panel Data." *China Economic Review* 23(2):385–95.

Douglass, Mike. 2006. "Global Householding in Pacific Asia." *International Development Planning Review* 28(4):421–46.

Douglass, Mike. n.d. "Global Householding and East Asia—Phantom or Phoenix?" Paper presented at International Conference on Global Migration and the Household in East Asia, Seoul, South Korea, 2–3 February.

Du, Fangqin, and Xinrong Zheng. 2005. *Women's Studies in China: Mapping the Social, Economic and Policy Changes in Chinese Women's Lives.* Seoul: Ewha Womans University Press.

Du, Julan, Yongqin Wang, and Yan Zhang. 2015. "Sex Imbalance, Marital Matching and Intra-Household Bargaining: Evidence from China." *China Economic Review* 35:197–218.

Durkheim, Emile. 1897. *Suicide: A Study in Sociology.* London: Routledge & Kegan Paul.

Eades, Jerry. 1999. "International Migration, Immobility and Development: Multidisciplinary Perspectives." *Journal of the Royal Anthropological Institute* 5(1).

Ebrey, Patricia Buckley. 1993. "Rites and Celebrations." In Ebrey, *The Inner Quarters, Marriage and the Lives of Chinese Women in the Sung Period.* Berkeley, CA: University of California Press.

Edwards, John N. 1969. "Familial Behavior as Social Exchange." *Journal of Marriage and the Family* 31:518–26.

Eitzen, Stanley, Maxine Baca Zinn, and Kelly Eitzen Smith. 2017. *Conflict and Order: Understanding Society.* London: Pearson Education.

Elder, Glen H. 1969. "Appearance and Education in Marriage Mobility." *American Sociological Review* 34(4):519.

Ellingsæter, Anne Lise. 1998. "Dual Breadwinner Societies: Provider Models in the Scandinavian Welfare States." *Acta Sociologica* 41(1):59–73.

Espiritu, Yen Le. 1997. *Asian American Women and Men: Labor, Laws and Love.* Thousand Oaks, CA: Sage Publications.

Esteve, Albert, Joan García-Román, and Iñaki Permanyer. 2012. "The Gender-Gap Reversal in Education and Its Effect on Union Formation: The End of Hypergamy?" *Population and Development Review* 38(3):535–46.

Esteve, Albert, Christine R. Schwartz, Jan van Bavel, Iñaki Permanyer, Martin Klesment, and Joan García-Román. 2016. "The End of Hypergamy: Global Trends and Implications." *Population and Development Review* 42(4):615–25.

Fan, C. Cindy, and Youqin Huang. 1998. "Waves of Rural Brides: Female Marriage Migration in China." *Annals of the Association of American Geographers* 88(2):227–51.

Farrer, Gracia Liu. 2004. "The Chinese Social Dance Party in Tokyo: Identity and Status in an Immigrant Leisure Subculture." *Journal of Contemporary Ethnography* 33(6):651–74.

Farrer, James. 2002. *Opening Up: Youth Sex Culture and Market Reform in Shanghai.* Chicago: University of Chicago Press.

Farrer, James. 2008. "From 'Passports' to 'Joint Ventures': Intermarriage between Chinese Nationals and Western Expatriates Residing in Shanghai." *Asian Studies Review* 32(1):7–29.

Farrer, James. 2010a. "A Foreign Adventurer's Paradise? Interracial Sexuality and Alien Sexual Capital in Reform Era Shanghai." *Sexualities* 13(1):69–95.

Farrer, James. 2010b. "'New Shanghailanders' or 'New Shanghainese': Western Expatriates' Narratives of Emplacement in Shanghai." *Journal of Ethnic and Migration Studies* 36(8):1211–28.

Farrer, James. 2011. "Global Nightscapes in Shanghai as Ethnosexual Contact Zones." *Journal of Ethnic and Migration Studies* 37(5):747–64.

Farrer, James. 2013. "Good Stories: Chinese Women's International Love Stories as Cosmopolitan Sexual Politics." *Sexualities* 16(1–2):12–29.

Farrer, James. 2014. "Love, Sex, and Commitment: Delinking Premarital Intimacy from Marriage in Urban China." In D. S. Davis and S. L. Friedman, eds., *Wives, Husbands, and Lovers: Marriage and Sexuality in Hong Kong, Taiwan, and Urban China,* 62–96. Stanford: Stanford University Press.

Farrer, James, and Sun Zhongxin. 2003. "Extramarital Love in Shanghai." *China Journal* 50:1–36.

Fernández, Raquel, Nezih Guner, and John Knowles. 2005. "Love and Money: A Theoretical and Empirical Analysis of Household Sorting and Inequality." *Quarterly Journal of Economics* 120(1):273–344.

Fincher, Leta Hong. 2014. *Leftover Women: The Resurgence of Gender Inequality in China.* London: Zed Books.

Fong, Vanessa L. 2002. "China's One-Child Policy and the Empowerment of Urban Daughters." *American Anthropologist* 104(4):1098–1109.

Forbes. 2012. "The World's Richest Women." *Forbes*, March 7. https://www .forbes.com/sites/erincarlyle/2012/03/07/the-worlds-richest-women/

Forbes. 2020. "Forbes Billionaires 2020." *Forbes*. https://www.forbes.com/ billionaires/.

Fox, Bonnie J., and Meg Luxton. 2001. "Conceptualizing Patriarchy." In D. M. Juschka, ed., *Feminism in the Study of Religion*, 314–33. New York: Continuum.

Frecklington, Cameron. 2014. "China: The Next Market for the World's Top Adultery Site." *Atlantic*, May 28. https://www.theatlantic.com/international /archive/2014/05/china-the-next-market-for-the-worlds-top-adultery-site/ 371687/.

Fryer, Roland G., Devah Pager, and Jörg L. Spenkuch. 2013. "Racial Disparities in Job Finding and Offered Wages." *Journal of Law & Economics* 56(3):633–89.

Fu, Xuanning, and Tim B. Heaton. 1999. "Implications of Status Exchange in Intermarriage for Hawaiians and Their Sovereignty Movement." *Sociological Perspectives* 42(1):97–116.

Giles, John, Albert Park, and Fang Cai. 2003. "How Has Economic Restructuring Affected China's Urban Workers?" *China Quarterly* 185:61–95.

Hakim, Catherine. 2011. *Erotic Capital: The Power of Attraction in the Boardroom and the Bedroom*. New York: Basic Books.

Harvey, David. 2012. *Rebel Cities: From the Right to the City to the Urban Revolution*. New York: Verso.

He, Qiao-Qiao, Zhen Zhang, Jian-Xin Zhang, Zhi-Guo Wang, Ying Tu, Ting Ji, and Yi Tao. 2013. "Potentials-Attract or Likes-Attract in Human Mate Choice in China." *PLoS ONE* 8(4):e59457.

Herrera, Gioconda. 2013. "Gender and International Migration: Contributions and Cross-Fertilizations." *Annual Review of Sociology* 39(1):471–89.

Hershatter, Gail. 2004. "State of the Field: Women in China's Long Twentieth Century." *Journal of Asian Studies* 63(4):991–1065.

Hershatter, Gail. 2007. *Women in China's Long Twentieth Century*. Berkeley: University of California Press.

Hershatter, Gail. 2019. *Women and China's Revolutions*. Lanham, MD: Rowman & Littlefield.

Heyl, Barbara Sherman. 2001. "Ethnographic Interviewing." In P. Atkinson, A. Coffey, S. Delamont, and L. Lofland, eds., *Handbook of Ethnography*, 369–73. Thousand Oaks, CA: Sage Publications.

Ho, Karen. 2009. *Liquidated: An Ethnography of Wall Street*. Durham, NC: Duke University Press.

Hoang, Kimberly Kay. 2014a. "Competing Technologies of Embodiment: Pan-Asian Modernity and Third World Dependency in Vietnam's Contemporary Sex Industry." *Gender & Society* 28(4):513–36.

Hoang, Kimberly Kay. 2014b. "Vietnam Rising Dragon: Contesting Dominant Western Masculinities in Ho Chi Minh City's Global Sex Industry." *International Journal of Politics, Culture, and Society* 27(2):259–71.

Hoang, Kimberly Kay. 2015. *Dealing in Desire: Asian Ascendancy, Western Decline, and the Hidden Currencies of Global Sex Work*. Oakland: University of California Press.

Hochschild, Arlie. 1983. *The Managed Heart*. Berkeley: University of California Press.

Hochschild, Arlie, and Anne Machung. 1990. *The Second Shift*. New York: Avon Books.

Hooff, Jenny van. 2016. *Modern Couples? Continuity and Change in Heterosexual Relationships*. New York: Routledge.

Huang, Kun. 2020. "'Anti-Blackness' in Chinese Racial-Nationalism: Sex/Gender, Reproduction, and Metaphors of Pathology." Trans. R. Chan, Roy, S. S. Yam. *Positions Politics*. https://positionspolitics.org/kun-huang-anti-black ness-in-chinese-racial-nationalism-sex-gender-reproduction-and-metaphors -of-pathology/.

Huang, Yanzhong. 2014. "The 2008 Milk Scandal Revisited." *Forbes*, July 16. https://www.forbes.com/sites/yanzhonghuang/2014/07/16/the-2008-milk -scandal-revisited/.

Hunter, Mark. 2010. *Love in the Time of AIDS: Inequality, Gender, and Rights in South Africa*. Bloomington: Indiana University Press.

Ingraham, Chrys. 1994. "The Heterosexual Imaginary: Feminist Sociology and Theories of Gender." *Sociological Theory* 12(2):203.

Ip, Po Keung. 2009. "Is Confucianism Good for Business Ethics in China?" *Journal of Business Ethics* 88(3):463–76.

Jeffreys, Elaine. 2008. "Advanced Producers or Moral Polluters? China's Bureaucrat-Entrepreneurs and Sexual Corruption." In D. Goodman, ed., *The New Rich in China: Future Rulers, Present Lives*, 243–91. London: Routledge.

Jeffreys, Elaine, and Wang Pan. 2013. "The Rise of Chinese-Foreign Marriage in Mainland China, 1979–2010." *China Information* 27(3):347–69.

Ji, Yingchun, Xiaogang Wu, Shengwei Sun, and Guangye He. 2017. "Unequal Care, Unequal Work: Toward a More Comprehensive Understanding of Gender Inequality in Post-Reform Urban China." *Sex Roles* 77(11–12):765–78.

Jiang, Quanbao, and Jesus J. Sanchez-Barricarte. "Bride Price in China: The Obstable to 'Bare Branches' Seeking Marriage." *History of the Family* 7(1):2–15.

Jin, Hong. 2012. "The Politics of Intimacy: Chinese Women's Marriage Migration to South Korea." PhD diss., University of Hong Kong.

Jones, Gavin, and Hsiu-hua Shen. 2008. "International Marriage in East and Southeast Asia: Trends and Research Emphases." *Citizenship Studies* 12(1):9–25.

Kang, Miliann. 2003. "The Managed Hand: The Commercialization of Bodies and Emotions in Korean Immigrant–Owned Nail Salons." *Gender & Society* 17(6):820–39.

Kawaguchi, Daiji, and Soohyung Lee. 2017. "Brides for Sale: Cross-Border Marriages and Female Immigration." *Economic Inquiry* 55(2):633–54.

Kay Hoang, Kimberly. 2010. "Economies of Emotion, Familiarity, Fantasy, and Desire: Emotional Labor in Ho Chi Minh City's Sex Industry." *Sexualities* 13(2):255–72.

Kay Hoang, Kimberly. 2011. "'She's Not a Low-Class Dirty Girl!' Sex Work in Ho Chi Minh City, Vietnam." *Journal of Contemporary Ethnography* 40(4):367–96.

Kim, Allen, and Karen Pyke. 2015. "Taming Tiger Dads: Hegemonic American Masculinity and South Korea's Father School." *Gender & Society* 29(4):509–33.

Kim, Elaine H. 1984. "Asian American Writers: A Bibliographical Review." *American Studies International* 22(2):41–78.

Kim, Minjeong. 2010. "Gender and International Marriage Migration." *Sociology Compass* 4(9):718–31.

Kim, Nadia Y. 2006. "'Patriarchy Is So Third World': Korean Immigrant Women and 'Migrating' White Western Masculinity." *Social Problems* 53(4):519–36.

Kimmel, Michael S. 2005. "Globalization and Its Mal(e)Contents: The Gendered Moral and Political Economy of Terrorism." In M. Kimmel, J. Hearn, and R. W. Connell, eds., *Handbook of Studies on Men & Masculinities*, 414–31. Thousand Oaks, CA: Sage Publications.

Kojima, Yu. 2001. "In the Business of Cultural Reproduction: Theoretical Implications of the Mail-Order Bride Phenomenon." *Women's Studies International Forum* 24(2):199–210.

Kong, Travis S. K. 2017. "Sex and Work on the Move: Money Boys in Post-Socialist China." *Urban Studies* 54(3):678–94.

Kuah-Pearce, Khun Eng, ed. 2008. *Chinese Women and the Cyberspace.* Amsterdam: Amsterdam University Press.

Lan, Pei-Chia. 2008. "New Global Politics of Reproductive Labor: Gendered Labor and Marriage Migration." *Sociology Compass* 2(6):1801–15.

Lan, Pei-Chia. 2011. "White Privilege, Language Capital and Cultural Ghettoisation: Western High-Skilled Migrants in Taiwan." *Journal of Ethnic and Migration Studies* 37(10):1669–93.

Lang, Graeme, and Josephine Smart. 2006. "Migration and the 'Second Wife' in

South China: Toward Cross-Border Polygyny (1)." *International Migration Review* 36(2):546–69.

Lee, Anru. 2007. "Subways as a Space of Cultural Intimacy: The Mass Rapid Transit System in Taipei, Taiwan." *China Journal* 58:31–55.

Le Espiritu, Yen. 2001. "'We Don't Sleep around Like White Girls Do': Family, Culture, and Gender in Filipina American Lives." *Signs* 26(2):415–40.

Levitt, Peggy. 2004. "Salsa and Ketchup: Transnational Migrants Straddle Two Worlds." *Contexts* 3(2):20–26.

Levitt, Peggy, and B. Nadya Jaworsky. 2007. "Transnational Migration Studies: Past Developments and Future Trends." *Annual Review of Sociology* 33(1):129–56.

Li, Li. 2008. "The 'Me Generation.'" *Beijing Review*. http://www .bjreview.com .cn/print/txt/2008–02/03/content_100662.htm.

Li, Norman P., J. Michael Bailey, Douglas T. Kenrick, and Joan A. W. Linsenmeier. 2002. "The Necessities and Luxuries of Mate Preferences: Testing the Tradeoffs." *Journal of Personality and Social Psychology* 82(6):947–55.

Li, Shi, John Whallet, and Chunbing Xing. 2014. "China's Higher Education Expansion and Unemployment of College Graduates." *China Economic Review* 30:567–82.

Lin, Jing. 2003. "Chinese Women under Economic Reform: Gains and Losses." *Harvard Asia Pacific Review* 7(1):88–90.

Lin, Xiaodong. 2019. "Young Rural–Urban Migrant Fathers in China: Everyday 'China Dream' and the Negotiation of Masculinity." *NORMA* 14(3):168–82.

Link, E. Perry, Richard Madsen, and Paul Pickowicz, eds. 2013. *Restless China*. Lanham, MD: Rowman & Littlefield.

Liu, Haoming. 2011. "Economic Reforms and Gender Inequality in Urban China." *Economic Development and Cultural Change* 59(4):839–76.

Liu, Melinda. 2001. "Second Wives Club." *Newsweek*. https://www.newsweek .com/second-wives-club-155079.

Liu, Monica. 2015. "Surrogate Dating and the Translation of Gendered Meanings across Borders: The Case of China's E-Mail-Order Brides." *Signs: Journal of Women in Culture and Society* 41(1):29–53.

Livingston, Gretchen. 2014. *Four-in-Ten Couples Are Saying "I Do," Again*. Pew Research Center's Social & Demographic Trends Project. https://www .pewsocialtrends.org/2014/11/14/four-in-ten-couples-are-saying-i-do-again/.

Logan, Trevon D. 2010. "Personal Characteristics, Sexual Behaviors, and Male Sex Work: A Quantitative Approach." *American Sociological Review* 75(5):679–704.

Luehrmann, Sonja. 2004. "Mediated Marriage: Internet Matchmaking in Provincial Russia." *Europe-Asia Studies* 56(6):857–75.

Mahler, Sarah J., and Patricia R. Pessar. 2006. "Gender Matters: Ethnographers Bring Gender from the Periphery toward the Core of Migration Studies." *International Migration Review* 40(1):27–63.

Mann, Susan. 2000. "Presidential Address: Myths of Asian Womanhood." *Journal of Asian Studies* 59(4):835–62.

Massey, Douglas S., Joaquin Arango, Graeme Hugo, Ali Kouaouci, and Adela Pellegrino. 1999. *Worlds in Motion: Understanding International Migration at the End of the Millennium*. Oxford: Clarendon Press.

McLelland, Mark J. 2000. "The Love between 'Beautiful Boys' in Japanese Women's Comics." *Journal of Gender Studies* 9(1):13–25.

Merkle, Erich R., and Rhonda A. Richardson. 2000. "Digital Dating and Virtual Relating: Conceptualizing Computer Mediated Romantic Relationships." *Family Relations* 49(2):187–92.

Merton, Robert K. 1941. "Intermarriage and the Social Structure: Fact and Theory." *Psychiatry* 4:361–74.

Meszaros, Julia. 2018. "Race, Space, and Agency in the International Introduction Industry: How American Men Perceive Women's Agency in Colombia, Ukraine and the Philippines." *Gender, Place, and Culture: A Journal of Feminist Geography* 25(2):268–87.

Miller, Toby. 1998. "Commodifying the Male Body, Problematizing 'Hegemonic Masculinity'?" *Journal of Sport and Social Issues* 22(4):431–46.

Mohanty, Chandra Talpade. 1984. "Under Western Eyes: Feminist Scholarship and Colonial Discourses." *Boundary 2* 12(3):333–58.

Mohanty, Chandra Talpade. 2003. " 'Under Western Eyes' Revisited: Feminist Solidarity through Anticapitalist Struggles." *Signs: Journal of Women in Culture and Society* 28(2):499–535.

Mojola, Sanyu A. 2014. "Providing Women, Kept Men: Doing Masculinity in the Wake of the African HIV/AIDS Pandemic." *Signs: Journal of Women in Culture and Society* 39(2):341–63.

Momesso, Lara. 2016. "Marriage Migration and State Interests: Reflections from the Experiences of Marriage Migrants from the People's Republic of China in Taiwan." *Asiatische Studien—Études Asiatiques* 70(3): 903–20.

Monto, Martin A., and Anna G. Carey. 2014. "A New Standard of Sexual Behavior? Are Claims Associated with the 'Hookup Culture' Supported by General Social Survey Data?" *Journal of Sex Research* 51(6):605–15.

Moore, Mignon R. 2008. "Gendered Power Relations among Women: A Study of Household Decision Making in Black, Lesbian Stepfamilies." *American Sociological Review* 73(2):335–56.

Moore, Mignon R., and Michael Stambolis-Ruhstorfer. 2013. "LGBT Sexuality and Families at the Start of the Twenty-First Century." *Annual Review of Sociology* 39(1):491–507.

Morgan, Stephen L. 2000. "Richer and Taller: Stature and Living Standards in China, 1979–1995." *China Journal* 44:1–39.

Moses, Julia, and Julia Woesthoff. 2019. "Romantic Relationships across Boundaries: Global and Comparative Perspectives." *History of the Family* 24(3):439–65.

Mu, Zheng, and Yu Xie. 2014. "Marital Age Homogamy in China: A Reversal of Trend in the Reform Era?" *Social Science Research* 44:141–57.

Novikova, I. 2000. "Soviet and Post-Soviet Masculinities: After Men's Wars in Women's Memories." In I. Breines, R. Connell, and I. Eide, eds., *Male Roles, Masculinities and Violence: A Culture of Peace Perspective*, 117–29. Paris: UNESCO.

Osburg, John. 2013. *Anxious Wealth: Money and Morality among China's New Rich.* Stanford: Stanford University Press.

Otis, Eileen M. 2008. "Beyond the Industrial Paradigm: Market-Embedded Labor and the Gender Organization of Global Service Work in China." *American Sociological Review* 73(1):15–36.

Otis, Eileen. 2012. *Markets and Bodies: Women, Service Work, and the Making of Inequality in China.* Stanford: Stanford University Press.

Padilla, Mark B. 2007. "'Western Union Daddies' and Their Quest for Authenticity: An Ethnographic Study of the Dominican Gay Sex Tourism Industry." *Journal of Homosexuality* 53(1–2):241–75.

Parish, William, and Sarah Brusse. 2000. "Gender and Work." In W. Tang and W. L. Parish, eds., *Chinese and Urban Life under Reform: The Changing Social Contract*, 209–31. Cambridge: Cambridge University Press.

Pessar, Patricia R., and Sarah J. Mahler. 2003. "Transnational Migration: Bringing Gender In." *International Migration Review* 37(3):812–46.

Pfeffer, Carla A. 2010. "'Women's Work'? Women Partners of Transgender Men Doing Housework and Emotion Work." *Journal of Marriage and Family* 72(1):165–83.

Pfeffer, Carla A. 2014. "'I Don't Like Passing as a Straight Woman': Queer Negotiations of Identity and Social Group Membership." *American Journal of Sociology* 120(1):1–44.

Pimentel, Ellen Efron. 2000. "Just How Do I Love Thee? Marital Relations in Urban China." *Journal of Marriage and Family* 62(1):32–47.

Ponzini, Adrianna. 2020. Educating the New Chinese Middle-Class Youth: The Role of Quality Education on Ideas of Class and Status." *Journal of Chinese Sociology* 7(1).

Portes, Alejandro, and Ruben G. Rumbaut. 2006. *Immigrant America: A Portrait.* Berkeley: University of California Press.

Press, Julie E. 2004. "Cute Butts and Housework: A Gynocentric Theory of Assortative Mating." *Journal of Marriage and Family* 66(4):1029–33.

Pyke, Karen D., and Denise L. Johnson. 2003. "Asian American Women and Racialized Femininities: 'Doing' Gender across Cultural Worlds." *Gender & Society* 17(1):33–53.

Randles, Jennifer M. 2013. "Repackaging the 'Package Deal': Promoting Marriage for Low-Income Families by Targeting Paternal Identity and Reframing Marital Masculinity." *Gender & Society* 27(6):864–88.

Raymo, James M., and Miho Iwasawa. 2005. "Marriage Market Mismatches in Japan: An Alternative View of the Relationship between Women's Education and Marriage." *American Sociological Review* 70(5):801–22.

The Richest. 2012. "World's Richest Self-Made Women Billionaires." https://www.therichest.com/world/forbes-richest-self-made-women-billionaires.

Ridgeway, Cecilia L., and Lynn Smith-Lovin. 1999. "The Gender System and Interaction." *Annual Review of Sociology* 25(1):191–216.

Robinson, Kathryn. 1996. "Of Mail-Order Brides and 'Boys' Own' Tales: Representations of Asian-Australian Marriages." *Feminist Review* (52):53–68.

Rosen, Stanley. 2004. "The Victory of Materialism: Aspirations to Join China's Urban Moneyed Classes and the Commercialization of Education." *China Journal* 51:27–51.

Rosenfeld, Michael J. 2005. "A Critique of Exchange Theory in Mate Selection." *American Journal of Sociology* 110(5):1284–1325.

Ru, Xin, Xueyi Lu, and Peilin Li, eds. 2010. *Blue Book of China's Society: Society of China Analysis and Forecast (2010).* Beijing: Social Sciences Academic Press.

Santos, Gonçalo, and Stevan Harrell. 2017. *Transforming Patriarchy: Chinese Families in the Twenty-First Century.* Seattle: University of Washington Press.

Schaeffer-Grabiel, Felicity. 2006a. "Flexible Technologies of Subjectivity and Mobility across the Americas." *American Quarterly* 58(3): 891–914.

Schaeffer-Grabiel, Felicity. 2006b. "Planet-Love.com: Cyberbrides in the Americas and the Transnational Routes of U.S. Masculinity." *Signs: Journal of Women in Culture and Society* 31(2):331–56.

Schaeffer[-Grabiel], Felicity. 2013. *Love and Empire: Cybermarriage and Citizenship across the Americas.* New York: New York University Press.

Schwartz, Christine R. 2010. "Earnings Inequality and the Changing Association between Spouses' Earnings." *American Journal of Sociology* 115(5):1524–57.

Schwartz, Christine R. 2013. "Trends and Variation in Assortative Mating: Causes and Consequences." *Annual Review of Sociology* 39(1):451–70.

Schwartz, Christine R., and Hongyun Han. 2014. "The Reversal of the Gender Gap in Education and Trends in Marital Dissolution." *American Sociological Review* 79(4):605–29.

Shaw, Ping, and Yue Tan. 2014. "Race and Masculinity: A Comparison of Asian and Western Models in Men's Lifestyle Magazine Advertisements." *Journalism & Mass Communication Quarterly* 91(1):118–38.

Shi, Lihong. 2017. *Choosing Daughters: Family Change in Rural China.* Stanford: Stanford University Press.

Shu, Xiaoling. 2004. "Education and Gender Egalitarianism: The Case of China." *Sociology of Education* 77(4):311–36.

Shu, Xiaoling. 2005. "Market Transition and Gender Segregation in Urban China." *Social Science Quarterly* 86(1): 1299–1323.

Silva, Tony. 2017. "Bud-Sex: Constructing Normative Masculinity among Rural Straight Men That Have Sex with Men." *Gender & Society* 31(1):51–73.

Siu, Kaxton. 2015. "Continuity and Change in the Everyday Lives of Chinese Migrant Factory Workers." *China Journal* 74:43–65.

Slater, Dan. 2013. *Love in the Time of Algorithms: What Technology Does to Meeting and Mating.* New York: Penguin.

Smith, Jim. 2017. *The Lazy Teacher's Handbook.* Carmarthen, UK: Crown House Publishing.

Snyder, R. Claire. 2008. "What Is Third-Wave Feminism? A New Directions Essay." *Signs: Journal of Women in Culture and Society* 34(1):175–96.

Song, Geng, and Derek Hird. 2014. *Men and Masculinities in Contemporary China.* Leiden: Brill.

Song, Geng, and Tracy K. Lee. 2010. "Consumption, Class Formation and Sexuality: Reading Men's Lifestyle Magazines in China." *China Journal* 64:159–77.

Song, Geng, and Tracy K. Lee. 2012. "'New Man' and 'New Lad' with Chinese Characteristics? Cosmopolitanism, Cultural Hybridity and Men's Lifestyle Magazines in China." *Asian Studies Review* 36(3):345–67.

Song, Shaopeng. 2011. "The Private Embedded in the Public: The State's Discourse on Domestic Work, 1949–1966" (in Chinese). *Research on Women in Modern Chinese History* 19:131–72.

Song, Shaopeng. 2012. "From Visible to Invisible: Housework in the Collectivist Period (1949–1966)" (in Chinese). *Jiangsu Social Sciences* 1:116–25.

Stack, Carol B. 1974. *All Our Kin: Strategies for Survival in a Black Community.* New York: Harper & Row.

Stanley, Phiona. 2012. "Superheroes in Shanghai: Constructing Transnational Western Men's Identities." *Gender, Place & Culture* 19(2):213–31.

Stark, Oded, and J. Edward Taylor. 1989. "Relative Deprivation and International Migration." *Demography* 26(1):1–14.

Starr, Emily, and Michele Adams. 2016. "The Domestic Exotic: Mail-Order Brides and the Paradox of Globalized Intimacies." *Signs: Journal of Women in Culture and Society* 41(4):953–75.

Stewart, Matthew. 2018. "The 9.9 Percent Is the New American Aristocracy." *Atlantic*, June. https://www.theatlantic.com/magazine/archive/2018/06/the-birth-of-a-new-american-aristocracy/559130/.

Streib, Jessi. 2020. *Privilege Lost: Who Leaves the Upper Middle Class and How They Fall.* New York: Oxford University Press.

Su, Lianling. 2012. "Cross-Border Marriage Migration of Vietnamese Women to China." Master's thesis, Kansas State University.

Sumra, Monika. 2019. "Masculinity, Femininity, and Leadership: Taking a Closer Look at the Alpha Female." *PLOS ONE* 14:e0215181.

Sweeney, Megan M. 2002. "Two Decades of Family Change: The Shifting Economic Foundations of Marriage." *American Sociological Review* 67(1):132–47.

Tajima, Renee E. 1989. "Lotus Blossoms Don't Bleed: Images of Asian Women." Pp. 308–17 In Asian Women United of California, ed., *Making Waves: An Anthology of Writings by and about Asian American Women.* Boston: Beacon Press.

Tang, Wenfang, and William L. Parish. 2000. *Chinese Urban Life under Reform: The Changing Social Contract.* Cambridge: Cambridge University Press.

Terry, Olufemi. 2019. "China's Woman Shortage Creates an International Problem." *ShareAmerica.* https://share.america.gov/dire-effects-of-chinas-woman-shortage/.

Thatcher, Melvin P. 1991. "Marriages of the Ruling Elite in the Spring and Autumn Period." In R. Watson and P. B. Ebrey, eds., *Marriage and Inequality in Chinese Society.* doi:10.1525/california/9780520069305.003.0002.

Thompson, Karl. 2017. "Modernisation Theory Applied to Gender Inequality." *ReviseSociology.* https://revisesociology.com/2017/03/22/modernisation-theory-applied-to-gender-inequality/.

Thornton, Arland, and Hui-sheng Lin. 1994. *Social Change and the Family in Taiwan.* Chicago: University of Chicago Press.

Tian, Xiaoli, and Yunxue Deng. 2017. "Organizational Hierarchy, Deprived Masculinity, and Confrontational Practices: Men Doing Women's Jobs in a Global Factory." *Journal of Contemporary Ethnography* 46(4):464–89.

To, Sandy. 2013. "Understanding *Sheng Nu* ('Leftover Women'): The Phenomenon of Late Marriage among Chinese Professional Women." *Symbolic Interaction* 36(1):1–20.

Treiman, Donald J. 2013. "Trends in Educational Attainment in China." *Chinese Sociological Review* 45(3):3–25.

Tsang, Eileen Yuk-Ha. 2019. "Reciprocating Desires: The Pursuit of Desirable East Asian Femininity in China's Commercial Sex Industry." *Deviant Behavior* 3F:1–19.

US Census Bureau. 2013. "American Community Survey 2013–2017 5-Year Data Release." https://www.census.gov/library/publications/2014/acs/acsbr13-02.html.

US Census Bureau. 2015. "Current Population Survey Annual Social and Economic Supplements" (CPS ASEC). https://www.census.gov/programs-surveys/cps.html.

Uretsky, Elanah. 2008. "'Mobile Men with Money': The Socio-Cultural and Politico-Economic Context of 'High-Risk' Behaviour among Wealthy Businessmen and Government Officials in Urban China." *Culture, Health & Sexuality* 10(8):801–14.

Väänänen, Ari, May V. Kevin, Leena Ala-Mursula, Jaana Pentti, Mika Kivimäki, and Jussi Vahtera. 2005. "The Double Burden of and Negative Spillover between Paid and Domestic Work: Associations with Health among Men and Women." *Women & Health* 40(3):1–18.

Villapando, Venny. 1989. "The Business of Selling Mail-Order Brides." In Asian Women United of California, ed., *Making Waves: An Anthology of Writings by and about Asian American Women*, 308–17. Boston: Beacon Press.

Vora, Kalindi. 2010. "The Transmission of Care: Effective Economies and Indian Call Centers." In E. Boris and R. S. Parreñas, eds., *Intimate Labors: Cultures, Technologies, and the Politics of Care*, 33–48. Stanford: Stanford University Press.

Wade, Lisa, and Myra Marx Ferree. 2019. *Gender: Ideas, Interactions, Institutions*. 2d ed. New York: W. W. Norton & Co.

Wang, Hong-zen, and Shu-ming Chang. 2002. "The Commodification of International Marriages: Cross-Border Marriage Business in Taiwan and Viet Nam." *International Migration* 40(6):93–116.

Wasserstrom, Jeffrey. 2014. "China and Globalization." *Daedalus* 143(2):157–69.

Watson, Rubie S. 2004. "Families in China: Ties That Bind?" Paper presented at conference, "The Family Model in Chinese Art and Culture," Princeton University, 6–7 November. http://catalog.ihsn.org/index.php/citations/51424.

Watson, Rubie S., Patricia Buckley Ebrey, and Joint Committee on Chinese Studies (US), eds. 1991. *Marriage and Inequality in Chinese Society.* Berkeley: University of California Press.

Wei, X., F. Meng, and P. Zhang. 2017. "Chinese Citizens' Outbound Destination Choice: Objective and Subjective Factors." *International Journal of Tourism Research* 19(1):38–49.

Whyte, Martin King. 2005. "Continuity and Change in Urban Chinese Family Life." *China Journal* 53:9–33.

Whyte, Martin King. 2012. "China's Post-Socialist Inequality." *Current History* 111(746):229–34.

Wolf, Margery. 1985. *Revolution Postponed: Women in Contemporary China.* Stanford: Stanford University Press.

Wolf, Wendy C., and Maurice M. MacDonald. 1979. "The Earnings of Men and Remarriage." *Demography* 16(3):389–99.

Wong, Alexandra. 2016. "Transnational Real Estate in Australia: New Chinese Diaspora, Media Representation and Urban Transformation in Sydney's Chinatown." *International Journal of Housing Policy* 17(1): 97–119.

Worldometer. n.d. "Coronavirus Update (Live)." https://www.worldometers .info/coronavirus/.

Wu, Angela, and Yige Dong. 2019. "What Is Made-in-China Feminism(s)? Gender Discontent and Class Friction in a Post-socialist China." *Critical Asian Studies* 51(4):471–92.

Wu, Jing. 2003. "From '*Long Yang*' and '*Dui Shi*' to Tongzhi: Homosexuality in China." *Journal of Gay & Lesbian Psychotherapy* 7(1–2):117–43.

Wu, X., and Z. Zhang. 2010. "Changes in Educational Inequality in China, 1990–2005: Evidence from the Population Census Data." *Research in Sociology of Education* 17:123–52.

Xiao, Suowei. 2011. "The 'Second-Wife' Phenomenon and the Relational Construction of Class-Coded Masculinities in Contemporary China." *Men and Masculinities* 14(5):607–27.

Xie, Yu. 2013. "Gender and Family Formation in Contemporary China." *PSC Research Report* (13):808–10.

Xie, Yu, and Xiang Zhou. 2014. "Income Inequality in Today's China." *Proceedings of the National Academy of Science of the United States of America* 111(19):6928–33.

Xie, Yuanchun. 2010. "The Linguistic Interpretation of Web Word 'Economic and Practical Man.'" *Journal of Ningbo Radio and TV University* 8:1–4.

Xu, Gary, and Susan Feiner. 2007. "Meinü Jingji: China's Beauty Economy:

Buying Looks, Shifting Value, and Changing Places." *Feminist Economics* 13(3–4):307–23.

Xu, Jing. 2017. *The Good Child: Moral Development in a Chinese Preschool*. Stanford: Stanford University Press.

Xu, Xiaohe, Jianjun Ji, and Yuk-Ying Tung. 2000. "Social and Political Assortative Mating in Urban China." *Journal of Family Issues* 21(1):47–77.

Yamaura, Chigusa. 2015a. "From Manchukuo to Marriage: Localizing Contemporary Cross-Border Marriages between Japan and Northeast China." *Journal of Asian Studies* 74(3):565–88.

Yamaura, Chigusa. 2015b. "Marrying Transnational, Desiring Local: Making 'Marriageable Others' in Japanese–Chinese Cross-Border Matchmaking." *Anthropological Quarterly* 88(4):1029–58.

Yan, Yunxiang. 2002. "Courtship, Love and Premarital Sex in a North China Village." *China Journal* 48:29–53.

Yan, Yunxiang. 2009. "Conclusion: The Individualization of Chinese Society." Presented at International Symposium on "The Rising Individuals and the Collective Morality: Social Transformation of Greater China in the Globalisation Age," 14 April.

Yan, Yunxiang, Arthur Kleinman Jing Jun, Sing Lee, Everett Zhang, Pan Tianshu, Wu Fei, and Guo Jinhua. 2011. *Deep China: The Moral Life of the Person: What Anthropology and Psychiatry Tell Us about China Today*. Berkeley: University of California Press.

Yang, Jie. 2007. "Re-employment Stars: Language, Gender and Neoliberal Restructuring in China." In B. S. McElhinny, ed., *Words, Worlds, and Material Girls: Language, Gender, Globalization*, 77–105. Berlin: Mouton de Gruyter.

Yang, Jie. 2011. "*Nennu* and *Shunu* : Gender, Body Politics, and the Beauty Economy in China." *Signs: Journal of Women in Culture and Society* 36(2):333–57.

Yang, Mayfair Mei-hui. 1994. *Gifts, Favors, and Banquets: The Art of Social Relationships in China*. Ithaca: Cornell University Press.

Yang, Mayfair Mei-hui. 1999. "From Gender Erasure to Gender Difference: State Feminism, Consumer Sexuality, and Women's Public Sphere in China." In Yang, *Spaces of Their Own: Women's Public Sphere in Transnational China*. Minneapolis: University of Minnesota Press.

Yang, Wen-Shan, and Melody Chia-Wen Lu, eds. 2010. *Asian Cross-Border Marriage Migration: Demographic Patterns and Social Issues*. Amsterdam: Amsterdam University Press.

Yarbrough, Michael W. 2018. "Very Long Engagements: The Persistent Authority of Bridewealth in a Post-Apartheid South African Community." *Law and Social Inquiry*: 43(3):647–77.

Yu, An, and Hoi K. Suen. 2005. "Historical and Contemporary Exam-Driven Education Fever in China." *KEDI Journal of Educational Policy* 2(1):17–33.

Yu, Jia, and Yu Xie. 2013. "Changes in the Determinants of Marriage Entry in Post-Reform Urban China." PSC Research Report 13–802 (September). Ann Arbor: University of Michigan.

Yuen, Nancy Wang. 2016. *Reel Inequality: Hollywood Actors and Racism*. Brunswick, NJ: Rutgers University Press.

Zeng, Junxia, Xiaopeng Pang, Linxiu Zhang, Alexis Medina, and Scott Rozelle. 2014. "Gender Inequality in Education in China: A Meta-Regression Analysis." *Contemporary Economic Policy* 32(2):474–91.

Zhang, Charlie Y. 2014. "Deconstructing National and Transnational Hypermasculine Hegemony in Neoliberal China." *Feminist Studies* 40(1):13–28.

Zhang, Chong, Xueyi Wang, and Dan Zhang. 2014. "Urbanization, Employment Rate and China's Rising Divorce Rate." *Chinese Journal of Population Resources and Environment* 12(2):157–64.

Zhang, Everett Yuehong. 2007. "The Birth of *Nanke* (Men's Medicine) in China: The Making of the Subject of Desire." *American Ethnologist* 34(3):491–508.

Zhang, Hong, Fei Teng, Darius K. S. Chan, and Denghao Zhang. 2014. "Physical Attractiveness, Attitudes toward Career, and Mate Preferences among Young Chinese Women." *Evolutionary Psychology* 12(1):97–114.

Zhang, Li. 2010. *In Search of Paradise: Middle-class Living in a Chinese Metropolis*. Ithaca: Cornell University Press.

Zhang, Weiguo. 2008. "State, Gender and Uxorilocal Marriage in Contemporary Rural North China." *China Journal* 60:111–32.

Zheng, Tiantian. 2006. "Cool Masculinity: Male Clients' Sex Consumption and Business Alliance in Urban China's Sex Industry." *Journal of Contemporary China* 15(46):161–82.

Zhou, Mucun, and Jin Lin. 2009. "China's Graduates' Employment: The Impact of the Financial Crises." *International Higher Education* 55.

Zhou, Xiao. 1989. "Virginity and Premarital Sex in Contemporary China." *Feminist Studies* 15(2):279–88.

Zulehner, Paul, and Rainer Volz. 1998. *Maenner im Aufbruch: Wie Deutschlands Maenner sich selbst und wie Frauen sie sehen. Ein Forschungsbericht* [Men in Emergence: How German Men See Themselves and How Women See Them: A Research Report]. Ostfildern: Schwabenverlag.

Zuo, J., and Y. Jiang. 2009. *Urban Women's Work and Family in Social Transition* (in Chinese). Beijing: Contemporary China Publishing House

Zurndorfer, Harriet. 2016. "Men, Women, Money, and Morality: The Development of China's Sexual Economy." *Feminist Economics* 22(2):1–23.

Zurndorfer, Harriet. 2018. "Escape from the Country: The Gender Politics of Chinese Women in Pursuit of Transnational Romance." *Gender, Place & Culture* 25(4):489–506.

Index

Note: page numbers followed by "f," "t," and "n" refer to figures, tables, and endnotes, respectively.

age-class-gender intersection, 57–58

age discrimination: erotic capital and, 55; marriage market and, 16; mistresses and, 53; as motive, 38–40; in service sector, 61

agencies. *See* dating agencies

agency as personal economic security, 119–20

bamboo ceiling, 114

beauty economy market practices, 13–14, 61, 158

Berg, Bruce, 28

breadwinner/homemaker model. *See* domesticity and breadwinner/ homemaker model

bride price, 85, 206n13

children's education. *See* education of children

China, Maoist/socialist: Cultural Revolution, 167, 201n3; double burden on women, 57, 75, 119; gender ideology, 128; labor market participation and social services, 13, 92; private property, prohibition against, 29, 92, 96; traditional values uprooted by, 167

China, postreform or postsocialist: entrepreneurial C-fem and, 119; female infidelity and, 170–71; gender ideology in, 14, 41, 57–58, 75–76; global rise of, 16–17, 21–22, 114; "iron rice bowl," smashing of, 67, 205n46; labor market shifts, 13–14; layoffs at state-owned

China (*cont*)
   enterprises, 13, 59, 207n16; moneymaking and materialism as public
   values in, 167; moral crisis in, 166–
   67, 170–71; patriarchy, changes
   to, 13; real GDP per capita, 201n7;
   structural inequality in, 33, 36,
   57–58, 92
China Doll stereotype, 140
class: billionaires, 114, 206n11;
   downward social mobility, 59,
   64, 68, 161, 190–91; increasing
   significance of, in mate selection,
   111–12; intersection with age and
   gender, 57–58; marriage rate and,
   74; "marrying up" vs. "marrying
   down," 57–58; masculinity and,
   41, 96, 207n2; mismatch in class
   positions, 75; nationality vs., 37,
   69; race, relationship with, 21–22,
   96, 113–14, 192–93; upward social
   mobility, 20–21, 44, 58, 62–63, 147,
   184–86, 190. *See also* financially
   burdened women; financially
   flexible women
Constable, Nicole, 141
contingent employment sector, 58–63
COVID-19 pandemic, 197–99
cultural capital, 152, 161, 180–81
Cultural Revolution, 167, 201n3

dating agencies: balancing profit
   with conscience, 174–79; courtship process, 11–13, 12f; COVID-
   19 pandemic and, 197–99; fee
   structure, 11, 169, 196; female client
   demographics, 5f, 37–38; financial
   pressure, quotas, and competitive

culture, 168; future of, 199; legal
   status and threat of shut-downs,
   169; male client demographics, 17,
   19t, 76, 208n11; men's complaints
   and negative reviews, fear of,
   171; moral regulation by, 171–74;
   post-1980s generation and, 194–95;
   power imbalance with Western
   companies, 168–69; professional
   training, lack of, 183; as relationship counseling centers, 6;
   responses to provider-love expectations, 85–89; turnover rate, 166,
   183; upward mobility and, 184–86;
   WeChat app, translation software,
   and, 196–97. *See also* marriage
   industry, global; translators
dating agency managers: Mr. Li case,
   6, 87, 183, 185; Ms. Fong case, 2–3,
   6–8, 29, 76, 85–86, 88, 108, 168, 177,
   183, 186–88, 195–97; Ms. Mei case,
   3, 6, 90–91, 156–57, 171–75, 178–79,
   183, 186
debt, 38, 63–65
Deng Xiaoping, 21, 46, 167
division of labor, gendered. *See* gendered division of labor
divorce laws in China, 170
divorce rates in China, 14, 42
domesticity and breadwinner/
   homemaker model: emphasized
   femininity and, 116, 117, 120, 130,
   133; entrepreneurial C-fem and,
   118–20, 122, 128, 130, 138; gender
   difference and, 57; individual- vs.
   group-level analysis and, 139–41;
   Joanne and Frederick case, 115–16,
   120–28, 133; Lindsay and Henry

case, 134–38; in postreform China, 75, 118, 206n3; separate spheres ideology, 82, 86–87, 127, 207n16; Susan and Tony case, 128–34; Western feminism and, 117. *See also* patriarchal bargain

Dong, Yige, 14

du suzhi (low quality), 208n10

Eastern Europe, 24

education of children: Beth and Edmond case, 155; Chinese expenditure on, 205n42; financially burdened women and, 64–66; Joanne and Frederick case, 122–23; as motive, 38, 39t

eHarmony, 15, 189

emotional labor, 179–83

emphasized femininity, 53, 116, 117, 120, 130, 133

English major graduates in China, 184, 211n28

entrepreneurial C-feminism: about, 14–15; breadwinner/homemaker model and, 118–20, 122, 128, 130, 138; Chinese modernization and, 24; controlling men's wallets, 149, 160, 191; gender equality, notion of, 16; marital dissatisfaction and, 160–61; physical appearance of women and, 154; social conditions in China vs. structural realities in U.S. and, 147; working brides and, 144, 147, 149, 154, 159–61

erotic capital: defined, 50, 101, 208n9; mistresses and, 50–51; as resource, 55; sexual competence, 103; trans-

national business masculinity and, 101, 103

family man image, 72–73, 75, 76, 112, 195

Farrer, James, 170–71

female clients. *See* financially burdened women; financially flexible women

femininity: bodies as commodities, 42; conventional, desire for, 16–17; emphasized, 53, 116, 117, 120, 130, 133; in postsocialist China, 14, 41; shared expenses as insult to, 87–88. *See also* gender

feminism, Chinese. *See* entrepreneurial C-feminism; noncooparative C-fem

feminism, Western or global, 17–18, 23–24, 191

financially burdened women: about, 23, 38; Beth case, 66, 153–56, 172; Daisy case, 36, 59–61, 156–60; debt and, 63–65; Emily case, 148–53; gender and labor market inequality and, 68; Joanne case, 64–65, 115–16, 120–28, 133, 164; Julia case, 173; Lindsay case, 63–64, 134–38; Margot case, 62; marital dissatisfaction and, 160–63; Meredith case, 142–48; Olivia case, 61–62; relative deprivation theory and, 59; Sally case, 177; single mothers, struggling, 64–66; Susan case, 60–61, 128–34; unemployment and low-wage jobs, 58–63; Zeena case, 62–63. *See also* domesticity and breadwinner/homemaker model; working brides

financially flexible women: about, 23,
38, 74; Angel case, 55–56; Anna
case, 89–90; billionaires, female,
206n11; Emma case, 87; gender
inequality and, 67; Grace case,
43–44, 82–83; Jennifer case, 48–54,
83–86, 154; Kristin case, 54–55,
110, 112, 171; Lucy case, 47–48,
111; middle-class professionals,
44–48; mistresses of rich men,
48–55, 83–85; Ms. Mei case, 90–91;
Ruby case, 35, 40–43, 71–74, 77–82;
Vivien case, 45–47, 93–95, 97–110,
178; wealthy women, 40–44, 77–
83; young women, 55–57. See also
provider masculinity; transnational business masculinity
financial support from men. See mistresses; provider masculinity
fiscal irresponsibility of men: as
motive, 38, 39t, 63–64; rejection of
failed Chinese masculinity, 68

gao bu cheng di bu jiu ("unfit for a
higher post and unwilling to take
a lower one"), 52, 58
gao suzhi (high quality), 208n10
gender: breadwinning and, 78; Chinese vs. Eurocentric conception
of gender equality, 16; financial
success and, 41, 67; intersection
with class and age, 57–58; Maoist
ideology, 128; patriarchal bargain and gender equality, 138–39;
social imaginary, gendered, 76–77,
206n8; in socialist vs. postreform
China, 14, 41, 57–58, 75–76. See
also femininity; masculinity;

patriarchal bargain; provider
masculinity
gendered division of labor: provider
masculinity and, 78, 87, 89; Western feminist perspective on, 117.
See also domesticity and bread-
winner/homemaker model
gender ideologies. See domesticity and
breadwinner/homemaker model;
entrepreneurial C-feminism; provider masculinity; transnational
business masculinity
geographic location and marital
satisfaction, 161
global business chain, 10–13, 11f
globalization: affluent capitalist class
under, 16; brides under China's
global rise, 16–17; grooms under
Western decline, 17–20, 190–92;
nationality vs. class and, 37, 69
"golden phoenix," 116–17

Hakim, Catherine, 101
Harvey, David, 16, 37
hegemonic male, 116, 129
Heyl, Barbara Sherman, 28
Hoang, Kimberly, 9
Hochschild, Arlie, 179, 182
homemaking. See domesticity and
breadwinner/homemaker model
home purchases, expectation of, 85,
194, 206n15
hukou (household registration
system), 165

immigration, 37, 204n6
infidelity in China: associated with
Chinese reforms, 41, 75–76; finan-

cially burdened women and, 60–
61; mistresses and, 51; as motive,
38, 39, 39t; self-esteem and, 60; as
socially acceptable in China, 42;
women's rates of, 170–71
intersectionality, 57–58, 68–69, 161
investment banker type, 102, 208n14.
See also transnational business
masculinity

Kimmel, Michael, 91

labor market in China: age discrimination in, 61; beauty economy
market practices, 13–14, 61, 158;
contingent employment sector
and low-wage jobs, 58–63;
inequality in, 68; layoffs, 13, 59,
202n20; postsocialist shifts in, 13–
14; rural workers, discrimination
against, 165
"leftover women" (*sheng nu*), 58,
203n31, 205n33

mail-order bride label, 35, 37
Mao Zedong, 201n3
marriage, agency-mediated: Anna
and Wayne case, 89–90; Beth and
Edmond case, 153–56; Daisy and
Peter case, 156–60; Emily and Joe
case, 148–53; ending in divorce,
108, 109–10; Joanne and Frederick
case, 115–16, 120–28; Lindsay and
Henry case, 134–38; managers
and translators marrying, 90–91,
184; Meredith and Robert case,
142–48; power imbalance between
Chinese and Western companies,

168–69; prenuptial agreements,
28, 131–32, 195, 209n22; rate of, in
financially flexible vs. burdened
women, 74, 161–62; Ruby and
Larry case, 77–82; Susan and
Tony case, 128–34; WeChat app,
translation software, and, 196–97;
Western models of marriage, 18;
women delaying, 107–8
marriage industry, global: COVID-19
pandemic and, 197–99; future of,
199; global business chain, 10–13,
11f; post-1980s generation and,
194–95; size of global business, 8.
See also dating agencies
"marrying up" vs. "marrying down,"
57–58
masculinity: Asian men, historical
stereotype of, 96; consumption of
female youth and sexuality, 41–42;
family man image, 72–73, 75, 76,
112, 195; financial success and, 41,
67; as fluid and situational, 112;
the hegemonic male, 116, 129, 192;
hegemonic power of Western
masculinity in China, 21–22, 113;
height and skin color in China
and, 101; hypermasculine sexuality and class, 207n2; partnership
marriages as threat to, 18; in
postsocialist China, 14, 41; pro-
gressive Western, 75, 91; rejection
of failed Chinese masculinity, 68;
Western men, Chinese ideal of,
71–72; White sexual capital, 96.
See also gender; provider masculinity; transnational business
masculinity

Match.com, 15, 189

men, Western. *See* marriage, agency-mediated; provider masculinity; transnational business masculinity

Meszaros, Julia, 24

middle-class professional women, 44–48

mistresses, 48–55, 83–85. *See also* transnational business masculinity

modernization, Chinese. *See* China, postreform or postsocialist

moral crisis in China, 166–67, 170–71, 210n5

moral regulation, 25, 171–74

moral values vs. profit, 174–79

motives for seeking Western husbands, 38–40, 39t. *See also* financially burdened women; financially flexible women

noncooparative C-fem, 14, 118, 203n31

nursemaids (*yue sao*), 62

One-Child Policy, 14, 118

Osburg, John, 205n46, 206n3

patriarchal bargain: alternative version of, 17; dysfunctional, 121–22, 127–28; emphasized femininity and, 117, 133; entrepreneurial C-fem and, 119–20; equity factors, 138–39; individual- vs. group-level analysis and, 139–41; long-run risks for women, 92; separate spheres ideology and, 127. *See also* domesticity and breadwinner/

homemaker model; gender; provider masculinity

patriarchy, Chinese, 13, 51

"picture bride" stereotype, 4, 179, 201n1

pinwei (taste), 152, 208n10

poverty, 58–59, 143–44

provider masculinity: agency responses to, 85–89; Anna and Wayne case, 89–90; definition of provider love, 78; Emily and Joe case, 150; Emma case, 87; gendered division of labor and, 78, 87, 89; Grace case, 82–83; the happily married minority, 89–91; hybrid masculine ideal, desire for, 91–92; indirect power and, 86–87; Jennifer case, 83–86; Joanne and Frederick case, 116, 127; mistresses and, 83–89; Ms. Mei case, 90–91; as performance among men, 87; postreform revival of traditional patriarchal ideology and, 75–76, 92; Ruby and Larry case, 71–74, 77–82; separate spheres ideology and, 82, 86–87, 207n16; shared expenses and, 87–90, 207n18; social imaginary, gendered, 76–77, 206n8; wealthy women and, 77–83; Western masculinity ideal, 71–73

race: anti-Black prejudice in China, 10, 202n10; class, relationship with, 21–22, 96, 113–14, 192–93; declining privilege associated with, 104; demographics, 10; educational attainment in US and, 208n17; whiteness and White sexual capital, 96, 192–93

relative deprivation theory, 59

Russia, 24

self-esteem, 53, 60, 128

separate spheres ideology, 82, 86–87, 127, 207n16

sexual assault, 105

sexually incompatible marriages: Beth and Edmond case, 153–56; Daisy and Peter case, 156–60; Emily and Joe case, 148–53

shared expenses, 32, 87–90, 192, 207n18

social imaginary, gendered, 76–77, 206n8

social mobility: downward, 59, 64, 68, 161, 190–91; upward, 20–21, 44, 58, 62–63, 147, 184–86, 190

social services, Western, 38, 39t

surrogate dating, 179–83

Thai, Hung Cam, 16

To, Sandy, 205n33

trafficking, human, 11, 169

translators: about, 20–21, 165–66; balancing profit with conscience, 164, 174–79; lack of experience, 183; Lingfang case, 164–66, 185; Liyi case, 177; Ming Ming case, 185; moral crisis in China and, 166–67, 170–71; moral regulation by, 171–74; personal and professional identity, detaching, 182–83; precarious position of, 166–70; role of, 164–65, 167–68; Sisi case, 176–77, 184–85; surrogate dating and emotional labor, 179–83; upward

mobility and, 184–85; Wenli case, 184, 197

transnational business masculinity: about, 95–96; Claire case, 112; confidence, assertiveness, and social skills, 101–4; erotic capital and, 101, 103; few male clients who embodied, 111–12; investment banker type, 102, 208n14; Kristin and Tim case, 110, 112; Lucy and Jin case, 111; race–class relationship and, 113–14; Tiffany, Barry, and Zihan case, 107–8; Vivien, John, and Kuan case, 93–95, 97–110, 178

utilitarian view of marriage. See entrepreneurial C-feminism

Vietnamese brides, 16

Vora, Kalindi, 182

whiteness and white sexual capital, 96, 192–93

working brides: Beth and Edmond case, 153–56; Daisy, Peter, and Anthony case, 156–60; Emily and Joe case, 148–53; entrepreneurial C-feminism and, 144, 147, 149, 154, 159–61; marital dissatisfaction and, 160–63; Meredith and Robert case, 142–48

Wu, Angela, 14

young women, as financially flexible, 55–57

youth culture, Chinese, 9, 180–82

yue sao (nursemaids), 62

Zelizer, Vivana, 9

GLOBALIZATION
IN EVERYDAY LIFE

As global forces undeniably continue to change the politics and economies of the world, we need a more nuanced understanding of what these changes mean in our daily lives. Significant theories and studies have broadened and deepened our knowledge on globalization, yet we need to think about how these macro processes manifest on the ground and how they are maintained through daily actions.

Globalization in Everyday Life foregrounds ethnographic examination of daily life to address issues that will bring tangibility to previously abstract assertions about the global order. Moving beyond mere illustrations of global trends, books in this series underscore mutually constitutive processes of the local and global by finding unique and informative ways to bridge macro- and microanalyses. This series is a high-profile outlet for books that offer accessible readership, innovative approaches, instructive models, and analytic insights to our understanding of globalization.

Children of the Revolution: Violence, Inequality, and Hope in Nicaraguan Migration
Laura Enríquez   2022

At Risk: Indian Sexual Politics and the Global AIDS Crisis
Gowri Vijayakumar   2021

Here, There, and Elsewhere: The Making of Immigrant Identities in a Globalized World
Tahseen Shams   2020

Beauty Diplomacy: Embodying an Emerging Nation
Oluwakemi M. Balogun   2020

The authorized representative in the EU for product safety and compliance is:
Mare Nostrum Group
B.V Doelen 72
4831 GR Breda
The Netherlands

www.ingramcontent.com/pod-product-compliance
Lightning Source LLC
Chambersburg PA
CBHW020852270326
41928CB00006B/672